Library of
Davidson College

*Monetary
Cooperation
Between
East & West*

ADAM ZWASS

Monetary Cooperation Between East & West

WITH AN INTRODUCTION BY GEORGE GARVY

 International Arts and Sciences Press, Inc.
White Plains, New York

Copyright © 1975 by International Arts and Sciences Press, Inc.
901 North Broadway, White Plains, New York 10603

Originally published in 1974 as
*Zur Problematik der Währungsbeziehungen zwischen
Ost und West,* Studien über Wirtschafts- und Systemvergleiche, Band 5,
by Springer-Verlag, Wien/New York. Copyright © F. Nemschak, Wiener
Institut für Internationale Wirtschaftsvergleiche.

Translated by Michel Vale

All rights reserved. No part of this book may be reproduced in any form
without written permission of the publisher.

Library of Congress Catalog Card Number: 73-92368
International Standard Book Number: 0-87332-057-3

Printed in the United States of America

Contents

Foreword to German-language edition   vii

Preface   ix

Introduction   GEORGE GARVY   xi

1 Money and credit in the USSR and Eastern Europe in the light of the economic reforms   1

2 Currency in the foreign trade of the CMEA countries   46

3 CMEA monetary institutions and steering instruments   97

4 Monetary steering instruments of East-West trade   159

5 The outlook for East-West monetary relations   234

Bibliography   258

Foreword
TO GERMAN-LANGUAGE EDITION

The fifth volume of the [Institute] series "Comparative Studies in Economics and Economic Systems" treats the problems of monetary relations between East and West.

The author, Dr. Adam Zwass, is especially well equipped to deal with this complicated subject. To it, he brings his extensive knowledge of monetary relations in Eastern Europe, gained while he held a number of posts in Poland and during his association with the CMEA Secretariat in Moscow. He already has to his credit a long list of publications concerning monetary matters (see his book, Pieniądz dwóch rynków [Money of Two Markets], Warsaw, 1968).

It was not the author's intention to draw up a master plan for closer cooperation between the two monetary systems, which differ widely in many respects. His main concern is the Eastern monetary system, and its instruments, institutions, and functions are subjected to a thorough analysis. Problems are pinpointed and suggestions made for improvements. Finally, Dr. Zwass considers the prospects for the development of a worldwide currency system.

It is hoped that his book will stimulate further research that would pave the way for productive cooperation between East and West in monetary relations.

Franz Nemschak
Editor

Preface

Rampant inflation has sent the Western monetary system reeling. Monetary and credit relations continue to be a nagging problem in the East. Both sides, therefore, have ample grounds for giving serious thought to the reordering of monetary relations between East and West with a view toward expanding economic relations without compromising the fundamental distinctions between their social and economic systems.

The present book deals with monetary and credit relations in Eastern Europe in the wake of the economic reforms; the role of currency in the foreign trade of the CMEA nations; the CMEA monetary institutions and steering instruments; and the general outlook for East-West monetary relations.

The author is especially indebted to the editor of the book, Prof. Dr. Franz Nemschak, who made this project possible and contributed to it many valuable suggestions.

Finally, he would like to thank his colleagues at the Vienna Institute for Comparative Economic Studies, and especially the Research Director, Dr. F. Levcik, for their assistance; the Deputy Director of the Institute for Advanced Studies and Economic Research, Dr. Erhard Fürst, and Dr. Fritz Schebeck of the Austrian Institute for Economic Research for editing the manuscript; the Austrian National Bank for its financial support; and, last but not least, his wife Friderike for gathering the source material and preparing the text.

Adam Zwass

Introduction
GEORGE GARVY

Trade between the socialist countries of the East and the developed countries of the West has been growing vigorously in recent years. Further rapid expansion has been predicted with monotonous insistence by spokesmen on both sides. Optimists claim that growth of trade will contribute to, or even insure, peace. Pessimists insist that trade is merely a consequence of, rather than a contributing factor to, peace. At least some realists believe that, foreign trade being the only significant point of contact between centrally directed and market economies, the growing exposure of the East, and particularly of the Soviet Union, to market forces is bound to focus on the weakest points of the system of the socialist economies and strengthen demands for reforming it.

Many of the inconsistencies, rigidities and wastes of the economies of Eastern Europe are most clearly visible in the area of foreign trade. It thus seems logical to assume that significant reforms to improve the performance of the socialist economies must involve, or even originate in, corrective measures aimed at improving the contribution of foreign trade to optimization of resources use and technological upgrading. This has already been demonstrated in several countries of Eastern Europe. By the same token, differences in the scope, thrust and speed of the reforms initiated since the mid-sixties demonstrate the need for overcoming the tendency still lingering since the cold war years to regard Eastern Europe as a "bloc" and to fail to recognize the important differences that have gradually developed in the way the broad principles and objectives of socialist economies are implemented in individual countries. Dr. Zwass's monograph makes a significant contribution toward dispelling the misconception that Eastern Europe is a monolithic bloc.

Without focusing specifically on the economic reforms, or systematically analyzing differences in what, in socialist countries, is called "steering of the economy," Dr. Zwass has succeeded in conveying the flavor of tendencies toward national divergencies from the original uniform pattern established after the communist seizure of power in each country. The original USSR model has changed least. And yet it is unrealistic to expect that significant moves toward incorporating market-oriented elements into the economic systems of the other socialist countries can make much further progress without at least tentative moves in this direction by the Soviet Union.

Foreign trade plays a very small role in the Soviet economy, whereas a very large part of the gross national product of every other country of Eastern Europe (ranging up to 40 percent in the case of Hungary) is exported. On the other hand, the Soviet Union may have reached a new threshold in its trade relations with the West, with imports assigned a much broader role than the gap-filling that was typical of the autarkic period of Soviet planning. The last few years have witnessed a broadening of the view of the role which imports are expected to play in the Soviet economy, with a prominent place given to large — as a matter of fact, typically giant — resource development projects and mass production facilities for basic materials (fertilizers, pulp) and durables (cars and trucks). At the same time, the emphasis on technology has been reinforced and broadened. Yet, expansion of trade to implement such projects will not necessarily mean a significant change in financing arrangements, which are essentially barter with an extended horizon. So far, in the case of the Soviet Union, they do not include recourse to the world capital market and financial loans which have become available to some of the smaller countries of Eastern Europe in recent years.

While Dr. Zwass does not discuss the commodity composition of trade and touches only lightly on the role of foreign trade in each of the CMEA countries, he broadened his subject to include a description of the basic features of the socialist monetary and banking system. In addition to discussing settlements for nonmerchandise exchanges, Dr. Zwass also reviews institutional arrangements for handling the money side of trade within Eastern Europe.

The use of a conventional jargon of Marxian derivation has gradually lost its dominant role in the writings of economists of Eastern Europe; and yet in many cases it requires the skill of a man with Dr. Zwass's background to bring out the real meaning of concepts and terms with a deceptively "Western" texture which, within the context of socialist economies, have a considerably different real meaning. Indeed, in spite of the similarity in terminology, the underlying processes are in many cases different in both substance and function, aside from differences in the legal framework. Dr. Zwass makes this abundantly clear in his discussion of transferability, credit and other relevant concepts.

Given the tight control over goods flows exercised in planned economies, the techniques of making payments related to trade and other international transactions have never presented a problem in East-West relations. They have been an adaptation of mechanisms and procedures used for trade among nonsocialist nations, with the unmistakable tendency since the sixties to replace bilateral arrangements (so important even among nonsocialist countries in the years following World War II) by settlements in convertible currencies. Special and at times ingenious and complex arrangements, known as switch trading, which sprang to life to bridge the excessive compartmentalization inherent in bilateral compensating accounts, by now have largely disappeared with the multilateralization of payments between East and West.

One can only wish that some other aspects of West-East relations would be as free of problems as those related to foreign exchange and to the payments mechanism. In fact, to the extent that there is a problem, it involves availability of credit to the

CMEA countries, and not the payments mechanism. Lack of convertibility of currencies of the individual countries of Eastern Europe and of the "transferable" ruble is a major problem for these countries themselves and for their domestic economies, rather than for their trade relations with the noncommunist countries; in the latter, they are willing to use "capitalist" currencies, which, according to their textbooks, are "inherently unstable" but, from a practical point of view, are irreplaceable.

Similarly, state trading does not seem to have interfered with the growth of the volume of trade, and, as the 1973 USSR-USA grain deal shows, at least some bureaucrats of state trading organizations possess great skills. But with the various branches of the economies of socialist countries moving to higher levels of technological sophistication and managerial efficiency, more and more policymakers in Eastern Europe might conclude that centralized trading might not be the most efficient organizational form for maximizing the contribution of foreign trade to an optimum allocation of physical and human resources.

Dr. Zwass does not dwell upon the special position of the Soviet Union, which as the second-largest producer and holder of not insignificant reserves of gold, is the only one of the socialist countries to have the alternative of settling in gold. The smaller socialist countries, in addition to tailoring imports from the West to exports to their trade partners, use a different balancing wheel — foreign loans beyond the narrow band of swing credits stipulated in bilateral trade agreements which provide the general framework for their trade relations with each Western country. Indeed, credit relations between some of the smaller socialist countries and the West have developed rapidly in recent years, as documented by Dr. Zwass.

The greater flexibility of the smaller socialist countries of Eastern Europe in many fields, including management and financing of foreign trade, is largely due to the fact that the political changeover came one generation later. The link with the past was never lost, and the soccer team of the National Bank of Hungary continues to play that of the Austrian National

Bank. The readiness of Austrian private bankers to resume their traditional interest in financing foreign trade of their former partner in the Hapsburg Empire was never in question.

In discussing financing of trade and investments among the socialist countries, Dr. Zwass is covering an area in which his rich practical experience shows. This and familiarity with pertinent literature in several languages permits him to fill in many a gap in the knowledge of the Western student. Beyond providing a contrast to, and thus a frame of reference for, discussion of East-West payments, intra-CMEA helps to focus on the central importance of the problem of price formation and price flexibility in socialist economies, internally and in their exchanges with similarly structured economies, as well as with market economies. Indeed, in no other area are the shortcomings of the Soviet-type price system more exposed than in its foreign trade. In holding that the "monetary veil" merely conceals the underlying real processes and relationships and that in the socialist economy money is (or should be) neutral in its effects on these processes, the leaders of Eastern Europe deprive their countries of the guiding hand of the price mechanism. Reading Dr. Zwass's book has reinforced my growing suspicion that the relevant and operational difference between socialist and capitalist economies is not so much ownership of the means of production as the role assigned to the price system.

When dealing with a complex picture, any monograph courts at least two dangers: to lack perspective by omitting, or relegating to the second plane, what has been superseded and thus has become part of history, and to become rapidly obsolete by failing to recognize harbingers of change that foreshadow future trends. Dr. Zwass cannot be faulted on either account. Whenever relevant, his discussion includes significant antecedents. His recognition of foreign trade as at least <u>one</u> of the ancestors of reforms, and of the price system as their touchstone, directs the reader's attention to what logically ought to be the lines of future developments.

There is always a difficulty in calibrating the issues in a rapidly changing setting — particularly when "détente" presumably represents merely the surface appearance of more deeply seated changes on both sides of what some of us who are well along in years remember as the iron curtain. How important are some of the possible institutional developments which intrigue Dr. Zwass, such as the socialist countries' joining the International Monetary Fund and the International Bank for Reconstruction and Development (which hardly can happen without the Soviet Union's taking the lead), or the ruble's becoming "convertible"? Certainly, joining the IMF would have a symbolic importance and, no doubt, bring the countries of Eastern Europe in a systematic manner into closer contact with the kind of monetary and fiscal problems which confront nonsocialist countries at various levels of economic development in controlling inflationary pressures and in managing their foreign exchange reserves. Participation in the periodic distributions of special drawing rights is an attractive feature. Membership in the IBRD, for which membership in the IMF is a precondition, would, among other things, permit the countries of Eastern Europe to bid for contracts for various projects around the world financed by the bank. But joining the Bretton Woods organizations is not likely to have any significant effect on the economic policies of the socialist countries.

The East and the West that are the subjects of Dr. Zwass's study are parts of the same cultural and historical context, which no curtain can separate; but these two areas are not the entire world. Nor is the split between the socialist countries of Europe and of Asia a historical necessity. One must be impressed by the similarity between the current phase in China and the Soviet Union of the twenties and thirties. China is moving much more rapidly in overcoming its original isolation and the resulting attitudes. Already, within a few short years, it has succeeded in establishing trade and cultural relations with the West that carry less of a deadweight of ideological struggles, which required considerable efforts by the Soviet Union to explain that Coca-Cola is now the opposite of what it used to symbolize only a few years ago. Already within a few years, without the help of committees with prestigious names and publicity trying to transform dreams into facts, Sino-American trade has reached a large volume. The Far East is not only red: it is rich in resources, natural and human; it is flexible, and it has the wisdom which the Russian revolutionaries who started it all perhaps never had, or which burned up in the fire of the civil war. It seems realistic to predict that, as time marches on, one of Dr. Zwass's next books will deal with payments related to an East-West trade enlarged into a triangle to include China.

New York, September 1974

Monetary Cooperation Between East & West

1 Money and credit in the USSR and Eastern Europe in the light of the economic reforms

Introduction

The economic reforms that have been carried out in the member nations of the Council for Mutual Economic Assistance (CMEA) have affected the monetary and credit systems of these nations. In accordance with the thrust toward decentralization in planning and administration, efforts are being made to relieve the banks of administrative tasks and to strengthen their economic functions.

Although the reforms may vary in scope from one country to another, they bear certain features in common. They carry nothing of the sensational about them; if anything, they foretoken a protracted process of change and adjustment. The various measures, both general and specific, that are being applied in the different countries, together with the problems that are being discussed, give a rough idea of the dominant trend of the reforms as well as the obstacles encountered by planned economies as they seek to augment the instruments of monetary and credit policy.

The evolution of the monetary and credit system in the Eastern bloc could pave the way for money to assume foreign trade functions in the planned economies, and thus developments in these countries are also of interest to economic circles in the West.

2 Monetary Cooperation Between East and West

1. The Function of Money

Originally, the ideologues of communism believed that it would be possible to eliminate money, and, indeed, the first economic model of the Soviet Union, war communism, did get along largely without it. The experiment failed, however, and the second system, the New Economic Policy (NEP), expanded the functions of money and credit. Yet even this policy was abandoned after a few years in favor of a centrally controlled and administered economy, although the latter was by no means imposed all at once, but rather was introduced by degrees. The monetary and credit systems were also modified accordingly.

Neither past experience nor the outlook for the foreseeable future indicates that a highly centralized, planned economy can dispense with money and credit. On the other hand, even Hungary, the most decentralized economy in the CMEA area, has been able to find only limited use for money and credit as a steering instrument.

In any planned economy, the growth and structure of the economy and the distribution of the national income are all determined by the plan. The input-output indicators (in terms of real magnitudes), rather than the financial resources of the individual enterprise or sector of the economy, are the basis on which production and investment patterns are shaped. The function of money is subordinate to the economic plan.

The socialist theory of money is a subject of debate in the CMEA nations. In official Soviet economic theory, which adheres to the abstract, historical interpretation, socialist money retains a close link with gold.

For economists who stress the distinctive feature of a planned economy — namely, the steering of economic activity and the distribution of the national product according to a plan — the functions of money are not only less important under socialism than under capitalism, they are also essentially different. (1)

But even in the market economies, money functions differently today than it did in the last century; money in a planned economy and money in a market economy have become even less amenable to comparison.

The most important function of money, that is, the aggregation and distribution of the national product, has been retained in the planned economy. Other major functions of money, however, such as its function as a standard of value or as a means of settlement or payment, are less developed in the planned economies than in the market economies.

The two monetary flows — notes and coin, and deposit money — move in parallel circuits among the enterprises within a state-controlled economy, traveling along channels and according to patterns unique to each. The possessor of cash can satisfy his desires and needs in accordance with his income and inclinations, although, of course, only within the scope of the limited facilities available on the seller's market. On the other hand, his access to the means of production is under the strictest control — if it exists at all. "Freedom of consumer choice should not be confounded with consumer sovereignty," observes G. Grossman. (2)

The imbalance between effective demand and supply on the consumer market is graphically evident in the recurrent shortages which the state attempts, insofar as it can, to eliminate.

Whereas money plays an important role on the consumer market, in interenterprise activities it has only a subordinate function geared to the meeting of plan targets. Nevertheless, economists in both East and West have underestimated the role of money in the production process.

As the contours of the planned economies became more finely drawn, money and credit did not diminish in significance as had been expected; on the contrary, they assumed a greater importance, even in the cases where state control of the economy was not later cut back. Some sort of system of monetary relationships seems to be an inevitable feature of every developed economy. An economic plan and its fulfillment can be aggregated only in monetary units, and economic efficiency can be expressed only in terms of money. The productivity of an economy therefore depends on the ability of money to function.

The planned economies, oriented toward quantity maximization by means of extensive development factors, have been able to restrict the economic functions of money; so far, however, such economies have not been able to dispense with money entirely. Every economic system that sets as its goals a high level of efficiency and an international division of labor must concede a place to monetary factors in economic activity.

Commodity exchange in natura may be appropriate in relatively underdeveloped economies or in certain emergency situations; but in a highly specialized economy, in which the structure of the social product and, in particular, the patterns of private consumption tend toward increasing differentiation, money is indispensable for the valuation, use, and distribution of the social product.

In planned as well as market economies, money functions as a mediator of commodity flows in the production and distribution processes; but it is not the driving force of economic activity in planned economies as it is in market economies, where the production unit also has entrepreneurial functions. In theory, the functions of money are limited to the tasks of economic cost accounting (called khozraschet). In the planned economies, the individual enterprise need not possess money to achieve plan targets, which are attainable even when money is in short supply.

Even the planned economies have been unable to devise a better criterion than profit by which to measure the efficiency of production. In all the planned economies, whatever their specific form, profit is becoming a universal standard for assessing enterprise performance. Experience has shown that peak performance cannot be expected unless a reasonable portion of the profit is left to the enterprise and its management. However, profit can fulfill the function intended for it only if other factors are also allowed some play, and one of the most important of these is prices, which must remain within striking range of the social value of the product.

The planned economies are steered not only by the plan and by steering instruments of economic activity, but also by means of money, in terms of which production results are aggregated and the efficiency of the economy assessed and promoted.

As the internal productive forces and foreign trade relations expand, modernization of the monetary system becomes more and more pressing; the drift toward autarky has been detrimental to both the structure and the efficiency of the planned economies.

Tourism, which until the mid-fifties was a negligible factor, has grown in some countries into a productive sector of the economy and an important source of foreign exchange. The domestic currencies, whose original purpose was to shield the planned economies from the elemental forces of the world market, are more and more becoming an impediment to the further economic growth of the CMEA countries.

2. The Function of Credit

In the literature, major stress is laid on the monitoring function of credit — that is, its contribution to the qualitative side of plan fulfillment (planned production costs and inventories, etc.). Actually, credit, like money, has important steering functions as well.

In the planned economies, just as in the market economies, credit continues to be the best means for raising money, whether in the form of deposit money for interenterprise payments or cash for consumer trade. The money supply can be adjusted to the needs of the economy by altering the terms of lending and repayment. The socialist banking system has developed appropriate instruments for coordinating credit relations with the overall planning process.

In a planned economy, in which borrower and lender both represent state property, credit cannot be granted on the basis of the criteria routinely applied on the capital market. In modern economies, bank credit is the primary source for raising money and, as such, performs two basic functions: it provides the funds for meeting economic objectives, and it creates money (the income and issuing functions of credit). The funds raised in this way enter the economy as enterprise deposits and privately held cash. The issuing and credit plan coordinates credit and monetary relations with the economic plan. Deviations from the economic plan show up as deviations of monetary and credit indicators from planned values.

Since a planned economy possesses no definite criteria for

directing credits to the enterprises, a clear distinction must be made between an enterprise's "own funds" and funds supplied in the form of loans from the State Bank. This distinction was a key aspect of the Soviet Union's credit reform of 1930-1931, which specified that the state budget was to provide the funds required by enterprises for current operations, while the banks were to finance needs attendant on seasonal fluctuations and similar events. The banks were endowed with appropriate economic and administrative instruments to support the enterprises in the fulfillment of their economic plans.

The State Bank does not have too great an influence over the activities of the enterprises, whereas the latter can compel the banks to supply needed funds. "Credit gives command over resources only if acquisition of the resources is foreseen in the plan, while plan allocation of resources carries with it an almost automatic claim on credit." (3) Even if an enterprise becomes insolvent, the financing bank cannot refuse credit for projects provided for in the plan. Since interenterprise credit transactions were abolished by the 1930-1931 reform, and wage payments and payments into the state budget have priority, the bank is obligated to bridge financing gaps by extending credit. Overdue loans are as negative a mark for a bank as is nonfulfillment of the plan target for an enterprise. To avoid placing the banks in an unfair position, new types of credit were developed. But even this measure has been unable to eliminate the fact that hitches in the economy cause excessive credit inflation.

The changes instituted in the credit system by the economic reforms should make it possible to utilize credits more efficiently, while the banks now have a more effective set of instruments and weapons at their disposal. The credit system has been reformed in all CMEA countries. Depending on the economic objectives of the particular country, each nation placed primary emphasis on either the managerial and technological or the economic aspects of the credit reform.

3. The Banking System

The centrally planned economies have incorporated the

nationalized banking system into their organizational hierarchy, modifying it as required.

The reorganization of the banking system in the Soviet Union (1930-1931) placed strong emphasis on the financing of fixed capital (machines, construction) and working capital (raw materials, semifinished and finished products, etc.) from different sources. Credits for working capital were to be provided by the State Bank, which also acted as an issuing and clearing center. The investment banks, conceived primarily as supervisory bodies of the Ministry of Finance, were to see that the investment funds were used prudently, and were made responsible for the financing of capital investments. The agricultural banks were to take care of the specific requirements of agriculture, while the savings banks were to be responsive to the needs of private households.

Special credit institutions, similar to their Soviet counterparts, were set up in the people's democracies, while those that already existed, such as the cooperative banks for artisans (Banken für Handwerk und Gewerbe) in the German Democratic Republic (East Germany), the savings and credit cooperatives and the Bank Pekao AG (Polska Kasa Opieki, a clearinghouse for foreign exchange remittances to resident citizens) in Poland, and so on, were continued.

In the mid-fifties, the banking system in the CMEA countries was reorganized in connection with the economic reforms. The purpose of the reorganization was to accommodate the new needs created by the restructuring of industrial administration, by the broader control granted to the individual enterprises over a part of their profits, and by the step-up of foreign trade relations.

The Soviet prototype was substantially modified in some countries, for example, the German Democratic Republic and later Bulgaria. In these countries, the new concept of a central bank as a banker's bank was counterposed to the traditional concept of a State Bank (National Bank) which not only regulates money circulation and credit policy but also engages directly in the extension of credits, the issuance of currency, and the transfer of payments through an extensive network of regional (oblast) administrative offices and local (raion) bank offices.

In the German Democratic Republic, this concept dates back

to a decision of the Central Committee of the Socialist Unity Party (December 1966), which set down the basic principles of the New Economic System and expanded the area of activity of the industrial associations (VVB, industrial associations of nationally owned enterprises). The reform of the banking system took effect in January 1968. The Notenbank (Bank of Issue) and Investment Bank were superseded by the State Bank and the Industry and Trade Bank. At the summit of the entire banking system was the State Bank, an issuing institution responsible directly to the government. The State Bank issues currency, regulates credit relations, and covers the credits of the other banks, but does not itself have a branch network. Business transactions are handled by the Industry and Trade Bank, which has 14 regional administrative offices, 180 local banking offices, and 50 offices for specific economic sectors. The Industry and Trade Bank, with its extensive branch network, takes care of all clearing and credit transactions of industry, trade, and the municipal sector of the economy and finances all investment ventures. In October 1968, a Bank for Agriculture and the Food Industry was established to cover corresponding operations in the area of agriculture.

The relationship between the State Bank and other banks was initially defined in the following decree of the Council of Ministers of the German Democratic Republic on December 22, 1971: "The president of the State Bank of the German Democratic Republic sets the guidelines for the deposit of free funds by other banks in the State Bank of the German Democratic Republic, including interest rates, subject to the approval of the Minister of Finance and the presidents of the other banks. The State Bank of the German Democratic Republic extends credits to cover funds tied up in loans or accepts freely moving funds as deposits from the commercial banks on the basis of the state credit plan and the established guidelines. These operations are effected by means of written agreements." (4) The president of the State Bank certifies the credit balances of the commercial banks and submits the overall credit balance to the Council of Ministers for approval.

A similar type of banking system was put into effect in

Bulgaria on April 1, 1969. Until 1972, Bulgaria's National Bank functioned as a central issuing bank and a banker's bank. Clearing and credit transactions, as well as the financing of investment projects, were undertaken by the Industrial, Trade, and Agricultural Banks. On January 1, 1972, however, Bulgaria returned to its earlier type of banking system.

The East German model was discussed in the other CMEA countries, but was ultimately rejected. It was concluded that, given the present structure of their economies, a banking system with those modifications would be unable to fulfill its economic functions. According to this view, there is no place in a planned economy for a money and capital market or for any interplay between bank deposits and credits.

The enterprises are not free to choose among different banks or to seek out the best credit terms. They receive credits on the basis of standard guidelines which are binding on enterprises and banks alike. A banking system of this type provides no possibility and hence no incentive to make profits or avoid losses. Thus, although it bears certain similarities to banking systems in a market economy, none of the credit mechanisms characteristic of the latter would be viable in it.

The following statement of the former president of the Polish National Bank probably typifies the views of the other national banks as well: "To achieve the full effect of cost accounting in bank organizations... requires the existence of a money and a capital market, as well as the use of money and capital in accordance with the rules of that market.... However, this could only be brought about by a thorough reorganization of the economic model...." (5)

Poland, Czechoslovakia, and Hungary have reorganized their banking systems by centralizing all financing of industrial enterprises, including investments, in the National Bank. The latter has also assumed the tasks of the now defunct Investment Bank (abolished in Czechoslovakia in 1958; in Poland, in 1970). (6)

The reorganization of the Hungarian banking system tends in the same direction but differs on a few points from the Polish and Czech approaches. Pursuant to a government decision of June 1971, the task of financing most of the capital investments made by the enterprises on their own account with their own funds or with bank credits was transferred to the National Bank, effective as of 1972. At the same time, a Bank for Economic Development was established to finance investments that are partially or wholly undertaken with budgeted funds or development loans pursuant to governmental decisions.

In the Soviet Union, the banking system was reorganized in 1960, with primary emphasis on the centralization of the financing of capital projects. Three investment banks were abolished, and the Industrial Bank was superseded by the Construction Bank (Stroibank). At the same time, the savings bank system was placed under the jurisdiction of the State Bank (Gosbank). With the expansion of foreign trade relations, the foreign trade banks were made into independent institutions. As joint stock companies, they had had only a very limited scope of operations after the war.

On January 1, 1962, the Soviet Union transferred all foreign trade operations to the already existing Foreign Trade Bank (Vneshtorgbank). Poland transferred foreign trade operations to the Bank Handlowy on January 1, 1964. Bulgaria's Foreign Trade Bank began its operations in 1964, while the Commerce Bank AG of Czechoslovakia and the Foreign Trade Bank of Romania were founded on January 1, 1965, and January 1, 1968, respectively.

The national banks of the CMEA countries remained responsible for planning the movements of foreign exchange and for the balance of payments.

4. The Function of the Banks

4.1. Basic Principles

In the planned economies, the banks maintain a close relationship with the enterprises, on which they place high demands. Every enterprise, without exception, must maintain an account with its associated bank and settle all its business through this institution.

Banking transactions are much less differentiated than in the Western industrial countries, however. There are no money and capital markets in the usual sense of the term, and foreign banks are barred. (7) An enterprise in the German Democratic Republic maintains connections with only one branch of the Notenbank, or Bank of Issue (a commercial bank). In the Soviet Union, Romania, and Hungary, ties are also maintained with an investment bank for the purpose of financing fixed assets. All settlements and credit transactions are carried out in the bank branches, which also provide the cash for loan payments.

Relationships among the individual banks are less developed than in the West. The investment banks and commercial banks (where they exist) deposit their liquid assets and obtain funds for their own business from the National Bank, which sets the guidelines for issuing and credit policy.

Deposits are not a prerequisite for granting credits. The size and availability of credits are stipulated in the credit plan of the State Bank.

The size of the credit balances of an enterprise in its bank account tells us nothing about its financial power, which is determined primarily by the banks' readiness to grant credit. If, as in Poland, for example, credits are entered in a current account rather than in a special account, an enterprise's liquid assets on deposit with its bank will be relatively less than when credits are placed in special accounts, as is the case in most CMEA countries.

The bank is a state administrative agency which, in the course of its operations, monitors the economic activity of the enterprises. Through the granting of short-term credits, it supervises inventories; by the performing of settlements, it watches over the movements of goods; it keeps check on project costs and construction deadlines in investment projects; and it sees that the wage fund is maintained at a proper level as it disburses wages and salaries, etc.

Short-term credits, which finance a part of the working assets of the national economy, constitute the major activity on the assets side of banking operations. The purposes for which credit may be used have been expanded and credit policy has become more diversified. The problems to which this has given rise will be dealt with in more detail in section 5.

4.2. Monetary Resources

Bank reserves consist of two principal components: funds from private households and funds from the socialized sector of the economy. The monetary funds from the economy are partially in the hands of central institutions (state budget, insurance agencies, investment funds, clearing accounts of foreign trade enterprises), and partially held by the enterprises and cooperatives.

The structure of bank resources in Poland is illustrated in the table below. The other CMEA countries show a similar structure.

The structure of monetary resources provides some useful insights into the breakdown of the unconsumed income generated by the production of socially useful goods. The relatively high share falling to the state budget (24.7 percent) is conspicuous and is due to the fact that surpluses that in some cases are not foreseen in the plan appear in the state budget. These surpluses represent mostly goods that do not fit the structure of demand, and usually end up as inventories of which it is difficult to dispose.

In Poland, the 1970 budgetary surplus, accumulated over several years, amounted to 37 percent of the total budget receipts for that year. In the assets column of the bank balance sheet, it is represented by credits for these inventories.

Structure of Monetary Resources in Poland, 1970
(in percent) (8)

Funds from the socialized sector		71.4
Enterprise settlement accounts	2.2	
Investment funds and other funds	26.4	
Bank funds	4.6	
State budget	24.7	
Funds from private households		28.6
Savings deposits	19.7	
Cash	8.9	
Total		100.0

The already slight, yet declining, share of enterprise settlement accounts in Poland's total volume of money is noteworthy. From 1960 to 1970, it decreased from 9.9 percent to 2.2 percent. The volume of settlement funds is directly related to the methods by which credit is granted. Before 1959, the enterprises had accounts for credits in addition to their settlement accounts (sight deposits). Thereafter, some enterprises experimentally instituted a policy of depositing credits in current accounts, and in 1966 almost all state-owned enterprises adopted this procedure. The volume of settlement funds of course diminished accordingly.

The large share of private money in total bank resources is also noteworthy. Thus, private households function as creditors, while the state sector, represented by the State Bank, functions as debtor.

4.3. Regulation of Total Money Circulation

The banking system in the socialist planned economies has developed appropriate steering mechanisms for deposit and cash money flows. As all enterprises are obliged to keep cash deposits with the banks and settle all payments through them, the banks are in a position to control the monetary resources of the enterprises. In addition, all payments of state-owned enterprises to private households are monitored by the banks.

In the case of noncash payment transfers, the banks monitor the money supply of the economy by adjusting lending terms and control the use of money by regulating clearing procedures. Banks are the sole legal lenders; up until now, interenterprise credits have been prohibited. Hungary is the only exception; in that country, limited interenterprise credits have been permitted since the economic reform of 1968.

The banking system supervises the relationship between payments and the flow of goods. The liquidity and solvency of the enterprises are not dependent on their monetary resources, which are relatively small, but on the readiness of the financing bank to grant credit.

The supply of cash money to private households is controlled through the wages fund, and, because trade is controlled, the return flow of money into the banks is insured. However, there are no means to directly influence how private households spend their cash funds.

By exerting influence on retail trade and encouraging saving, the banks, together with the administrative authorities, take care that a balance is maintained between cash incomes and expenditures, and hence that the amount of cash money in circulation does not exceed the ceiling (currency issue directives) set by the plan.

Both monetary flows — that is, cash money and deposit money — begin and end in the banks. The proceeds from retail sales and the savings banks' receipts return to the banks, where they are converted into deposit money. Only a part ends up as private cash holdings, and this portion is balanced out by printing more money.

4.4. Interenterprise Settlements

The traditional settlement system of the banks of the CMEA countries is based on the following principles.

All payments are made through the banks. The customary form of payment is the collection mandate system whereby the supplier authorizes his bank to collect on his claim. The purchaser must declare his agreement within three days. A tacit acceptance is sufficient. The purchaser's bank then debits his account after a period of ten days has elapsed (three days are allowed for the acceptance and seven days for procuring the necessary funds). If the supplier's claim is not collected in due time, the payment is considered overdue and charged with punitive interest.

If an enterprise becomes insolvent, its obligations are generally met in the following sequence of priorities: first wages, then payments to the budget, then payments to the bank, and finally payments to its suppliers. From the mid-fifties on, suppliers' claims were settled before due bank credits. An enterprise that got into payment difficulties had only a small sum which it could dispose freely.

In cases of chronic insolvency, the banks did have the power to suspend the enterprise's right to dispose over goods that were not paid for, although this sanction was seldom imposed.

Over the past ten to fifteen years, the bank settlement system was made more functional in several important respects through economic as well as technical and organizational changes.

The economic aspects of the changes introduced in the settlement system stand out most clearly in Hungary. As a result of the economic reform, in 1971 the banks lost the right of disposal over an enterprise's bank balance. The relations between a bank and an enterprise are now spelled out in the agreement defining the terms governing the opening of a new account with the bank. The enterprise decides on the type and terms of payment, but payment may not take place later than thirty days after delivery. Interenterprise credits are now possible in Hungary, whereas under the former settlement and credit system they were not.

In the other CMEA countries, the settlement system was reformed much earlier, if not as extensively as in Hungary. In Poland, the enterprises were given full control over the funds in their settlement accounts by a decree of July 1, 1958. (9) Creditors could demand punitive interest of up to 12 percent for overdue claims.

Early in 1959, Czechoslovakia replaced the traditional system of payment priorities with a chronological system, in which bills are payable in the order received. The enterprises were given full powers of disposal over 20 percent (in some cases, up to 50 percent) of their daily receipts.

An enterprise's decision on payment priorities is influenced by a differentiated punitive interest scale (36 percent for overdue budget payments, 18.6 percent for delivery orders, and 10.8 percent for bank credits).

Bulgaria has retained the traditional system of priorities. However, pursuant to a decree of July 1, 1968, the enterprises now have the right to unrestricted utilization of 50 percent of their daily receipts.

The changes made in the settlement system in the German Democratic Republic in 1961 and in Romania in 1962 were very similar. The supplier is credited with the amount due the day after an authorization to collect is submitted. The purchaser's bank debits his account and grants credit if its client is unable to pay. The client has the right to refuse acceptance within twenty days if the supplier has not met the terms; the sum in question is then returned. Further changes were made in the German Democratic Republic in 1964 (10) and 1968. (11) The enterprises were granted the right to choose their own form of settlement. However, immediate payment, under the rules described above, continued to be preferred.

This form of payment, with a few modifications, is also used in Romania. The supplier receives for his direct use only the production costs (minus depreciation allowance) of the goods sold. Depreciation allowance and profit are indicated separately on the invoice and credited to a special account.

The Soviet Union has not changed the economic aspects of its settlement system. Any modifications have been exclusively of a technical and organizational nature. Pursuant to the government decree of April 3, 1964, the settlement procedure was expanded to include deferred acceptance by the purchaser. However, if the supplier repeatedly fails to meet the standards agreed upon for the goods, the purchaser can postpone payment until after he has inspected the goods.

The punitive interest for overdue payments was raised from 0.01 percent to 0.03 percent. At the same time, the purchaser's solvency was strengthened by permitting credits to be granted.

4.5. The Organization of Cash Flow (12)

While supply and demand on the producers' "market" can be steered by a central plan, the consumer demand for commodities, whatever their type, cannot be centrally regulated. This task became even more difficult when the income of individual groups within the population grew beyond the subsistence level and their demands became more diversified. The market, traditionally dominated by the seller, must increasingly heed the buyer's wishes.

This being the case, it became difficult for the government to maintain responsibility for both the planning of incomes and expenditures in the household sector and for the currency issue directives of the State Bank. The traditional practice of making the bridging of gaps between bank incomes and expenditures contingent upon the approval of a higher-ranking banking institution had to be abandoned, since such a practice would have given rise to unreasonable delays in wage payments.

In principle, the institutional planning methods were retained. But in practice, technical and organizational measures were supplanted by economic instruments.

As before, cash flow is controlled by two plans: first, by an estimate of net movements of private receipts and expenditures — that is, a central plan covering all private transactions drawn up by the planning commission and approved by the Council of Ministers; and second, by the State Bank's cash plan (see Table 1, page 38), which contains the major sources of cash receipts (retail sales receipts, savings bank receipts, post office receipts, etc.) and cash expenditures (wages, pensions, advances for official travel, advances for payments for agricultural products, etc.).

In Poland, Hungary, and the other people's democracies, the policy of having every local banking office and regional administrative office submit proposals for the cash plan was abandoned as a result of the reforms. These proposals had served as the foundation for the central cash plan, which was broken down by local offices to which the plan gave specific issuing directives.

Since mid-1969, Poland has had a central cash plan that functions as a kind of nonbinding forecast for the entire country; it is no longer broken down by local banking offices. The local offices are supposed to analyze economic trends in their areas to determine the amount of circulating currency required, and endeavor to establish as close collaboration as possible with the local administrative agencies and enterprises. (13) In addition, a number of administrative regulations, such as requiring a permit from a higher banking authority for any additional issuance of money, were abolished.

Similar reforms were instituted in the other people's democracies (with the exception of Romania). The Soviet Union found a better way to cover the discrepancies between bank cash receipts and expenditures. Now estimates of net movements of private receipts and expenditures covering entire regions serve as the basis for steering retail turnover and currency circulation. These estimates are binding on both the State Bank, as the central issuing institution, and the local administrative authorities.

An important change was also introduced into the State Bank's procedure for putting currency into circulation when cash expenditures exceed current revenues. Formerly, permission from a higher-level banking authority was required. Now, the regional administration can obtain the short funds within the limits set down by the plan. In addition, needs not foreseen in the plan can be met if reimbursement is guaranteed. (14)

4.6. Monitoring the Wage Fund

Wages, a basic factor in the overall economic plan, are quantitatively the most important item in the cash plan. The banks not only issue the funds for wages but also function as a state supervisory office over them in that they reward the enterprises in proportion to their performance. The wage fund is increased if the plan is overfulfilled and decreased by an appropriate amount if it is not fulfilled. For example, in the Soviet Union wages are adjusted by factors of ±0.6 percent to ±0.9 percent for every percentage point of plan overfulfillment or nonfulfillment.

In some countries, the economic reforms brought certain changes in the system of wage fund control. In Hungary, wage raises were made contingent upon increased productivity. For a productivity (profit + wages/number of employed) increase of 1 percent, the wages are usually increased by 0.3 percent. If these norms are exceeded, the enterprises are subjected to a progressive tax: 150 percent for an excess of 0.5 percent, and as much as 400 percent for excesses of 2 percent. (15) These measures are designed to prevent inflationary trends.

In Poland, the control of the wage fund was modified in 1971. The adjustment factor for wage payments is set by the chairman of the Committee for Labor and Wages in agreement with the chairman of the Planning Commission and the president of the State Bank.

The controlling bank has the authority to contest any additional expenditures on wages if the goods produced in excess of the plan cannot be disposed of. The enterprise can be required to refund the excess payments in wages within a certain specified time. If this happens, the payment from the bonus fund to the administrative personnel is reduced to 50 percent. (16)

4.7. Cash Holdings and Savings of Private Households

The rise in incomes and the increased demand for consumer goods have considerably altered the composition of money in the household sector in the Eastern bloc. The state has also revised its savings policy.

Compulsory savings in the form of obligatory participation of the population in state loans was discontinued in the mid-fifties, and private savings increasingly became the basis of consumer credits.

Nevertheless, for several reasons, compulsory saving still exists in the Eastern bloc. Occasional regional supply problems, shortages, and inordinately high prices for high-demand consumer goods amount in practical terms to compulsory saving.

The promotion of individual and collective housing construction has encouraged saving among the population. Private savings and consumer credits, which the state encourages, have contributed to the gradual emergence of a consumer's market in all CMEA countries.

The statistics from the German Democratic Republic, Poland, and Czechoslovakia (statistics exist only for these countries) given in the table on page 20 will provide some idea of how the composition of household funds has changed from 1960 to 1970.

The relative share of cash holdings and savings deposits in the total volume of money in the hands of private households depends on the living standards and saving habits of the population. The existence of private enterprises is also a factor. As might be expected, the share of savings deposits is greatest in the German Democratic Republic and smallest in Poland, although in all countries the share of savings deposits in total volume of money in private hands is growing.

Composition of Private Household Funds (at year-end)

	GDR			Poland			Czechoslovakia		
	1960	1965	1970	1960	1965	1970	1960	1965	1970
(In billion units of the national currency)										
Cash	4.5	5.2	7.4	26.3	39.4	58.6	7.3	10.2	17.8
Savings deposits	17.5	31.3	52.1	16.2	51.3	114.8	19.4	35.6	63.5
Total	22.0	36.5	59.5	42.5	90.7	173.4	26.7	45.8	82.3
(In percent)										
Cash	20.6	14.2	12.4	61.9	43.4	33.8	27.5	22.3	21.9
Savings deposits	79.4	85.8	87.6	38.1	56.6	66.2	72.5	77.7	78.1
Total	100.0	100.0	100.0	100.0	100.0	100.0	100.0	100.0	100.0

Source: Statistical yearbooks of the German Democratic Republic, Poland, and Czechoslovakia.

A comparison of funds (cash and savings deposits) per capita is interesting. The following table shows money per capita for the three countries mentioned (in rubles, based on the exchange rate for noncommercial payments set in the Prague agreement of February 8, 1963; see Chapter 2):

Money per Capita, 1970

	GDR	Poland	Czechoslovakia
In the national currency	3491	5319	5664
In rubles	1091	348	602
GDR = 100	100	31.8	55.1

Changes in the ratio of money in private households to the produced national income in the three countries are also illuminating:

Ratio of Monetary Resources in Private Households to
Produced National Income, 1960-1970 (in percent)

	1960		1965		1970	
GDR	31.0	100.0	42.9	100.0	55.6	100.0
Poland	11.1	35.8	17.8	41.5	25.3	45.5
Czechoslovakia	16.6	53.5	25.8	60.0	29.1	52.3

Source: Statistical yearbooks of the German Democratic Republic, Poland, and Czechoslovakia; the national income is given in comparable prices.

From 1960 to 1970, the share of private monetary resources in the produced national income grew in all three countries. The growth was greatest in Poland and least in Czechoslovakia. Private households in the German Democratic Republic have by far the most money in both absolute and relative terms.

Savings deposits also grew in the other CMEA countries: for example, by 122 percent in Bulgaria, 147 percent in the Soviet Union, and 106 percent in Hungary from 1965 to 1970. (17) Consumer credits underwent a simultaneous increase, and, by the end of 1968, constituted 15.4 percent of the savings deposits in Bulgaria, 37.0 percent in the German Democratic Republic, 13.7 percent in Czechoslovakia, and 34.5 percent in Poland.

5. Credit Policy

5.1. Basic Principles

Credit policy was modified even more substantially by the economic reforms than was the banking system. The credit policy reforms took place in coordination with reforms in overall state finance policy, which constituted the core of the economic reform. Interventions in credit policy varied in scope among the different countries but were the most far-reaching in Hungary and the German Democratic Republic. In these countries, enterprises are no longer required to transfer the major part of their profits to the state or their industrial association as they had been formerly; instead, profits are now taxed but remain in principle at the disposal of the enterprises and their associations, to be used for further growth and expansion.

In Hungary, for example, the profit shown on the balance sheet is subject to a 6 percent tax, which goes to the local administration. The remaining profit is divided into two main portions, a consumer fund and a fund for economic development, which are also taxed, but at different rates.

The consumption fund is used for raising wages and salaries; the development fund, for expanding fixed assets and working assets (raw materials, semifinished and finished products, etc.). The enterprise management has control over both funds. In addition, self-financing from profits was introduced in the German Democratic Republic and Bulgaria in 1971. In these two countries, it is primarily the industrial associations, rather than the enterprises themselves, that decide to what use profits are to be put.

In the German Democratic Republic, the industrial associations of nationally owned enterprises are the immediate partners. Through them, all enterprise profits are transferred to the state. The associations can use a part of the profits for their own projects.

The interest on fixed and working capital, as well as the state's share of export profits (30 percent) is paid into the state budget from the gross profits of the enterprises. The enterprises can freely utilize the net profit remaining after subtraction of the differentiated tax (40-70 percent). All rates for deductions from the gross profits usually remain in force for a five-year period, and only the Council of Ministers can change these rates.

In Bulgaria, the industrial associations, which were reduced in number from 120 to 66 in 1971 (18), have been transformed from purely administrative organs into independent economic bodies serving industry. They now dispose over the total profits and settle their accounts directly with the state budget, bypassing the enterprises they manage. The individual enterprises have become mere subsidiaries of these associations, with only limited powers.

In the East German and Bulgarian systems, only the incentive funds are dependent on profit, in contrast to the Hungarian system, in which wage increases too are linked to profit.

There is a growing body of opinion in the other CMEA countries as well that it is no longer appropriate to transfer the total profits to the state budget and to distribute them entirely over budget items. In these countries, too, the enterprises are retaining increasingly larger portions of the profits. However, their control over these funds is so limited that they are able to exert no notable influence on investments. (19) As before, investment decisions are made centrally, and the enterprises usually retain merely the function of carrying out the directives of the central authorities.

Any increased power that has been given the enterprises has been confined largely to matters bearing on modernization of machinery and equipment.

In those countries where the profits remaining after taxes are left in the hands of the enterprises to use for their own development, investments are no longer financed predominantly from budget funds. The development and modernization of equipment have been made the responsibility of the enterprises.

In these countries, the most important substantive change brought about by the economic reforms has been the elimination of the separation between financing of fixed capital and financing of working capital, and the transfer of important decision-making powers to the enterprises.

The methods of financing capital projects were also modified in the other CMEA countries, but the enterprises have only slight influence over investments. The state now makes less direct use of the budget to control investments and relies more on manipulating the terms under which credits are granted and repaid. Decisions concerning the modernization and expansion of the fixed capital of enterprises have been left in the hands of the central planning authorities and the industrial associations. But the scope of the reforms in these countries should not be underestimated, since here, too, credits promote technological progress.

Credit policy on working capital also underwent some changes.

Two different credit methods were developed, depending on the extent of the economic reform. In cases where profit is the principal criterion of economic effectiveness and a prerequisite for the growth of an enterprise, more stress is laid on self-financing of working capital, while credits are deemphasized; but in those countries where the state is trying to increase its use of credit to control enterprise activities, it has expanded its range of influence.

5.2. Priority to Investment Credits

Investment activity was unsatisfactory in all CMEA countries. The construction terms were too long, and many construction projects remained incomplete for long periods. Inadequate financing methods were considered to be the major cause of this defect. Since the subsidies allotted by the budget did not have to be paid back, there was no incentive to use the funds efficiently and to complete the construction projects on time.

The economic reform attempted to make enterprise expansion dependent on the realization of profit by the enterprise. At the same time, the banks augmented their influence over construction by the use of larger credits and by appropriately geared interest rates.

Approaches differed in detail. It is interesting to look at the financing methods employed in those countries in which the economic reforms have continued to flourish. The system in which credits and profit are used to finance capital projects is most popular in Hungary and the German Democratic Republic.

In Hungary, investments are financed primarily from the enterprise development funds. If necessary, credit is made available. Credits can also be granted from the state budget, but only when there is a reasonable possibility that the investment credits can be paid off from profits within a period of ten years. Long-term bank credits are made available upon application. Initially, the credit applicant had to guarantee that the investment projects would bring at least 7 percent return. But because the demand for this type of credit was very great, the required return was increased to 15 percent [20], and the applicants were required to assume 30 percent of the risk themselves with their own funds. Enterprises that are involved in some kind of cooperative venture are permitted to enter into credit contracts with one another and in this way share in the borrower's profits.

The progressive nature of the Hungarian reform is also reflected in the fact that the financial power of an enterprise is the deciding factor in its investment projects. In Hungary, supplies of materials are not subject to a quota, nor are there any set limits to the expansion of enterprise investments. (21)

In the German Democratic Republic, only capital projects relevant to the structure of the economy (30-40 percent of total investments) are financed from the budget. So that investments might be better controlled, interest-free credits are granted; these must be covered from budgetary funds after the investment project is completed.

In principle, the enterprises must finance their outlays for development from their own resources. The investments projected for industry and construction in the 1971-1975 five-year plan are to be financed on the following schedule: 40 percent from the depreciation fund, 30 percent from the net profit, and 30 percent from bank credits. (22) Pursuant to the government decree of December 22, 1971, credits are granted for the following capital investment projects: improvement in working conditions and living conditions; domestic and foreign cooperative projects; measures aimed at regional coordination, etc. (23) Investment credits must be paid back within five years.

The financing of capital investments in Bulgaria resembles the system in the German Democratic Republic. The principal sources of financing are the development fund and the fund for technological progress. In 1970, 75 percent of the total capital investments will be financed from profits and credits (in 1968, the figure was 48 percent). (24) In the future, only capital investments for the infrastructure and public institutions are to be financed from budgetary funds.

The use of profits and credits to finance investments has increased in the other CMEA countries as well, although economic conditions have not permitted the enterprises to exercise broader decision-making powers.

Poland serves as an example of this type of investment policy. In that country, the share of budgetary funds in total financing resources decreased from 41 percent in 1966 to 18.3 percent in 1970, and the share of credits increased from 10.3 percent to 45.8 percent, while the share of the enterprises' own funds decreased only slightly, from 42.5 percent to 35.9 percent during that same period. (25) The general guidelines laid down in 1970 actually narrowed the decision-making powers of the enterprises. The Chairman of the Board of the Polish National Bank, J. Szyrocki, ventured the opinion that the present financing system leaves the enterprises no say at all in determining their development and noted that the enterprises acted in a decision-making capacity in only 10 percent of investment projects (renovations and minor modernization measures). (26) Decisions on all other investments lay in the hands of industrial associations, the Ministry, or the Council of Ministers.

In the Soviet Union, credits now play a greater role than they did formerly in the control of investment activity and the promotion of technical progress. Whereas, before 1966, centrally planned investments were financed exclusively through the state budget, since that time they have also been financed through credits.

Credits are granted by the Construction Bank (Stroibank) for centrally planned investments if the given enterprise is able to pay back the credits within five years. If it cannot, the investment projects are financed insofar as is necessary through the state budget.

Capital projects that are independently planned by an enterprise or industrial association are financed by the Fund for the Development of Production, which is formed from the enterprise's profits, and, if the latter is not sufficient, by credits from the State Bank. As a result of the reforms, the term for repayment of credit has been extended from the original one year to two to six years. The State Bank grants credits solely for the expansion of consumer goods production and the enlargement and modernization of technical equipment. (27)

N. Barkowski, former Member of the Board of the State Bank, has criticized the fact that, although investment financing and the granting of investment credits are functions of both the Construction Bank and the State Bank in a 60:40 ratio, this ratio was not established on the basis of economic criteria. He proposes that all investment financing be concentrated in the hands of the Investment Bank. (28) This proposal differs from the policies pursued in the other CMEA countries, where, since the reforms, investment financing and financing of working capital have been concentrated in the hands of the State Bank.

In Romania, credit policy for investments underwent only slight changes. Credits should promote technological progress; they are granted when they can be repaid from profits within three years. The State Bank grants credits up to one million lei, and the Investment Bank, up to five million lei.

In Czechoslovakia, credit terms have tightened and credit volume has shrunk over the past few years. According to the explanation offered by S. Potač, President of the State Bank (29), during the period from 1971 to 1975, only a certain portion of the total costs of a project will be financed by credit; specifically, up to 40 percent of the investment projects planned by the federal government, and up to 60 percent of those planned by investment associations, provided they do not exceed a cost of 1.5 million koruny.

The State Bank is steering a deflationary course and intends successively to reduce the increase in the volume of investment credits from 8.8 billion koruny in 1971 to 2.3 billion koruny in 1974. By 1975, an absolute reduction of 1.5 billion koruny in the total credit volume is even foreseen.

5.3. Credits for Working Assets in a Centrally Planned Economy

In the traditional centrally planned economy, the granting of credits was incorporated into the overall system of controls. As compared with the allocation of budgetary funds, credits had the advantage that they procured financing funds and created money at the same time. Credit was better suited than budget financing for calling attention to production cost overruns due to payment bottlenecks and made it easier for higher-level authorities to intervene in good time.

In this system, credit and budgetary funds each had well-defined uses. The central authorities decided on questions of economic development; in their hands were concentrated the total profits, over which they had exclusive control. Budgetary funds were thus used to finance all investment activity, while the use of credits was limited to the financing of working capital. Credits finance only a portion of the working assets, however; the remainder is provided from the enterprise's own funds.

An enterprise was supposed to have its own funds available for absolutely necessary inventory (normative stocks), while credits could be obtained for what was needed in addition (above-normative stocks).

The working assets (raw materials, semifinished and finished goods, etc.) were itemized in detail and allocated by the central authorities. But only a certain portion of the above-normative stocks could be covered by credits. Every credit granted was deposited in a special account and was to remain available for as long as the planned above-normative stocks were on hand.

Lending terms differed for industry, agriculture, trade organizations, purchasing agencies for agricultural products, and even for special individual branches of industry; moreover, the guidelines were quite specific. Before the economic reform, there were sixteen different types of credit in Poland and twelve in Romania.

Despite the stringent regulations for the extension of credits, credits were not a prerequisite for production; in fact, they were granted after it was decided what was to be produced, and how. If credits were not made available, either the supplier would not be paid or the state would receive less in taxes and profits. This would have given rise to a long line of unmet payment obligations. Such a disastrous consequence was avoided by making credit automatic. Only those enterprises that do not fulfill their plans encounter difficulties, and even then they face various administrative sanctions rather than a refusal of credits or an increased interest rate, the weapons usually used by banks. Indeed, an increased interest rate would be meaningless, since profit has to be transferred to the budget anyway. This practice was given legal status for well-functioning enterprises by the Decree of the Soviet Government No. 1789 of August 21, 1954.

The credit policy outlined above had been followed for over a quarter of a century and had been accompanied by a steady stream of progressively weaker regulations and decrees; it was therefore only a matter of time until a fundamental reform in credit policy came about.

In some CMEA countries, such as the Soviet Union and Romania, the reforms placed key emphasis on technical and organizational measures; in other countries, especially Hungary and the German Democratic Republic, the reforms went much further and availed themselves of a more sophisticated set of economic weapons. In practice, the credit reforms of all countries contained both technical and organizational as well as economic elements, with main emphasis placed on one or the other according to the specific needs and practices of the individual country.

5.4. Stress on Self-financing and Restriction of Short-Term Credit

In all countries, the economic reforms brought about a greater differentiation of credits for working capital. Increased stress on enterprise self-financing and the restriction of short-term credit are characteristic of Hungary, the German Democratic Republic, and Czechoslovakia.

The economic reform made greater changes in credit policy in Hungary than in any of the other CMEA countries. Hungarian enterprises have been accorded such a wide scope for independent action that by and large they have a free hand over their own monetary resources. Under these conditions, credit is largely able to fulfill its economic function.

The Hungarian National Bank defines the function of credit as follows: "The credit policy directives propose to strengthen selective credit policy and to accelerate repayment of credits, to lay more emphasis on frugality in enterprise management, and, finally, to curb the accumulation of stocks." (30) Credit should above all stimulate production; that, in fact, is the keynote of the entire credit policy. One of the chief functions of credit is to compensate for seasonal fluctuations in the demand for working capital. Current needs should be financed from the development fund, which is formed from profits, rather than from the budget.

The director of the board of the Hungarian National Bank, J. Fekete, has described credit conditions explicitly as follows: "Credit will be granted to enterprises which are profitable, whose products are in demand, and which regularly meet their obligations on maturity." (31) Thus, the enterprises are to resort to credits to finance current needs only in exceptional cases, and, when they do, they must repay this credit within three years with resources from the development fund.

The Hungarian system is aimed especially at maximizing enterprise profit and helping the enterprises accumulate their own funds, that is, at limiting the demand for credit. The share of credits in the total resources for financing working assets was reduced from 45 percent to 20-25 percent as a result of the reform.

Short-term credit is no longer used exclusively for inventory items specified in the plan, as was the case before the reform; it is now used impartially to cover any seasonal needs. As a general rule, it must be repaid within ninety days. If the term is longer, the interest rate is increased by 1 percent for each subsequent ninety-day period, with a ceiling of 10 percent. (32)

In the Hungarian economic system, money can also play an independent role, that is, it is not bound unconditionally to a preset purpose. Clearing money can be converted into bank deposits and subjected to an interest rate of 3 to 7 percent; the interest rate will depend on the term of the obligation. These deposits serve as resources for investment credits, which, in turn, are subject to 7-8 percent interest.

The Hungarian credit system most closely resembles the reformed credit system of the German Democratic Republic. The economic aspects, however, are not as strongly emphasized in the German Democratic Republic as they are in Hungary. In East Germany, the central plan still figures as strongly as before. The government decree of December 22, 1971, places great value on the planned allocation of credit: "The nation's credit fund shall be employed in accordance with the credit plans." (33) The industrial associations of nationally owned enterprises have important powers in the area of financing. They dispose over large sums and are able to pursue an autonomous financing policy, and even to finance large projects.

As in Hungary, credit is viewed only as an extra source of assistance for the enterprises, which actually are supposed to finance themselves. However, the industrial associations, which are largely autonomous, and not the enterprises, dominate in the German Democratic Republic, and the financing bank is more of a partner in the enterprise than a superior authority. The financial counterpart of the enterprise is the commercial bank; its interest rate for credits must be lower than the enterprise's profit rate but high enough to insure that the commercial bank remains profitable.

Credit terms are adjusted to enterprise performance, and the enterprises must see to it that credits are repaid within the specified time. Otherwise, the liquidity of the commercial bank is imperiled, since it finances its own funds through the State Bank and must pay interest rates of 4.5 to 6 percent.

Relations between banks and enterprises are regulated by a credit agreement. In making its credit commitment, the bank gives the enterprise a green light to draw up its operating plans. The agreement stipulates the amount of credit, interest rate, terms of repayment, and consequences of nonfulfillment of the agreement.

As in Hungary, the monetary assets of East German enterprises now play a more important role than they did formerly. Clearing money can be converted into bank deposits and can bear interest.

Nevertheless, there are important differences between the East German and the Hungarian systems. In the German Democratic Republic, specified proportions must be maintained between an enterprise's own funds and credit. The enterprise must finance at least 50 percent but no more than 90 percent of its working capital. On the average, the self-financing figure varies between 50 percent and 70 percent. (34)

In the German Democratic Republic, the controlling function of bank credit stands out more prominently than it does in Hungary. The above-cited government decree requires, as a precondition for the extension of credit, that an enterprise meet the "state planning criteria and the accounting indices for the national economy, as well as the indices of economic effectiveness set by the competent authorities in conjunction with the bank." (35)

The bank gives primary consideration to the following two enterprise inventory indices: the standard turnover rate of working capital (commodity production/average level of stocks) and the standard for assessing the profitability of stocks (gross profit/average level of stocks).

Not only does the bank serve to meet the planned needs of an enterprise, but it can also grant "credits for financing working capital that has been temporarily inflated in the interests of the economy as a whole," or "for emergency assistance for temporary liquidity difficulties." (36) In carrying out these functions, a bank employs a number of administrative weapons in addition to variable interest rates.

Like Hungary and the German Democratic Republic, Czechoslovakia also places considerable value on enterprise self-financing. The 1967-1968 economic reform gave primary emphasis to the use of economic instruments for formulating and implementing credit policy. The Czechoslovak State Bank not only tried to enhance the importance of monetary assets, it was also the first CMEA bank to introduce bank bonds (37), which were intended to circulate among the enterprises and serve as mortgage for bank credits. The prohibition on credit relations between enterprises was also lifted, as was later done in Hungary as well.

These plans remained unrealized, however; the reforms never got beyond their embryonic stages. Only a few measures were able to achieve a lasting effect. For instance, the bank interest rate did continue to perform the important function of a steering instrument for planning that had been established by the reform. For working assets, the enterprises are permitted to obtain long-term as well as short-term credits if they do not have enough of their own funds to meet their current needs. These credits are repaid from future profits. Relationships between bank and enterprise are regulated by credit agreements.

In the last two years, credit policy has pursued predominantly anti-inflationary goals. Credits are once again being limited or granted on the basis of control indices just as before the economic reform. The growth in credit has been pegged at an annual average of no more than 9.5 billion koruny in the five-year period from 1971 to 1975, as opposed to 14.5 billion koruny in the last five-year period, while credit should comprise about the same share — 39 percent — of the total resources for financing working assets for the years 1971 to 1975.

This restrictive credit policy is intended to influence inventory stocks. In the next five-year period, inventory should grow by only 43 billion koruny, as opposed to 61 billion koruny in the five-year period from 1966 to 1970. At the same time, a three-day acceleration in the turnover cycle of working assets is targeted (it had slowed by four days over the last decade). (38) Enterprises that increase their productivity receive more favorable credit terms, while credit terms have been made more unfavorable for inefficient enterprises. Credit interest rates are reduced by 50 percent if an enterprise achieves its planned indices and are raised if an enterprise is operating inefficiently.

The method by which credit is granted also depends on enterprise performance. Efficiently operating enterprises receive unlimited credits in a current account, while those which operate inefficiently receive credits in a special account under rigid supervision. In 1970, credits in current accounts comprised 45.6 percent of the total credit volume. (39) The higher-ranking industrial associations decide on the lending procedure in agreement with the financing bank.

5.5. Stepped-Up Control by Means of Short-Term Credit Arrangements

Especially in Poland, but also in Bulgaria and Romania and, to a certain extent, the Soviet Union, credits have been broadened in scope to allow better control over the enterprises. Aside from this common feature, however, credit policy varies quite considerably among these countries.

A unique credit policy was developed in Poland in accordance with the economic reform. In 1957 and 1958, many changes were introduced into the financing and credit system that were later adopted by other CMEA countries. First, the cumbersome and inefficient method of allocating working assets on the basis of norms for specific inventories set at higher administrative levels was abolished. Further, the practice of settling deficits and surpluses in circulating funds with the state budget was abandoned. The enterprises were permitted to set a figure for the volume of their own funds and to represent themselves in negotiations with their bank. They put their profits into a development fund from which planned growth in working assets and the investments of the enterprise were financed.

Later, the itemized allocation of credits for specific stocks was abolished, and the number of different types of credit was reduced from sixteen to five. In addition, the differentiated interest rates were scaled to the efficiency of the enterprise to a greater degree than formerly. The Polish National Bank introduced the first notable improvement in the traditional credit procedure by booking credits in current accounts.

Since 1958, however, the credit policy in Poland has made but little progress. The reforms were not enough to insure that credits would be granted according to economic criteria. Credits were merely broadened to step up control over enterprises. The enterprises must cover 40 percent of the working assets with credits; 60 percent of the planned stocks and all unplanned stocks must be financed from the enterprises' own funds.

As a result of these measures, the share of credits in the total working assets of Polish industry was increased from 31.9 percent in 1961 to 48.9 percent in 1967. This is a much greater proportion than that in Hungary or Czechoslovakia. (40)

As mentioned above, in 1970 the financing of working and fixed capital was placed in the hands of the banks. At the same time, two sources of financing were created from the hitherto single enterprise development fund. One was to finance working assets; the other, the enterprise's capital expenditures. A paradoxical situation thus arose: The new bank structure covered both investment financing and financing of working assets, while at the enterprise level the two sources of financing were separate. (41)

In the Soviet Union, Bulgaria, and Romania, the former credit policy was also substantially revised. Improved flexibility in the allocation of working assets relieved the banks of many supervisory functions. The norms for the allocation of an enterprise's own funds are now set by the enterprises themselves, instead of at higher levels, as was formerly the case. In Bulgaria, an enterprise need only inform its parent industrial association of the norms it has set. In Romania, the industrial associations set only the volume of total working assets, while determination of their specific composition in terms of raw materials, semifinished and finished goods, etc., is left to the enterprises. In the Soviet Union, the enterprises decide on both the volume and the composition of their working assets. If one may judge from a statement by N. Barkowski, former Member of the Board of the State Bank, however, these measures apparently have not been effective: "Enterprise norms are revised for the purpose of receiving a higher credit, which is granted much too liberally. The equilibrium of the financial plans is thereby imperiled." (42)

The new policy has improved relationships between enterprise and bank, and the volume of limited credit has become smaller. Various branches of the economy still continue to follow their own special guidelines, although these remain of minor importance. Deliveries are usually paid for directly out of special credit accounts, which are maintained by the foodstuffs industry, purchasing agencies for agricultural products, trade agencies, and, more and more frequently, by heavy industry. Heavy industry and all nonseasonal sectors of industry in the Soviet Union and Bulgaria received so-called turnover credits which are used to cover the most important operating costs. These turnover credits are granted by the financing bank, and constitute 40 to 50 percent of the total working assets in the Soviet Union and 30 percent in Bulgaria.

In all these countries, interest is beginning to play an increasingly greater role as an instrument of credit policy. Within the past few years, the average interest rate has been increased from an original 2 percent in all nations to 6 percent in the

Soviet Union, 5 percent in Bulgaria, and 4 percent in Romania.

* * *

This modest presentation has attempted to show that the economic reforms made in the monetary and credit systems of Eastern Europe since the mid-fifties exhibit certain specific characteristics unique to the various countries as well as general features common to all; these specific characteristics are attributable to differences in the respective levels of development as well as to the historical peculiarities of the different countries.

The banking system has become much more differentiated. In the German Democratic Republic and Bulgaria, the attempt was made to create a banking system similar to those in the West. In the German Democratic Republic, the omnipresent State Bank no longer extends credits directly or engages in clearing operations; these functions are now carried out by the newly founded commercial banks.

In the other CMEA countries, with the exception of the Soviet Union, Romania, and Hungary, all enterprise financing, including the financing of investments, was placed in the hands of one bank, the State Bank, and direct financing of investments through the state budget has been almost universally abandoned. In Hungary, the German Democratic Republic, and Bulgaria, credits and the enterprises' own funds became the major sources of investment financing. In these countries, the enterprises and the industrial associations decide on the scope and composition of their investments.

In some countries, the economic reforms placed a wider array of economic weapons at the disposal of the banks. The interest rate has again become respectable in Eastern Europe. Credit policy has become more sophisticated. Hungary, the German Democratic Republic, and, to a certain extent, Czechoslovakia have restricted credit and are now emphasizing profit maximization for the enterprises. Other countries, such as the Soviet Union and Poland, are attempting to exert better control over enterprise activity by forcing credit.

Relatively broad changes have also been made in money circulation. In Hungary and Poland, the amount of issue is no longer regarded as a binding directive. Efforts are made to influence money circulation through economic intervention. The banks' powers of disposal over the monetary assets of the enterprises has been curtailed.

The Eastern European monetary and credit system has been stimulated through greater diversification, and the end of this process is not yet in sight.

Appendix

Table 1

Items in the Operative Cash Plan of the Polish National Bank

I. Cash income
  Retail sales receipts
  Receipts from:
    Services
    Transportation
    Recreational institutions
    Other economic units
  Taxes, insurance payments, and other fees
  Other receipts
  Inpayments
    To postal accounts
    To accounts of social organizations
    To current accounts of private industry and private households
    To accounts of agricultural collectives
    To savings accounts
  Increase in money circulation (balance)

II. Cash outlays
  Wages
  Pensions, grants in aid, and payment for damages
  Purchase of agricultural goods
  Expenses for official travel
  Outlays for services
  Purchase of goods and materials
  Payments
    To the post
    From accounts of social organizations
    From current accounts of private industry and households
    From savings accounts
  Decrease in money circulation (net balance)

Source: Z. Fedorowicz, Finanse w gospodarce socjalistyczej, Warsaw, 1970, p. 613.

Table 2

Long-Term and Short-Term Credits in Bulgaria
(at year-end; in million leva)

	1960	1965	1970
Total	2,088.8	3,573.5	8,247.7
Long-term credits	451.1	859.9	3,305.7
For the public economy	322.9	540.1	2,718.6
For private households	128.2	319.8	587.1
Short-term credits	1,637.7	2,713.6	4,942.0
For the public economy	1,637.5	2,690.8	4,857.0
For private households	0.2	22.8	85.0

Source: Statistical Yearbook of the People's Republic of Bulgaria, 1971, p. 228.

Table 3

Short-Term Credits by Branch of Industry in Bulgaria
(at year-end; in million leva)

	1960	1965	1970
Total	1,637.5	2,690.9	4,857.0
Including:			
Industry	610.8	1,017.6	1,676.7
Agriculture	143.5	86.4	444.1
Construction	24.9	267.1	705.4
Domestic trade	854.2	1,312.8	2,006.3

Source: Statistical Yearbook of the People's Republic of Bulgaria, 1971, p. 229.

Table 4

Circulating Funds and Financing Sources of Enterprises in Poland (at year-end; in million zlotys)

	1961	1965	1970
Total assets	406,057	567,488	924,179
Including:			
Inventories	232,697	329,803	195,073
Claims on customers	86,006	117,885	195,289
Clearing accounts	7,763	4,152	8,355
Total liabilities	406,057	567,488	924,179
Including:			
Own funds	111,677	142,205	233,021
Bank credits	134,717	211,534	343,884
Obligations	43,008	56,496	88,115

Source: Rocznik statystyczny, 1971, p. 616.

Table 5

Credits of the State Bank by Industrial Branch in Czechoslovakia (at year-end; in million koruny)

	1960	1965	1970
Total	41,145	56,794	117,111
Including:			
Industry	21,151	32,928	70,720
Construction	2,838	3,437	4,100
Agriculture	3,112	5,186	5,936
Purchasing agencies for agricultural goods	1,784	2,646	6,322
Domestic and foreign trade	11,919	11,696	22,287
Other	341	901	7,746

Source: Statisticka ročenka ČSSR, 1971, p. 197.

Table 6

Financing Sources for Working Capital in the National Economy of Czechoslovakia (at year-end; in percent)

	1960	1965	1970
Resources	100.0	100.0	100.0
Including:			
Own funds	71.8	59.9	23.8
Bank credits	24.6	35.8	38.1
Other	3.6	4.3	38.1

Source: Statisticka ročenka ČSSR, 1971, p. 197.

Table 7

Working Capital and Financing Sources in the National Economy of the USSR (at year-end; in percent)

	1960	1965	1970
Total working capital	100.0	100.0	100.0
Including:			
Inventories	77.2	78.5	77.2
Money	6.2	6.5	7.8
Claims on customers	9.2	7.8	7.2
Other	7.4	7.2	7.8
Total financing sources	100.0	100.0	100.0
Including:			
Own funds and permanent liabilities	38.8	38.3	34.1
Bank credits	44.3	47.1	45.9
Creditors	14.0	11.5	13.3
Other	2.9	3.1	6.7

Source: Narodnoe khoziaistvo SSSR, 1970, p. 709.

Table 8

Working Capital and Financing Sources of Industry
in the USSR (at year-end; in percent)

	1960	1965	1970
Total working capital	100.0	100.0	100.0
Inventories	80.4	82.5	80.2
Money	4.8	4.0	6.6
Claims on customers	11.2	9.9	8.5
Other	3.6	3.6	4.7
Total financing sources	100.0	100.0	100.0
Own funds and permanent liabilities	47.7	45.7	38.9
Bank credits	39.2	42.6	43.6
Creditors	10.6	8.6	9.0
Other	2.5	3.1	8.5

Source: Narodnoe khoziaistvo SSSR, 1970, p. 709.

Table 9

Working Capital of Enterprises by Branch of Industry
in the USSR (at year-end; in millions of rubles)

	1960	1965	1970
Total	91,966	137,168	212,356
Including:			
Industry	36,088	53,653	79,683
Agriculture	6,495	11,859	21,341
Transportation and post	2,538	3,238	5,373
Construction	5,889	9,207	19,285
Purchasing agencies for agricultural goods	4,663	7,153	10,505
Trade	25,732	37,261	50,097

Source: Narodnoe khoziaistvo SSSR, 1970, p. 709.

Notes

1) W. Brus, "Money in a Socialist Economy," Ekonomista, 1963, No. 5, p. 913.
2) Money and Plan, University of California Press, 1968, p. 5.
3) George Garvy, Money, Banking and Credit in Eastern Europe, Federal Reserve Bank of New York, 1966, p. 16.
4) Gesetzblatt der Deutschen Demokratischen Republik, December 22, 1971; January 26, 1972, p. 47.
5) L. Siemiatkowski, "Reform of the Banking System," Gospodarka planowa, 1969, No. 1, p. 8. See W. Jaworski, Banki i kredyt v krajach socjalistycznych [Banking and Credit in Socialist Countries], Warsaw, 1971, p. 62.
6) In Czechoslovakia, the institution that bears the name of Investment Bank is engaged in the administration of foreign and domestic securities.
7) The branches recently established by the large Western banks in the Soviet Union are unable to integrate with the Soviet banking system because of the nonconvertibility of the ruble.
8) M. Kucharski and W. Pruss, Pieniądz i kredyt w socjalizmie [Money and Credit Under Socialism], Warsaw, 1971, p. 134.
9) Dziennik ustaw PRL, 1958, No. 44, Position 215.
10) Gesetzblatt der DDR, 1964, Vol. II, No. 99.
11) Ibid., 1968, Vol. II, No. 64.
12) The circulation of notes and coin is defined identically in a planned economy and in a market economy. This concept refers to the total amount of cash money existing among the general population and in the cash reserves of the enterprises and various economic organizations, with the exception of the cash holdings of the bank of issue.
13) See Bank i kredyt, 1971, No. 2, pp. 51-54.
14) See Den'gi i kredit, 1971, No. 3, p. 48.
15) See Finanse, 1970, No. 2, pp. 51-53, and Bank i kredyt, 1971, No. 5, pp. 205-206.
16) See Kucharski and Pruss, op. cit., pp. 359-360.
17) Statisticheskii ezhegodnik stran-chlenov SEV [Statistical

Yearbook of the Member Nations of the CMEA], 1971, p. 53.

18) Planovoe khoziaistvo, 1971, No. 2, p. 27.

19) In Czechoslovakia, the distribution of profits instituted by the economic reform as a part of the net national income was abolished on January 1, 1972. Fifty to 75 percent of enterprise profits are now transferred to the state budget (see Finance a úvěr, 1972, No. 1, p. 23).

20) See Den'gi i kredit, 1971, No. 10, p. 86.

21) The results of the new investment policy were unsatisfactory according to the report of Prime Minister Jenö Fock. During the years 1970-1971, investments increased twice as fast as the national income. The same rate of growth was planned. Investment costs were 13 percent higher in 1971 than in 1970. The fact that 80 percent of the annual investments remained incomplete was a cause for concern. (Handel zagraniczny, 1972, No. 4, p. 147.)

22) See Voprosy ekonomiki, 1972, No. 3, p. 125.

23) See Gesetzblatt der DDR, January 28, 1972, p. 43.

24) Den'gi i kredit, 1970, No. 9, p. 78.

25) Finanse, 1971, No. 2, p. 40.

26) Bank i kredyt, 1971, No. 5, p. 174.

27) From 1965 to 1970, the State Bank increased its credits for the expansion of consumer goods production from 685 billion rubles to 861 billion rubles; and for technological renovation and modernization, from 681 million rubles to 1,900 million rubles. (The total value of investment projects in the Soviet Union in 1970 was 82.0 billion rubles; of this, 29.7 billion rubles represented investments in industry.) (Narodnoe khoziaistvo SSSR, 1970, pp. 483 and 736.)

28) See Den'gi i kredit, 1970, No. 2, p. 42.

29) See Finance a úvěr, 1972, No. 2, p. 77.

30) Economic Bulletin of the National Bank of Hungary, May 1969, p. 15.

31) "Monetary and Credit Policy in Hungary," in Grossman, op. cit., p. 78.

32) Economic Bulletin of the National Bank of Hungary, May 1969, p. 16.

33) Gesetzblatt der DDR, January 28, 1972, p. 41.

34) See Finanse, 1971, No. 11, p. 106.
35) Gesetzblatt der DDR, January 28, 1972, p. 41.
36) Ibid.
37) One alternative was supposed to be bank bonds for enterprises that had free funds available but could not invest them favorably. The president of the State Bank, S. Potač, noted in a lecture in Vienna (June 7, 1972) that these bonds have not caught on in either the enterprises or private households.
38) According to the report of the president of the State Bank, S. Potač. See Finance a úvěr, 1972, No. 2, p. 76.
39) Statisticka ročenka ČSSR [Statistical Yearbook of Czechoslovakia], 1971, p. 197.
40) See Kucharski and Pruss, op. cit., p. 245.
41) See ibid., p. 272.
42) See Den'gi i kredit, 1970, No. 2, p. 36.

2 Currency in the foreign trade of the CMEA countries

1. Foreign Trade in a Planned Economy

1.1. The Autarkic Foreign Trade Model

In the Soviet model of a planned economy, essentially the sole function of foreign trade was to fill in the gaps in supplies on the domestic front. The primary task of exports was to procure the foreign exchange necessary to pay for critical imports. Indeed, this concept, which tended toward autarky, seemed more or less justified if one considers that the Soviet Union was spread out over a vast area, possessed enormous manpower reserves, had access to all the raw materials, energy sources, and agricultural products necessary for the development of a highly diversified economy, and, on top of all this, not only felt itself threatened from without by the surrounding capitalist countries but was at the same time convinced that capitalism and capitalist society would perish in the foreseeable future as a result of their own internal contradictions. Furthermore, this belief was reinforced by the disastrous worldwide economic crisis and the dismal currency situation in the period between the world wars.

At no time in its history has the Soviet Union been able to afford to neglect foreign trade. It has, however, succeeded to a high degree in becoming autarkic. By 1939, the foreign trade of the Soviet Union had shrunk in volume to 12 percent of its 1913 level. (1) Soviet foreign trade comprised barely 4 percent of the national product in 1972, although the Soviet Union had considerably expanded its trade with the other CMEA countries. For many years after World War II, the victorious Soviet Union held fast to its original concept of foreign trade. Yet, at the same time, it was able to develop its intellectual and material resources, construct a diversified modern economy, rise to the position of the second greatest economic power in the world, and become one of the two military superpowers of our time. Thus, viewed in the total perspective, the Soviet Union, with its special brand of socialist planned economy, can boast of some outstanding achievements, at least up to now. It is understandable, therefore, that the USSR is inclined to cling to its time-tested economic system, even though the Soviet planned economy must become increasingly less suited to meet the manifold needs and requirements of a highly developed industrial world society that is dissolving all national boundaries and tending toward worldwide cooperation. It is equally understandable that the Soviet Union should tend to proceed cautiously in instituting urgent economic reforms, to tailor these reforms as much as possible to the specific features of the Soviet economy, and, in so doing, to take no steps that would jeopardize its sphere of influence.

The people's democracies of central and southeastern Europe, on the other hand, which fell under the sway of the Soviet Union after World War II, found themselves in a totally different situation from that of the Soviet Union. (2) Their natural circumstances and level of technological development favored their integration into the world market, which offered broad opportunities for development even to the smaller nations, provided specialization was fittingly administered and comparative cost advantages were utilized properly. Such a course, however, was barred for reasons that need no elaboration. Some of the people's democracies that had intended to participate in the Marshall Plan and to join the Organization for European Economic Cooperation (OEEC) in Paris in 1948 withdrew their applications; ultimately, all the central and southeastern European people's democracies adopted the Soviet concept of foreign trade in keeping with the principles of a socialist planned economy.

1.2. Production Aspects

In a highly centralized planned economy, imports are not expected to compete with or stimulate domestic output; their sole function is the provision of critical items which are produced domestically either in insufficient quantities or not at all. The principle is to replace imports wherever possible by domestic products, often without regard for cost. Exports are not viewed as a sector of the economy with its own justification, but are conceived basically as a means through which absolutely necessary imports may be obtained. For many reasons, including the West's embargo against the East, the main emphasis in foreign trade in the Eastern bloc shifted to intrabloc trade, which now comprises about two-thirds of the total trade of the CMEA countries. This geographical about-face, which was not made without considerable effort, is reflected in the figures given in the table opposite.

Intra-CMEA trade and East-West trade have evolved different commodity structures. In the former, the Soviet Union is the principal supplier of raw materials, fuels, and semifinished products to the people's democracies. The latter, in turn, supply the Soviet Union with finished products, mainly machines and equipment. The West supplies the USSR with sophisticated products such as modern machines as well as know-how which promote technological progress; in return, Western countries receive mainly raw materials, fuels, and agricultural products. Despite growing foreign trade relations, the Eastern bloc has so far been unable to develop into a unified, integral economic area, since some important prerequisites for such a development are lacking. For example, supranational economic planning does not exist, nor are there any competent supranational agencies that could formulate and put through a common economic policy. The prices current in intrabloc trade have no real basis, and since none of the national currencies are convertible, multilateral trade relations remain impossible. The long-term economic plans of the individual CMEA countries are only very imperfectly coordinated: each country works out its own credit, monetary, and price policies. Trade relations

Foreign Trade Relations of the Eastern European
CMEA Countries (in percent)

	USSR	CMEA countries (total)	Other
Bulgaria			
1937	1.0	9.0	90.0
1970	53.0	74.4	25.6
Czechoslovakia			
1937	1.0	10.0	89.0
1970	32.7	64.0	36.0
GDR			
1937	—	17.0	83.0
1970	39.0	67.3	32.7
Hungary			
1937	—	13.0	87.0
1970	34.0	62.1	37.9
Poland			
1937	1.0	6.0	93.0
1970	37.0	63.1	36.9
Romania			
1937	1.0	17.0	82.0
1970	27.0	49.3	50.7
USSR			
1937	—	11.0	89.0
1970	—	55.6	44.4

Source: Międzynarodnowe stosunki ekonomiczne, Warsaw, 1964, p. 74; Statisticheskii ezhegodnik stran-chlenov SEV, 1971, p. 342; and the statistical yearbooks of the various countries.

and economic cooperation among the member nations are based primarily on bilateral agreements (on prices, settlement procedures, credits, etc.). Furthermore, the "Comprehensive Program for the Further Intensification and Improvement of Collaboration and the Development of Socialist Economic Integration of CMEA Member Nations," ratified at the Twenty-Fifth Session of the Council of the CMEA held in July 1971 in Bucharest, basically did nothing to change this situation.

A unique feature of foreign trade in the Soviet planned economy is the complete separation of production and trade. The enterprises manufacture goods for export under the same conditions as for domestic consumption. They have no need to gear their production to the exigencies of international competition and the struggle for markets. (3)

As a result of the economic reforms, however, this fundamental separation between production and trade has now been abandoned in some people's democracies that are especially dependent on foreign trade. Major enterprises have been given the right to engage in foreign trade transactions and conclude agreements.

1.3. Monetary Aspects

In a planned economy, monetary relations are generally considered subordinate to the quantitative input-output indicators. However, as capital-extensive* factors of economic growth are gradually depleted, the efficiency of the economy begins to play a more important role and economic relationships become more complex; money begins to serve as an economic steering instrument, and, in so doing, once again assumes a function that goes far beyond the mere aggregation of economic values and the distribution of the social product.

But while money is again resuming a part of its market function in the domestic economy, foreign trade continues to be

---

*"Extensive" refers to the excessive increase in low-productivity labor input from the countryside and an excessive rate of investment.

pursued without its own monetary medium. A planned economy obviously could not place its money on the world market as a commodity or adjust its exchange rate to fluctuations on the international monetary market; nor could it continually attune the domestic economy to the needs of foreign trade. In the traditional model of a planned economy, money is not convertible. This, of course, also rules out the possibility of a functioning money and credit market, either in internal CMEA trade or in trade with the Western market economies.

Since in the socialist countries money functions only within the domestic economy, these nations were unable to develop a multilateral foreign trade and were consequently committed to bilateral clearing from the very outset. This clearing procedure, which in a market economy is regarded as an emergency solution when currencies become unconvertible, was even given theoretical justification and praised as a unique virtue of a planned economy. (4) Nevertheless, even in the planned economies, bilateral trade remained unable to overcome "the clumsiness, inconvenience, and inefficiency that barter entails." (5)

Attempts were made to change this unsatisfactory situation by developing a multilateral clearing system in CMEA trade and by settling transactions with the market economies through foreign exchange. But while this modification did much to facilitate the technical aspects of business transactions, it did almost nothing to alter the bilateral character of foreign trade.

1.4. The Comparative Advantages and Practical Implementation of Foreign Trade in a Planned Economy

In a market economy, the nation's industries assess the world market because they expect advantages from the international division of labor. Various theories of foreign trade have attempted to justify this expectation, but the most convincing is the classical theory of comparative costs. This theory has been modified over time, becoming broader in scope and more sophisticated. B. Ohlin, co-author of the modern theory of foreign trade (the Heckscher-Ohlin or Heckscher-Ohlin-Samuelson model), represents the view that "the classical theory of international trade is still the most universally recognized. No one will dispute this statement, since no other theory in fact exists." (6)

Official Soviet economic theory at one time rejected the classical theory of comparative costs. Recently, however, noted economists both in the Soviet Union and in some of the people's democracies have acknowledged the usefulness of the rational core of this theory. (7) But a socialist economy has no parameters that are authoritative enough to permit a comparison of the national costs structure with the terms of trade on the world market, nor does it have at its disposal the economic instruments that would permit the adjustment of internal value relations to the international standards.

The Marxist theory of value is equally unable to deal adequately with the extremely complicated mechanisms of price formation on today's world market. (8)

The average, socially necessary expenditure of labor is no longer a useful concept in dealing with the highly diversified commodity structure of world trade today. The CMEA countries are not even able to set prices for intra-CMEA trade that would accurately reflect their respective internal production conditions. They, too, must refer to world market prices, which are themselves distorted by monopolistic influences and the division of the world into highly developed industrial nations and developing countries.

The implementation of this conception of foreign trade and its monetary relations in the socialist planned economies is in the hands of a powerful state currency and foreign trade monopoly. How this monopoly operates will be the subject of the next section.

2. The Foreign Trade and Currency Monopoly

2.1. The Concept and Basic Principles

The foreign trade and currency monopoly is exercised by institutions attached to the Ministry of Foreign Trade. These are among the oldest and most tradition-bound of the institutions of the planned economy. In the Soviet Union, foreign trade and foreign exchange transactions were declared a state monopoly quite early, on April 22, 1918, a measure frequently referred to as "nationalization" or "converting into state property" — and not only in the Western literature. In the socialist system, however, foreign trade and foreign exchange came to function quite differently from the other sectors of the economy, especially industry. Production enterprises were made state property, yet within certain limits they were still able to maintain their own interests. Enterprises were obliged to set up a system of cost accounting which enabled them to assess their own efficiency. Accordingly, prices, profit, money, and credit have retained a certain role at the enterprise level — a role, it might be added, that has been growing in recent years. Foreign trade transactions, on the other hand, were removed completely from the jurisdiction of the enterprises. Foreign trade was also nationalized, but it was not considered an organic part of overall enterprise activity. In the traditional model, the enterprises are permitted to sell or purchase export or import goods only through the foreign trade organizations, not directly. Only the latter, in their capacity as central state agencies, cultivate and maintain direct contacts with foreign countries in their own name and on their own responsibility. Hence, the state monopoly means not only that the foreign trade flows are steered by the state, but also that business is transacted through state foreign trade organizations.

In the more recent Soviet literature, this organizational concept is portrayed as a kind of division of labor between production and sales, and is adduced as a proof that the socialist economic system is superior to a market economy. Thus, the Soviet expert V. Pekshev observed: "The present organization of Soviet foreign trade incorporates the progressive trend, typical of large-scale commodity production, toward a separation of the sales apparatus from the production apparatus, with all the advantages and benefits that that entails." This tendency, Pekshev stresses, "is also discernible in the capitalist world, but only socialism is able to utilize to the fullest extent the advantages that this objective process offers." (9) The organizational form of Soviet foreign trade is designed structurally to exclude foreign trade from the enterprises' sphere of influence. Foreign trade is under the direct control of the central economic authorities.

This arrangement flows directly from the basic tenets of foreign trade monopoly set forth by the October (1925) Plenum of the Central Committee of the Communist Party of the Soviet Union and still in force today. These declare that the state itself "shall conduct foreign trade through an agency created specifically for that purpose, the People's Commissariat [Ministry] for Foreign Trade." This agency shall stipulate "which organizations in which branches of industry shall engage directly in foreign trade and to what extent they shall do so" and shall specify "the kinds and quantities of goods that may be exported or imported. The People's Commissariat for Foreign Trade manages exports and imports directly through a licensing and quota system." (10)

The organizations encharged with foreign trade are subordinate to the Ministry of Foreign Trade. In the summer of 1968, there were forty-five foreign trade organizations in the Soviet Union dealing in goods and four dealing in services. (11) The activities of most are confined to transactions involving a specific group of goods. Along with the organizations under the Ministry of Foreign Trade, the State Committee for Foreign Trade Relations also transacts business abroad, with primary emphasis placed on the delivery of entire plants to newly established enterprises in socialist countries and developing nations. One of the most important agencies in the system of foreign trade organizations is the trade mission, which is active in all socialist and almost all capitalist countries. Although the trade missions usually constitute a part of the diplomatic corps, they are subordinate to the Ministry of Foreign Trade.

Regardless of the form in which a given foreign trade transaction is carried out, the state itself is always the legal partner in trade. The December 16, 1947, decree of the Presidium of the Supreme Soviet of the USSR gave the Ministry of Foreign Trade exclusive authority to cultivate and maintain contacts with foreign representatives on matters bearing on trade relations. The same decree empowered the Ministry to set down for those economic organizations authorized to operate independently on the foreign market, a system of formal guidelines for establishing contact with the trade representatives or trade attachés of foreign diplomatic missions within the Soviet Union. (12)

The foreign trade system described above has remained unchanged in the Soviet Union, but it has been reformed in some people's democracies. Section 6 will take up this question in more detail.

2.2. The Currency Monopoly as an Inherent Feature of Planned Economies

The foreign exchange and settlement system corresponds to the foreign trade concept peculiar to the planned economies. In the commerce of the Eastern countries, in which the producer of export goods and the consumer of import goods do not themselves participate in foreign trade operations, the national unit of currency is also cut off from the international monetary system.

The domestic markets of planned economies, on which money has only limited functions and the enterprises engage in no foreign business, cannot be integrated into the world market in the traditional manner.

The currency monopoly of a socialist state may be likened to a certain extent to total control over foreign exchange, as is sometimes practiced in market economies. But the Polish economist Kamecki underscores the differences between foreign exchange policy in the Eastern countries and the restrictive practices of a capitalist economy. (13) The latter ordinarily stem from balance of payments difficulties and are conceived essentially as temporary. In contrast, the monopoly on foreign exchange in the socialist economies is implied by the very nature of the economic system.

2.3. Control of Foreign Exchange (14)

In the Soviet Union and the other socialist countries, only the state may possess and dispose over foreign exchange. Organizations engaged in foreign trade operations are required to sell all their foreign exchange receipts from exports to the foreign trade bank for domestic currency.

Import of foreign exchange and precious metals (gold, silver, platinum, etc.) and remittances in foreign currency from abroad are permitted. The export of foreign exchange by Soviet citizens and foreigners, on the other hand, must be approved by the Ministry of Finance. Foreign currency held in special accounts or registered with Soviet customs authorities when it is brought into the country is an exception to this rule. No more than two months may elapse between the import and the use of such currency, however.

The import and export of Soviet currency is also regulated. Soviet citizens traveling abroad are permitted to take with them only 30 rubles per person, which, however, they may not spend abroad. A partial exception is the CMEA countries, where a Soviet citizen may convert 10 rubles into the national currency of the respective country. (15) Only citizens of the socialist countries may import Soviet currency into the Soviet Union. They purchase from their national banks rubles which the latter have procured from the Foreign Trade Bank of the Soviet Union.

Apart from the motivations behind its adoption, the above-described system differs from restrictive policies of market economies only in the degree of control exercised. The restrictions imposed on monetary functions by the foreign exchange monopoly create problems in settlement and credit relations with other countries.

2.4. The Clearing System

The nonconvertible currencies of the planned economies cannot be traded on the Western market; they can serve neither as a standard of value nor as a means of payment in international trade. Payments between the Soviet Union and the capitalist countries are made in foreign currencies rather than in rubles under the terms of the foreign exchange monopoly. (An exception is Finland, which uses the clearing ruble to settle its accounts with the Soviet Union.)

The various national currencies are not used as a means of payment in transactions among socialist countries. The so-called clearing ruble, which had served as the medium for commodity exchange among the socialist countries before the founding of the International Bank for Economic Cooperation (IBEC), now functions solely as an accounting unit for trade between the CMEA countries and the other socialist countries.

Trade within the CMEA is cleared with the transferable ruble. The clearing ruble and the transferable ruble have the same parity as the Soviet ruble. But neither of these accounting units reflects the true prices of goods based on internal value relations; they merely translate the prices on the world market into rubles.

Because of the foreign exchange monopoly, trade among the planned economies can be settled only on a clearing basis, so that despite the many efforts to introduce multilateral payments, trade ultimately remains bilateral. The general principle — namely, that there can be no multilateral relations without currency convertibility — maintains its full force in the Eastern bloc as well. The socialist countries must use the currency of the foreign party in their dealings with the West.

The convertible currency reserves of the planned economies are kept in foreign banks. The money of the planned economies can neither serve as nor be converted into a reserve currency. As a result of the exclusion of the national currencies from the international monetary system, the Eastern bloc is to a large extent cut off from the Western market.

2.5. Credit Relations with Foreign Countries

The present currency monopoly of the planned economies is especially restrictive in the area of credit relations. The domestic currency, which cannot even be used as a means of payment in dealings with foreign countries, is even less fit as an instrument for international credit relations. The East German professor Karl-Heinz Domdey has described this situation as follows: "Currency relations are otherwise ordinarily tied to real movements of goods and services. Short-term and middle-term credits as well as long-term government credits are usually transferred in the form of goods." (16) Credits tied to goods deliveries also occur in credit relations among the Western countries, but this relationship is not the necessary consequence of the economic and currency system; moreover, it affects only a portion of the credits granted.

The underdeveloped banking system and the lack of a monetary and capital market in the CMEA countries prevent the development of a credit demand comparable with that in the West. In intra-CMEA trade, credits have a purely technical function of bridging gaps in payments; investment credits granted by one CMEA country to another or extended to the developing countries are generally tied to deliveries. The CMEA countries are obtaining an increasing volume of credits from the Western industrial nations, which they repay punctually; but they are unable to extend credit to the latter in return.

The currency monopoly creates obstacles not only for credit relations between East and West but also for the flow of credits within the CMEA itself. The credit system instituted by IBEC permitted the financing only of temporary deficits in the balance of payments. Even after the founding of the International Investment Bank (IIB), investment credits continued, as before, to be granted either in transferable rubles — that is, ultimately in commodity form — or in convertible currencies, and then only within a very limited scope.

3. Domestic Currency and Its Standards of Value

The different forms of ownership over the means of production and the restricted function of foreign trade in the planned economies would not be sufficient in themselves to sever the CMEA market from the world market. The separation is above all the result of the isolation of the monetary system, and hence the standards of value, of the CMEA area from those of the rest of the world.

Of course, even in the Western countries price levels and

price structure are not determined exclusively by the world market. Many goods and services are not traded at all on an international basis; moreover, the foreign trade relations that have developed among the Western countries vary widely in extent. There are also other factors peculiar to each country that influence price formation, such as resources in raw materials, social structure, the tax system, etc. Still, the Western nations that are more or less vitally dependent on foreign trade cannot protect themselves over the long term from international price fluctuations. In the short term, world market price fluctuations affect only the profits of firms that are especially vulnerable to international competition. Over the middle term, however, these fluctuations have repercussions throughout the entire economy, since the affected sectors react with changes in production, investments, and wages; under certain circumstances, adjustments in the exchange rates may even occur.

The exclusion of the currencies of the planned economies from the international monetary system is an inherent, and not just a temporary, feature of the socialist system. Of course, it also has its advantages. For example, the currencies are not subject to the chronic fluctuations in exchange rates on the international monetary markets. The balance of payments situation of the CMEA countries does not force changes in parity; no outside pressure can be exerted. When the exchange rates fluctuate on the world market, however, the Eastern countries adjust the exchange rates of their currencies to maintain a parity with gold. Nevertheless, such an adjustment — as was made, for example, in connection with the worldwide currency realignment of December 1971 — has no immediate influence on trading within the CMEA, although it does affect tourist trade, in which the national and foreign currencies come into contact with one another, foreign exchange reserves, and credits obtained from the West. (17) Although the planned economies are indeed able to avoid some of the negative influences of the world market, in exchange they must forego some of its positive effects as well. Domestically, the enterprises are shielded from the vicissitudes of the world market by the foreign trade organizations, the results of whose transactions are accounted for in the state budget.

No intrinsic connection exists between price relations in planned economies and world market price relations such as might be expected to ensue from the interplay of prices with exchange rates. In planned economies, price formation takes place according to different rules from those in force in market economies. In planned economies, prices are set in accordance with state cost accounting and are based on production costs. Other factors influencing price formation are the profit rates and turnover tax set by the central authorities (the turnover tax is levied primarily on consumer goods). Unequal production conditions in industry are balanced out by varying the profit rate. Since all enterprises are owned by the state, it is possible to keep prices for producer goods at relatively low levels and prices for consumer goods at high levels by making appropriate adjustments in the profit rates and turnover taxes for the two. In some CMEA countries, the profit rate is high for the manufacture of producer goods, while consumer goods production has a high turnover tax. The net effect, then, is an accelerated growth of heavy industry at the expense of the consumer goods industry.

The table on the opposite page shows the various factors involved in price formation in the principal sectors of industry in the Soviet Union.

Since in most CMEA countries consumer goods prices are relatively higher than those for production goods, a special exchange rate has been set for the tourist trade (see section 4).

Autonomous price formation, shielded from the world market, has the advantage that economic plans can be fulfilled under conditions of relative price stability. However, a disadvantage is that changes in supply and demand are not reflected in price fluctuations.

The economic reforms in the CMEA countries have introduced certain modifications into the basic principles of price formation. As an experiment, the "cost model" was tentatively replaced by a "capital model" in which profit appears as a function of invested capital. Payments to the state budget, which comprise 5 to 6 percent of the enterprise funds, are now an

Structure of Wholesale Prices in Soviet Industry
(in percent)

	1965			1970		
	All industry	Heavy industry	Light industry and food industry	All industry	Heavy industry	Light industry and food industry
Wholesale prices of industry Including:	100.0	100.0	100.0	100.0	100.0	100.0
a) Production costs of industry and costs of sales enterprises	74.7	81.3	67.6	73.0	77.0	68.0
b) Profits of industry and sales enterprises	9.4	11.6	7.1	14.2	18.1	9.3
c) Turnover taxes	15.9	7.1	25.3	12.8	4.9	22.7

Source: Narodnoe khoziaistvo SSSR v 1970 godu, p. 178.

important component of prices. These payments are intended to aid in economizing on the use of the means of production. (18) Price formation on the world market is also taken into greater consideration than formerly. The setting of prices is now more elastic. This is especially true in Hungary, where the "new economic mechanism" instituted on January 1, 1968, makes a distinction between maximum prices, interval prices, and freely moving prices, and narrows the range of state intervention in the area of prices. The different types of prices carry different weights according to the category of goods (see table on page 62).

Relative Weight of the Different Types of Prices in Hungary,
in Percent of Planned Turnover for 1968

	Fixed price	Maximum price	Interval price	Free price
Raw materials and typical semifinished products (e.g., energy carriers, steel products, textile fibers)	30	40	2	28
Products of the processing industries (e.g., machines, textiles)	3	16	3	78
Consumer goods	20	30	27	23

Source: Wochenbericht des Deutschen Institutes für Wirtschaftsforschung, August 24, 1972, p. 308.

Even in Hungary, where the planned economy is now the most decentralized, prices are not a dominant steering instrument for the economy. The centralized price-setting system has been relaxed, but supply and demand still do not play a significant role in price formation. As before, prices are still instruments for the implementation of centrally preferred alternatives for growth. Although the Hungarian economic policy gives some consideration to world market prices, money still does not constitute a uniform standard of value for the domestic economy nor an adequate basis for a uniform rate of exchange on foreign markets.

4. Limited Function of the Exchange Rate

4.1. Exchange Rate for Commercial Payments

The planned economies do not place their currencies on the world market as a commodity, as is done in the market economies; rather, they serve only the domestic economy. The prices of

Gold Parities and Exchange Rates, March 1974

Country	Unit of currency	Gold content in grams	Rubles per 100 units	Dollars per 100 units
Bulgaria	lev	0.759548	81.81	103.09
Czechoslovakia	koruna	0.123426	13.22	16.74
GDR	mark	0.399902	27.82	35.20
Poland	zloty	0.222168	25.41	30.03
Romania	leu	0.148112	15.89	20.12
Hungary	forint	0.075758	8.62	10.92
USSR	ruble	0.987412	—	126.58

Source: Data from the individual countries and Monthly Bulletin of Statistics, March 1973, p. 218.

their currencies have no economic underpinnings. Consequently, the exchange rates and gold parities of Eastern currencies are not recognized internationally, nor are they supported on the world market by the central banks of the Eastern nations. The CMEA countries set the gold parities of their currencies autonomously, and these parities serve as the basis for determining the official exchange rate.

The table above shows the present gold parities and exchange rates of the CMEA nations against the dollar and ruble. The gold parity, and hence the foreign exchange rate, have been readjusted several times since World War II in connection with currency reforms in the CMEA countries. Without changing the gold parity, the CMEA exchange rates for the U.S. dollar and other Western currencies were revaluated after the monetary realignment of December 1971 and the dollar devaluation in February 1973.

In none of the CMEA countries does currency have important economic functions; its exchange rate is irrelevant for price formation. The unilaterally set ratios of CMEA currencies to foreign currencies can be construed as exchange rates in the Western sense only within a very limited scope. (19) They are attuned to the domestic economy and need not be accepted by a foreign party in trade. Because of the unique status of foreign trade in a planned economy, the prices of currencies function in an entirely different manner than do the domestic prices. At the enterprise level, the exchange rate is not an economic magnitude that must be taken into account; it has practically no influence on enterprise operations.

As in a market economy, in a planned economy the foreign exchange receipts from export transactions are converted into domestic currency by the central banks, which also supply the necessary foreign currency for imports in exchange for domestic currency. Interenterprise foreign exchange transactions, which also play no notable role in market economies, are prohibited in a planned economy. Furthermore, unlike the practice in a market economy, the Soviet enterprises, and to a certain extent enterprises in some of the other CMEA countries, handle no foreign exchange whatsoever in their export and import transactions. The exchange rate bears no relation to the prices of the enterprises. For the individual enterprises, at least in the Soviet Union, foreign business has the character of a domestic transaction and is settled in domestic currency.

The monetary flows in foreign trade are integrated into the national accounting system. In traditional foreign trade practices, this integration is not effected directly at the enterprise level: the enterprises need not be concerned over the relationship between domestic prices and foreign exchange rates. Nor is the foreign trade activity of the central institutions (Ministry of Foreign Trade, Ministry of Finance, Central Planning Commission, etc.) directly influenced by the exchange rate. Foreign exchange receipts from exports are expressed in domestic currency by multiplying by the official exchange rate or a conversion factor and then counterposed to the cost of the exported goods in domestic currency. Similarly, the foreign exchange spent for imports is computed in terms of domestic currency by using the same conversion factor and then compared with the receipts for imported goods in domestic money. The net sums of these figures are balanced out in the state budget.

These relationships can be expressed in the following formulas:

$$E_{de} \cdot k = E_b \qquad D_{be} = E_b - K_{ie}$$

$$D_{bi} = I_b - E_{ii}$$

$$A_{di} \cdot k = I_b \qquad D_b = D_{bi} - D_{be}$$

E_{de} — foreign exchange proceeds from imports
A_{di} — foreign exchange expenditures in imports
E_b — export proceeds in domestic currency
I_b — import expenditures in domestic currency
D_{be} — budget equalization payment in export
D_{bi} — budget equalization payment in import
D_b — netted out balance budget equalization payment
K_{ie} — domestic costs of exported goods
E_{ii} — domestic proceeds for imported goods
k — conversion factor

In practice, it is almost always the case that the budget equalization payment in exports (D_{be}) is negative, while that in imports (D_{bi}) is positive. Given fixed values for E_{de}, A_{di}, K_{ie}, and E_{ii}, the budget deficit in exports and the budget excess in imports will be smaller, the higher the conversion factor, and vice versa.

In the traditional foreign trade model, financial transactions are executed exclusively by the three agencies of the central economic authority — namely, the state foreign trade enterprises, the state bank, and the state budget — without the participation of the exporting and importing enterprises.

The socialist state shields the economy from fluctuations in the exchange rate and speculation in foreign currency. Since economic disequilibria are therefore not reflected in fluctuations in the exchange rates, there are no signals or regulatory mechanisms to point out or correct undesirable trends, as in a market economy. In a planned economy, the exchange rate is not an indicator of how the domestic economy is faring in international competition.

To a certain extent, the planned economies have institutionalized the stability of their currencies. In practice, the national currencies of the socialist countries are continuously being devaluated or revaluated; this ongoing process is reflected in a deteriorating (or improving) ratio between the costs of exported goods, in domestic currency, and the foreign exchange receipts. This ratio deviates considerably from the official exchange rate, which is maintained at a stable level over the years.

Of course, the individual CMEA countries possess no precise statistical data on fluctuations in the ratios between their national currencies and the currencies of their trading partners. Such figures are not published in the official statistics. There are, however, a few publications that provide information on the real purchasing power of the national currencies of Czechoslovakia, Hungary, and Poland.

Statistics of this sort are based on the relationship between foreign trade prices and the domestic prices for exported goods, and reflect the financial results of foreign trade. In Czechoslovakia, the domestic costs of foreign currency obtained from exports are called reproduction costs. This relationship is expressed by the following formula:

$$K_f = \frac{\sum P_a}{\sum P_b} \times 100$$

where K_f is the financial returns, P_a is the foreign trade price, and P_b is the domestic price of the exported goods.

The statistics on the foreign trade receipts of these three CMEA countries are not complete, nor are they directly comparable with one another, given the different commodity composition of the foreign trade of these countries.

In Czechoslovakia, the ratios between the foreign exchange receipts obtained from exports to the West and the domestic prices for the same goods deteriorated considerably over the years, as the following indicators show: (20)

1953	1960	1965	1966	1967
100	70.0	61.4	59.4	42.3

Correspondingly, the reproduction costs for procuring U.S. dollars through goods exports rose steadily:

Reproduction Costs of U.S. Dollar in Koruny (21)

1950-1952	1955	1966	1967	1968
10.40	14.90	18.72	30.96*	31.39

*At 1966 prices: 24.04.

While the official exchange rate was 7.2 koruny in 1968, Czechoslovakia had to sell goods for 31.39 koruny to obtain one U.S. dollar. The official exchange rate of the koruna was thus more than seven times as high as the actual rate. The official rate was revaluated in the realignment of December 1971 and in the aftermath of the dollar devaluation of February 1973.

A similar trend may be observed in Hungary, where the official exchange rate was 11.60 forints per dollar from the time of the monetary reform in 1950 until the international realignment in 1971. In practice, however, foreign exchange receipts have been computed domestically at a rate of 60 forints per dollar since the institution of the economic reforms on January 1, 1968; at 55.26 forints per dollar since the international realignment; and at 50 forints per dollar since the dollar devaluation in February 1973. Including the subsidies paid to the various branches of industry by the budget (22), the effective forint equivalents of the dollar in 1968 in the various branches of Hungarian industry were the following: (23)

Industry	Forint equivalent of 1 U.S. dollar
Mining	73.3
Metalworking	67.4
Construction materials	63.8

Industry	Forint equivalent of 1 U.S. dollar
Machine tool	70.8
Chemistry	70.1
Textiles	79.9
Foodstuffs	70.3
Average	72.4

Thus, the different branches of Hungarian industry obtain different exchange rates for the forint in their exports.

The situation is somewhat different in Poland. Since 1959, Polish exporters have received 24 zlotys per dollar for their foreign currency receipts from the Foreign Trade Bank, whereas the official exchange before the realignment was only 4 zlotys. The bank received the necessary funds from the state budget. On the other hand, enterprises producing for export receive the domestic price for their products, which is generally higher than the export returns expressed in domestic currency. This difference is also cleared in the state budget.

The effective dollar/zloty ratio has changed several times over the years. In 1962, goods worth 49.6 zlotys had to be exported to obtain one dollar. (24) In the years following, this ratio was changed only slightly: (25)

	1965	1966	1967	1968
Zloty/dollar	46.4	47.2	46.8	48.0

The above figures represent averages for the total sum of Poland's exports throughout the world. Proceeds from trade relations with the socialist countries were 28 percent higher than from trade with the West. (26) While the financial proceeds from Polish exports as a whole improved during the years 1965 to 1969, the proceeds from exports to the Western countries declined during that same period. (27)

Polish exports brought in the following receipts in 1971-1972 (broken down by economic area):

Intra-CMEA trade 1 dollar = 40 zlotys
Trade with developing countries 1 dollar = 52 zlotys
Trade with developed industrial countries 1 dollar = 60 zlotys

As in Hungary, financial results varied depending on the economic area: (28)

Dollar/Zloty Ratio for Polish Exports in 1968

	Total	Machinery and equipment	Raw materials, fuels	Agricultural products, foods	Industrial consumer goods
Zloty equivalent of 1 U.S. dollar	48.0	36.0	44.8	83.2	51.2

Statistics for the reproduction costs of foreign exchange through exports are scanty for the other CMEA countries. In the German Democratic Republic, the average conversion factor for export receipts in marks has been pegged at a much lower level since January 1, 1965. As a rough estimate, the depreciation for trade with the West amounts to about 73 percent. (29)

In the Soviet Union, the "kilogram prices" of machinery exported to or imported from the West provide some idea of the efficiency of Soviet foreign trade.

Kilogram Price of Exported and Imported Machines
(SITC Position 711-732) in U.S. Dollars (30)

	1961	1965	1968
Exports of USSR to Western Europe	1.13	0.94	0.79
Exports of Western European countries to USSR	2.26	3.49	3.65

Because there is such a difference between the kinds of goods imported and exported, it would be meaningless to compare absolute prices. In terms of quantity, however, the trends in exports and imports for the years 1961-1968 did show marked differences. Soviet export prices fell about 30 percent, while Soviet import prices rose by over 60 percent during this period.

A similar pattern is evident in Poland's foreign trade. Thus, the Polish Premier P. Jaroszewicz stated at the Sixth Party Congress (December 1971): "For the machinery and equipment we import from the capitalist countries, we pay per kilo three times more than we obtain from exports because our products require more material resources and less brain power, and embody a relatively smaller portion of skilled labor." (31)

From what has been said, it is evident that the exchange rates of CMEA currencies, which have been shielded from foreign trade and have been stable for many years, have in the course of time lost any relevance as a ratio between domestic and foreign currencies. A planned economy that has failed to create the preconditions for making its currency convertible is also unable to adjust its exchange rate to the changing economic circumstances. Even though the socialist state is able to eliminate the usual factors causing fluctuations in the exchange rate — supply and demand, balance of payments, disequilibria, etc. — the most crucial factor determining the exchange rate, namely, purchasing power, remains fully in force. Changes in purchasing power are inevitably reflected as changes in the ratio between the domestic prices and the foreign prices for exported goods. Because of this, even a planned economy must make appropriate adjustments if excessive use of budgetary funds is to be avoided and a smoothly running and balanced national economy is to be insured.

The official exchange rate remained meaningless as long as the central authorities remained in exclusive control of settling foreign exchange transactions and managing their receipts. However, as soon as some CMEA countries attempted to integrate foreign trade more fully into the economy and tie it in some way to enterprise cost accounting, the official exchange rate was no longer able to serve even as a conversion factor.

In its place, some CMEA countries worked out separate coefficients for their CMEA partners and for the West. These coefficients are based on the average ratio of domestic to foreign currency in exports, and provide the enterprises with a standard for measuring their capacity to compete on an international scale. At the same time, they have a crucial influence on the size of enterprise profits from domestic and foreign dealings. Today, the official exchange rates in many of the CMEA countries remain relevant only for foreign trade statistics.

4.2. Special Exchange Rates for Noncommercial Payments (32)

4.2.1. Significance and Area of Application

The planned economies were not able to isolate the national unit of currency from the other currencies in tourism and other services as they had been in commodity trade. The days are long past when the only foreigners eligible to receive services in a planned economy are the official representatives of other countries. A flourishing tourist trade and a strong foreign demand for other services in the socialist states have been developing since the middle of the 1950s. The number of foreigners traveling to CMEA countries rose from 3.5 million in 1960 to 26.0 million in 1971. The rise in the number of foreign tourists in the past decade was especially steep in Bulgaria (from 0.2 million to 2.7 million) and Hungary (from 0.2 million to 6.1 million persons). (33)

There was an especially significant relaxation of restrictions on personal travel and exchange of national currencies among the CMEA countries. In 1971, the German Democratic Republic and Poland attempted to open their common border completely, and during the first six months of 1972, 3.5 million Poles and 2.5 million Germans crossed. Money exchange was also completely free for tourists between the two countries until the end of 1972. During the first six months of 1972, the Poles had exchanged 1 billion zlotys and the Germans the equivalent of 350 million zlotys. (34) At the end of 1972, however, restrictions were again imposed on travel and currency exchange between the two countries.

4.2.2. Special Rates for Western Tourists

The Western tourist must be able to buy the currency of the Eastern country he intends to visit and the Eastern tourist traveling in the West must be able to exchange his Eastern currency for the currency of a Western country. (35) In contrast to commodity exchange, in which the domestic and foreign currencies are kept completely separate in each country, in the tourist trade this separation cannot be maintained. Therefore, even in practical terms, it is impossible to ignore economic facts, such as respective purchasing powers, in pegging the exchange rate. The inconvertibility of the Eastern currencies has caused distortions in this area as well. The special tourist exchange rates of Eastern currencies were established on the basis of unilateral pegged prices for money to be used exclusively for tourist purposes. Eastern currencies can be purchased legally only in the CMEA countries. Over the short term, foreign demand has no influence on the exchange rate; the tourist rate is changed only after a demand has persisted over a long period.

The exchange rates of Eastern currencies for payments in transactions dealing with services are usually higher than the official rates. The Soviet Union is an exception: there, after the rate change of January 1, 1961, a uniform exchange rate was introduced and maintained for foreign trade in goods and services. (See table opposite.)

The tourist rate of exchange from CMEA currencies into U.S. dollars is still not an authentic currency exchange rate, but it is at least more than a traditional conversion factor. The level at which it is pegged influences the flow of Western tourists, which the Eastern countries have a strong interest in maintaining. In 1971, the percentage of Western tourists in the total number of tourists was highest in Bulgaria (45.1 percent), followed by the USSR (36.1 percent), Romania (18.8 percent), Poland (17.9 percent), Czechoslovakia (16.9 percent), and Hungary (14.3 percent). The relatively large share of Western tourists in the tourist trade of the German Democratic Republic (55.9 percent) constitutes a special case, since large numbers of citizens from West Germany and West Berlin travel to the

U.S. Dollars per 100 Units of National Currency, March 1974

Country	Unit of currency	Official rate	Tourist rate
Bulgaria	lev	103.09	60.60
Czechoslovakia	koruna	16.74	9.55
GDR	mark	35.20	35.21
Poland	zloty	30.03	3.01*
Romania	leu	20.12	6.51
Hungary	forint	10.92	4.27
USSR	ruble	126.58	126.58

*For the exchange of 50 U.S. dollars, an extra 16 zlotys is given per dollar in Poland, and 100 zlotys are exchanged for 2.77 U.S. dollars.

Source: Data from the individual countries and Monthly Bulletin of Statistics, 1973, No. 3, p. 218.

German Democratic Republic. (36)
The share of the CMEA countries in total world income from tourist trade was 3 percent, or $453 million, in 1969, but this is much lower than the share of these countries in the total number of tourists (10 percent). (37) In Bulgaria and Romania, where in 1969 the income from tourism was already 3.6 percent and 3.5 percent, respectively, of the income from the export of goods (38), an attempt was made to attract more foreign tourists by offering a favorable exchange rate. The other people's democracies have also considerably reduced the tourist exchange rates for their currencies, prompting the German Institute for Economic Research to observe that they "were usually more favorable for the citizens of the Federal Republic than would have been expected on the basis of monetary parities in the area of consumer goods." (39)
The tourist trade is the most important source of foreign exchange after commodity exchange, but it is not the only other source, nor is the tourist exchange rate the only one whose

function is to procure Western currency. The chronic scarcity of foreign exchange forces the CMEA countries to seek out other possibilities for its procurement, provided the conditions and terms are sufficiently favorable.

The most prominent of these is so-called internal exports. These are currency remittances from foreign relatives of citizens and official Eastern representatives in the Western countries. The foreign currency acquired through these channels is usually used by the recipients to purchase goods that are difficult to obtain domestically. The exchange rate for this foreign exchange is more favorable than the tourist rate. In the Polish PKO bank the dollar was rated at 72 zlotys before the realignment in December 1971; this was approximately double the exchange rate for Western tourists, which was itself favorable.

The Czech counterpart of the Polish PKO bank is Tusex, which rates the koruna at a level approximately five times higher than the tourist exchange rate. In the Soviet Union, the official exchange rate is 1 U.S. dollar = 0.77 rubles, but in the Soviet Posyltorg one receives approximately four times the amount of goods for the ruble equivalent of a U.S. dollar as in ordinary shops.

As a result of the total economic control over foreign exchange and the typical overevaluation of most Eastern currencies, a black market in foreign currency has developed. Western currencies are in special demand from private enterprises — insofar as they exist — and from prospective Eastern tourists. The Western currency supply comes from foreigners and native citizens in possession of foreign currency. The difference between the black market rate and the tourist rate is relatively large, and reveals something of the discrepancy between supply and demand.

4.2.3. Special Exchange Rate for Noncommercial Payments of the CMEA Countries

At the Prague Convention of February 8, 1963, twelve socialist countries (in addition to the presently active CMEA members, Albania (40), the People's Republic of China, North Vietnam, and North Korea also participated) agreed on a special exchange rate (basic rate with additions and deductions) among themselves and a new clearing procedure for noncommercial payments. Until 1956, transactions dealing in services among the socialist countries were settled predominantly by bilateral clearing at the world market prices. But before that time, payments were of negligible importance for purposes other than goods deliveries in any case. In 1956, it was agreed that certain services had to be paid for by the foreigner at the current domestic prices in the host country and that these payments were to be transferred to the clearing account by means of special conversion factors. In 1959, the first steps were taken to institute multilateral payments for trade in services; these measures found their favorable culmination in the Prague Convention of February 8, 1963.

In contrast to trade with the West, in which only a unilateral conversion of foreign currency into the national currency of the CMEA country is possible, a bilateral exchange system at a special tourist rate is maintained for tourist trade among the twelve socialist countries.

The Prague Convention set exchange ratios in accordance with the purchasing powers of the various CMEA currencies, purchasing power being determined on the basis of a standard market basket containing thirty-three foods and semiluxuries, twenty-two industrial products, and fourteen services.

The parities obtaining against the ruble are shown in the table on the following page.

An important aspect of the Prague Convention was the agreement upon a conversion factor of 3.4, which was intended to correlate payments for services, converted into Soviet rubles, with payments accruing from the sale of goods. At year's end, each CMEA country's balance for invisible trade payments is transferred to an account with the International Bank for Economic Cooperation; for non-CMEA members, the balance is transferred to their respective clearing accounts. The conversion factor, established on the basis of the ratio between the Soviet domestic price and foreign prices for the standard market basket, was considerably overvalued, and hence was especially

100 rubles = 8.372	Albanian leks		
100	Albanian leks	=	1.19 rubles
100 rubles = 78	Bulgarian leva		
100	Bulgarian leva	=	128.21 rubles
100 rubles = 1.311	Hungarian forints		
100	Hungarian forints	=	7.63 rubles
100 rubles = 192	Vietnam dongs		
100	Vietnam dongs	=	52.08 rubles
100 rubles = 320	GDR marks		
100	GDR marks	=	31.25 rubles
100 rubles = 418	Mongolian tugriks		
100	Mongolian tugriks	=	23.92 rubles
100 rubles = 129	Chinese yuan		
100	Chinese yuan	=	77.52 rubles
100 rubles = 144	North Korean wons		
100	North Korean wons	=	69.44 rubles
100 rubles = 1.530	Polish zlotys		
100	Polish zlotys	=	6.54 rubles
100 rubles = 830	Romanian lei		
100	Romanian lei	=	12.05 rubles
100 rubles = 965	Czech koruny		
100	Czech koruny	=	10.36 rubles

Source: A. Zwass, Pieniądz dwóch rynków, Warsaw, 1968, p. 456.

unfavorable to those tourist countries which had been able to enter a positive balance for themselves. The equivalent of the excess, expressed in transferable rubles, is disproportionately low. Czechoslovakia resisted particularly strongly and, through bilateral agreements, was able to get through a reduction of the conversion factor from 3.4 to 2.0-2.2. In 1971, a multilateral adjustment was made. The annual debit and credit balances of payments for services are now converted with a factor of 2.3 instead of the former 3.4. (41) Even though the CMEA tourist exchange rates were not dictated exclusively by economic criteria, they still permitted some sort of de facto convertibility in this sector. Moreover, they clearly differ from exchange rates for trade in services with the West. Their connection with the domestic economy, however, is tenuous.

The tourist countries correctly point out that the costs of the requisite infrastructure and investments for hotels and tourist establishments are also factors to be taken into account in setting a tourist exchange rate. These exchange rates, which are arbitrarily fixed and hence prevent exchange rates and prices from exerting any mutual influence on one another, had the net effect of creating unequal conditions for the signatories of the Prague Convention.

5. Need for Reform in the Foreign Trade Policy of the CMEA Countries

The lines along which foreign trade is organized in the Eastern bloc follow logically from state ownership of the means of production, although that is not the only factor involved; they are also partly determined by the peculiar economic structure of the Soviet Union, which even before the revolution was only marginally integrated into the world economy. And, indeed, during the years of economic warfare, with its embargoes and credit refusals, organization of foreign trade along the lines described was entirely adequate for the people's democracies. In fact, in the trade and monetary chaos that reigned in Europe between the world wars as well as directly after World War II, the controlled trade of the planned economies, with its bilateral settlement system, could even chalk up some points in its favor. It is perhaps understandable, then, that the first wave of reforms from 1956 to 1958 changed little in the foreign trade monopoly. In addition, the enterprises in the Eastern economies still had scarcely any latitude within which they were permitted to function independently; it was not until the sixties, when some enterprises were granted a greater degree of autonomy to dispose over their own resources, that an alternative to totally centralized foreign trade appeared.

An even greater contrast, however, was evident between the Eastern concept of foreign trade, which flirts with autarky, and the spirit of the Bretton Woods Agreement and the General

Agreement on Tariffs and Trade, both of which set sights on maximally free trade and unrestricted convertibility of the Western currencies. The West was able gradually to achieve these goals with the aid of the Marshall Plan and the European Payments Union. Multilateral trade, and with it monetary and capital trade, experienced an unprecedented upswing.

The Eastern European countries tried to achieve multilateralism in foreign trade by setting up a clearing office for the CMEA area and by settling accounts with the West through foreign exchange. However, these efforts were thwarted by the backward monetary system. At the same time, there was a growing awareness that the goal of CMEA integration and the targeted growth rates could only be achieved through increased international specialization. The founding of joint enterprises within the CMEA area was even considered. Yet even this goal remained beyond reach as long as the economies of these countries had no equivalent standards of value or effective settling instruments. Thus, the material situation urgently demanded reform of the existing foreign trade policy.

6. Reform of the Foreign Trade System

6.1. Clearing the Way for the Enterprises to Engage in Foreign Trade Transactions

The keynote of the foreign trade reform was the relaxation of the stringent system of foreign trade monopoly and the granting of permission to the enterprises and industrial associations to engage in foreign trade operations. At the same time, the concept of foreign trade was entirely rethought, and initiatives were taken to place it on solid theoretical and ideological foundations, especially in the smaller CMEA countries, which were highly dependent on foreign trade. It would be pointless to discuss whether the reforms have brought merely outward modifications in the lines along which foreign trade is organized or whether they have introduced fundamental changes in the system itself. (42) The fact remains that something has been set in motion. To be sure, the reforms are pursued with varying enthusiasm in the different countries. Yet one objective is shared by all: to permit the enterprises to engage in foreign trade — although the degree to which they are able to influence foreign trade varies from country to country. Delegation of some responsibilities in foreign trade to the enterprises can be effective only when they already possess a certain range of independence in matters bearing on production.

Only in the Soviet Union, where the foreign trade enterprises are under the Ministry of Foreign Trade, do they remain the sole executors of the state foreign trade monopoly. In all other European CMEA countries, the function and area of influence of the central foreign trade enterprises have been restricted to some degree. Many large enterprises and industrial associations have been granted the right to carry out foreign trade transactions on their own behalf and even to dispose over foreign exchange. So far, this policy has been pursued most consistently in Hungary and the German Democratic Republic.

With the introduction of the new economic mechanism in 1968, the central foreign trade enterprises in Hungary lost their monopoly over foreign trade. Now every enterprise certified by the Ministry of Foreign Trade is authorized to engage in foreign trade. (43) On January 1, 1970, there were 111 enterprises in Hungary authorized to engage in foreign trade; in each case, the type of foreign trade transactions open to them is precisely specified. (44) In terms of value, however, the foreign trade carried out directly by the enterprises is still modest: about 23 percent of the exports and 11 percent of the imports. (45) Transactions undertaken on a commission basis have been given a considerable range. The foreign trade enterprise concludes an agreement with the foreign firm on instructions from the producing enterprise. However, the risk is assumed jointly by the manufacturer and the foreign trade enterprise. The manufacturer also has the right to change from one foreign trade enterprise to another. As a rule, a commission contract is concluded for one year, but can be extended for a longer period (up to three years). There are at present 40 foreign trade enterprises working exclusively on commission contracts. (46)

The German Democratic Republic has retained its centralized economic system fundamentally intact, although it, too, has instituted a number of organizational reforms. The new German Democratic Republic constitution contains a clause stipulating that foreign trade is a state monopoly. (47) Nevertheless, like Hungary, the German Democratic Republic has given industry some range within which it may directly engage in foreign transactions. Initially, there were only certain specifically designated exceptions in individual branches of industry, but later two large enterprises — the Carl Zeiss Company, Jena, in 1965, and the Ruhla Watch Combine in 1967 — were authorized to conclude foreign trade transactions on their own responsibility.

In 1967-1968, the first foreign trade enterprises were placed under the direct jurisdiction of various branches of industry in the German Democratic Republic. The Deutsche Pharmazie Export und Import GmbH attached to the industrial association of the pharmaceutical industry was founded on January 1, 1967, and the foreign trade enterprise Schiffkommerz attached to the industrial association for the ship-building industry was founded on January 1, 1968. (48)

Further measures transferring direct responsibility for foreign trade to industry have been instituted on a gradual but consistent basis.

At present, foreign transactions are carried out by the following agencies in the German Democratic Republic:

— Foreign trade enterprises, directly subordinate to the Ministry of Foreign Trade, working mainly on a commission basis.

— Sales enterprises that are integrated with the industrial associations. Here it is important to maintain a distinction between the sales departments of the combines and large factories and the export agencies or sales cooperatives of industries coordinated on a district basis.

In the other people's democracies, the reforms have gone in the same direction as in Hungary and the German Democratic Republic, but have not been pushed so far. In Czechoslovakia, some reforms were made retroactive.

Poland was the first CMEA country that began to reform its foreign trade system. As early as 1963, advisory committees were encharged with coordinating trade problems among sales and production enterprises. The right to engage in foreign trade has been granted successively to various large enterprises, for example, the textile machinery plant Befama, the machine-tool factory Rafamat, the metal-processing factory Cegielski, the electronics enterprise Elwro, etc. Further steps in this direction were taken in 1970-1971. Twenty-five foreign trade enterprises were subordinated directly to the industrial associations, themselves organized by industrial branch (Metal-export, Bumar, Metronex), or placed directly under the jurisdiction of the appropriate ministry (e.g., Ciech was placed under the Ministry for Chemical Industry and Textilimport under the Ministry for Light Industry). (49) The fifteen foreign trade associations directly subordinate to the Ministry of Foreign Trade were responsible in 1971 for one-third of the total sales with the CMEA countries and one-half of total sales concluded with the West.

Czechoslovakia established a special relationship between production and foreign trade. Joint stock companies were founded comprising foreign trade enterprises, the industrial associations, and the financially involved banks. The foreign trade transactions of the most important trade enterprises, such as Technoexport, Strojimport, Investa, Menrkuria, Chemapol, Centrotex, Exico, etc., are cleared through this organizational form. (50) The number of enterprises authorized to engage in foreign trade has risen from twenty-eight in 1968 to fifty in 1972. However, these are more thoroughly controlled than formerly by the central authorities.

Production and foreign trade activities are also being coordinated in Bulgaria and Romania. Bulgaria's foreign trade organizations carry out commission business for several branches. Some major producers (e.g., Rodopa, Bulgarplod, Bulgartabak, Balkancar, Bulgarska Sachar, Bulgarsko Pivo) have been granted the right to establish direct relations with foreign firms. (51) However, Bulgaria's social and economic plan for the five-year period 1971-1975 stipulates that the state foreign trade monopoly will continue to remain in the hands of the Ministry of Foreign Trade.

In Romania, the restructuring of the foreign trade system was instituted by the "Law for Foreign Trade Activity and the Economic and Scientific-Technological Cooperation of the Socialist Republic of Romania," March 19, 1971. (52) In a clear departure from the traditional concept of foreign trade, the preamble of the law reads: "Foreign trade, as a part of the economy, must be integrated into the overall national economic system of planning and management." In addition to the foreign trade enterprises under the Ministry of Foreign Trade, which are still able to export on their own account, other organizations have also been authorized by the Council of Ministers to carry out foreign trade operations.

The following information should shed some light on the progress made by the economic reforms in the various CMEA countries. The number of enterprises engaged in only the movement of merchandise has increased in the seven European CMEA countries from 270 in 1968 to 368 in 1972. The growth was greatest in Hungary (from 52 to 75) and Romania (from 22 to 56), and it was about the same in Czechoslovakia and the German Democratic Republic (from 28 and 33, respectively, to 55). In Poland, where the number of foreign trade organizations had already risen sharply before 1968, the total decreased from 42 in 1968 to 41 in 1972. In the Soviet Union, the number increased from 46 to only 50. Bulgaria diverges from this general trend. In that country, the number of foreign trade enterprises decreased from 46 to 36 in connection with the amalgamation of production and trade enterprises. (53)

The increase in the number of enterprises authorized to conduct foreign trade varied from branch to branch. No noteworthy changes occurred in the raw materials, fuels, and foodstuffs industries, in which the state wants to maintain its monopoly position. The number of foreign trade enterprises in the machine-tool and consumer goods industries, on the other hand, increased from 90 in 1968 to 170 in 1972.

The average turnover of foreign trade enterprises varied from country to country. In 1971, it reached over $500 million in the USSR, $160 million to $200 million in the German Democratic Republic, Poland, and Czechoslovakia, over $100 million in Bulgaria, and about $75 million in Romania and Hungary. (54)

Foreign trade transactions were most highly decentralized in Hungary, while in the Soviet Union, where the number of foreign trade organizations (50) is about the same as in the German Democratic Republic and Czechoslovakia and even less than in Hungary and Romania, they are the most centralized.

6.2. Decentralization of Authority in Foreign Currency Transactions

The specific powers transferred to industry in the area of foreign trade also vary from country to country. Hungary was the only country to abolish the obligatory export and import quotas for many branches of industry and to make the production enterprises responsible for determining the scope of foreign trade operations and the choice of supply and delivery countries. The Ministry of Foreign Trade sets the overall goals of trade policy and analyzes international business trends and fluctuations in the terms of trade.

Exports and imports must be approved by the Ministry of Foreign Trade; ordinarily this approval is obtained within thirty days. (55) The possessor of an import permit can purchase the necessary foreign currency from the Hungarian National Bank without any further formalities; or, put more precisely, on the basis of this permit, the bank obligates itself to meet the terms of payment of the transaction. (56)

Whether a given agreement is economical from the standpoint of the individual enterprise plays no role in the decision to approve a trade transaction; rather, the decision is made from the perspective of the economy as a whole, for example, whether the transaction makes a positive contribution to the balance of payments or makes possible the fulfillment of trade agreements. (57)

In the other CMEA countries, some foreign trade enterprises have been incorporated into the industrial associations, but in important questions concerning the conditions and geographical pattern of foreign trade, and so on, they remain subordinate to the Ministry of Foreign Trade, and in all questions bearing on prompt delivery and timely ordering, they are still under a ministry for the appropriate industry.

In the German Democratic Republic, "it is the responsibility of the Ministry of Foreign Trade, in the name of the Council of Ministers, to look after general government interests in matters of foreign trade." (58) Price limits and terms of payment are set for the production enterprises, which guarantee to make good any foreign exchange losses suffered by the foreign trade enterprises. (59) They may dispose over a small portion of their foreign exchange receipts themselves, however, especially when they have been able to earn more foreign exchange than had been provided in the state plan.

In Poland, the Ministry of Foreign Trade determines overall trade policy: the flows of goods and payments, the indices for assessing the efficiency of foreign trade, measures to promote exports, etc. (60) The central plan remains dominant. The Polish minister of foreign trade has made the following observation on this point: "The plan must be the principal steering instrument; it sets the main goals and provides the enterprises with the means necessary to achieve these goals." (61)

The strict and detailed quotas prescribed for imports have been relaxed somewhat in Poland, however. Whereas it had been the procedure to set import quotas in terms of quantity, now they are set in value terms, with the exception of those for basic materials and raw materials (30-40 percent of the total trade). (62) The import of machinery and equipment from the CMEA member nations has been completely unrestricted since 1972. (63) For machinery imports from the capitalist countries, however, there are still upper limits set for foreign currencies. Recently, the process was liberalized even further when the enterprises received foreign currency advances with which they were able to conclude import agreements for 1973 and 1974 on the basis of their own assessments. They need not account for the use of the currency until afterward.

Poland took another important step toward the relaxation of controls over foreign exchange with Government Decree No. 49

of February 18, 1972. The managers of major enterprises and industrial associations were authorized to set up and manage a foreign exchange fund to be built up from the following sources:
— 10 percent of the growth in exports over the preceding year;
— 30 percent of the foreign exchange receipts from export of their own licenses and technical expertise;
— 30 percent of the foreign exchange receipts from the export of documents and studies bearing no relation to commodity exchange.

In Czechoslovakia, certain powers were delegated in connection with the reforms; later, however, central control over foreign trade was reasserted. Late in 1970, the State Bank was assigned the responsibility of restructuring foreign trade along more efficient lines and, pursuant to this task, was given broad powers of intervention, extending even into the license and patent trade.

In Romania, the Council of Ministers is responsible for foreign trade relations. It determines the organizational form and decides, in particular, which units of the economy shall be permitted to engage in foreign trade (Article 21 of the law of March 19, 1971, on foreign trade activity and economic and technical-scientific cooperation). The functions of coordination and control were transferred to the Ministry of Foreign Trade (Article 34). Accordingly, the minister of foreign trade "may issue guidelines for all ministries, central agencies, and other economic units as regards foreign trade activities" (Article 35).

The economic units in Romania entrusted with carrying out foreign trade activities may not utilize the receipts from foreign trade but must remit these to the state through the Foreign Trade Bank. They may use freely only that income in foreign currency exceeding the sum stipulated in the annual plan.

In the countries where the central plan still plays a dominant role — such as Poland, and especially Romania and Bulgaria, but more recently even Czechoslovakia — the reforms have given the enterprises more autonomy in foreign trade transactions than they have in domestic transactions. It is quite possible that the experience gained in the area of foreign trade will have an influence on the economic system as a whole.

6.3. Integration of Foreign Trade Receipts into Enterprise Accounting

The restructuring of foreign trade can achieve its declared objective of raising the efficiency of the economy as a whole only if the proceeds from foreign trade transactions are made an integral part of enterprise operating accounts. This would mean that the profits and losses from foreign trade would fall to the account of the enterprises, whereas previously they had been accounted for in the budget and had nothing further to do with the enterprises.

The relationship between domestic price and cost ratios and those on the world market requires a realistic exchange rate which can be used in enterprise cost accounting. As long as Eastern currencies lack broad mutual convertibility or convertibility with Western currencies, it is hardly possible to arrive at exchange rates based on economic criteria. Up till now, internal conversion coefficients have been used; these have at least maintained a distinction between intra-CMEA trade and trade with the West.

These internal conversion coefficients have the net effect of devaluing the transferable ruble to a level below both the officially set exchange rate and the rate of exchange between the transferable ruble and the dollar used in IBEC.

In Hungary, the institution of the new economic mechanism transferred the responsibility for foreign trade accounting to the enterprises. One result was that prices became an important steering instrument of trade policy. The present price system has three principal components:

1) Coefficients of the relative value of foreign currencies which establish a connection between domestic and foreign prices. In transactions with CMEA countries, 1 transferable ruble is worth 40 forints, while in transactions with Western countries, 1 dollar is worth 50 forints since the dollar devaluation of February 1973.

2) Customs tariffs that apply to all foreign trade partners outside the CMEA area. These were established in accordance with the Brussels nomenclature and set forth in three columns. (64)

The first column lists the so-called preferential customs duties, which are placed on goods deliveries from developing countries that do not discriminate against Hungary in trade and which have a smaller per capita income than Hungary. The second column lists duties for goods deliveries from countries from which Hungary receives a most-favored-nation status. Finally, the third column is for countries that have refused Hungary that status.

3) The tax and subsidy system, which is connected to the relative value coefficients. This system is based on the average results from foreign trade. Enterprise receipts often diverge considerably from the average. Excessive discrepancies are then compensated by imposing varying tax burdens or subsidies. Subsidies vary between 15 percent and 30 percent of export proceeds. (65) This "state reimbursement" is based on an enterprise's total export activity rather than on individual products or product categories whose production yields no profits. (66)

Whereas in the previous procedure, all foreign trade was set off in one comprehensive sum in the budget, in this new form of budgetary subsidization of foreign trade, only those enterprises which meet certain minimal profitability requirements are compensated for their losses. Joint Decree 11/1967 (FAZ12) of the Ministry of Foreign Trade and the Ministry of Finance states explicitly: "An excessively unprofitable export activity, which moreover cannot be expected to improve even in the future, is not eligible for compensation." (67)

In 1971, 70 percent of the exports settled in dollars and 50 percent of the exports cleared in rubles had roots in the common interest of production and trade enterprises in the profits accruing therefrom and in its distribution. (68)

In Czechoslovakia, the equalizing factors between the foreign trade and domestic prices that had been introduced in connection with the economic reform are still in force: 18 koruny for 1 transferable ruble vis-à-vis the socialist countries and 27 koruny for 1 dollar for trade with the capitalist countries. (69) The equalizing factor set for the convertible currency area was unrealistic from the outset, however, and was therefore later raised by 15 percent. This eliminated the discrepancy between the values of the Czech koruna in intra-CMEA trade and its value in trade with the West. The equalizing factors are based on the average value of total foreign trade. As in Hungary, tax deductions and subsidies or additional tax burdens are provided where discrepancies are relatively great. The government has the power to alter the equalizing factors if economic policy or price trends so require.

The German Democratic Republic instituted a price reform before foreign trade proceeds were integrated into enterprise operating accounts. The purpose of the reform was to bring domestic prices in line with cost expenditures and then gradually, through realistic conversion factors, with foreign prices as well. A first effort to integrate foreign trade receipts into enterprise operating accounts by means of the old clearing procedures failed. Since 1968, the industrial enterprises authorized to conduct foreign trade have been permitted to employ foreign prices as standards of value for settlement purposes.

In late 1967, the German Democratic Republic introduced a special exchange rate for tourist trade with the West (1 dollar = 4.2 marks) that was to function over and above the official exchange rate (1 dollar = 2.2 marks). This rate has been used as an internal accounting factor for foreign trade transactions. It, too, has overvalued the mark since the end of the sixties. To achieve "realistic enterprise results," as it is called in East Germany, the internal accounting factor was pegged at 7.28 marks per dollar and 6.07 marks per ruble. (70)

In Poland, efficiency coefficients, so called, were established in 1966 for the most important goods and services obtained from abroad; these were internal clearing indices for foreign trade accounting. (71) In 1971, Poland made the first attempt to incorporate the results from foreign trade into enterprise operating accounts by means of an average conversion coefficient. This experiment affected no more than a few enterprises, however, and was confined to determining prices for goods that could be exported at a profit and for imported machinery and equipment that could not be produced domestically. (72) F. Kubiczek — quoted above — conjectures that in Poland foreign trade accounting will be merged with overall operating accounts within two years. (73)

Currency in the Foreign Trade of CMEA Countries

In the other people's democracies, the reform of foreign trade accounting has not yet passed beyond the experimental stage. This is especially true of Romania. In Bulgaria, profits and losses from imports continue to be balanced out in the budget. On the other hand, export receipts now appear on the balance sheets of the foreign trade enterprises. The difference between foreign trade prices, expressed in terms of the domestic currency, and domestic prices is covered by either the overall profits of the branch industrial association or by the state budget.

From the preceding presentation, it should be clear that the Eastern concept of foreign trade has become more flexible. The direct participation of the enterprises stimulated their interest in conducting foreign trade at a profit and encouraged them to participate more widely than before in the international division of labor. Economic policy makers have not been satisfied with the results, however. Polish Minister of Foreign Trade Olechowski observes: "The reforms should integrate production and foreign trade both organizationally and economically. However, as yet we have been unable to create the conditions necessary to effectively integrate foreign trade and production at the enterprise level." (74)

The primary shortcoming of the reforms is that they have failed to forge organic links between foreign trade accounting and accounting for domestic production at the enterprise level. Although the internal conversion factors make it possible to perform simple arithmetic operations and calculate production and foreign trade proceeds together, they are not able to reflect the dynamic interplay between the price of goods and the exchange rates in the economic process. Even the reformed accounting procedures have not created the necessary preconditions for optimal allocation of resources in a planned economy.

The results of foreign trade may be organically incorporated into the production returns of the enterprises by applying the rules governing the exchange rates of convertible currencies. Several Eastern European countries have now put their sights on convertibility. J. Bognar has stated this problem succinctly for Hungary, whose economy is more decentralized than that of any other CMEA country: "The Hungarian economy is moving toward convertibility, but it is not yet clear under what circumstances this will be achieved." (75)

Romania, with an extremely centralized economy, is moving in the same direction: "The necessary preconditions for the future transition to convertibility are being created." (76) Since December 1972, Romania has been a member of the International Monetary Fund and the International Bank for Reconstruction and Development. The eminent East German scholar Professor Domdey considers currency convertibility in the socialist countries to be fully compatible with a planned economy: "There is no question that nonconvertibility, which has characterized socialist currencies up to the present, is not an inherent feature of the socialist mode of production." (77)

Recently, H. Reuss, Chairman of the Subcommittee for International Economics of the Joint Economic Committee of the U.S. Congress, came out in favor of the Soviet Union's membership in the International Monetary Fund and the World Bank.

It is also interesting that the top leader in the Soviet Union, Leonid Brezhnev, outlined a vision of substantial long-term economic cooperation between East and West on his visit to the Federal Republic of Germany in 1973, and proclaimed grandly that the Soviet Union had abandoned its autarkic tendencies: "We shall not pursue a course that would isolate our country from the rest of the world."

The prerequisites for the integration of Eastern currencies into the international monetary system are examined in the following chapters.

Notes

1) Vneshniaia torgovlia SSSR 1919-1940 [Foreign Trade of the USSR 1919-1940], Moscow, 1960, p. 14.

2) The well-known Soviet economist Professor O. T. Bogomolov has pointed out the considerable difficulties involved in the integration of socialist countries that are at different levels of development: "The creation of the socialist system and the development of a new kind of international relations is a complicated

process that takes place simultaneously at many different levels." See O. T. Bogomolov, Theorie und Methodologie der internationalen sozialistischen Arbeitsteilung, East Berlin, 1969, pp. 11-12 (translated from the Russian).

3) The extremely different positions of enterprises with regard to foreign trade in a market economy and in a planned economy are characterized by Professor Haberler as follows: "The state enterprises are becoming more and more nationally oriented. They act patriotically in the economic sense, for which the price is a lack of flexibility. On the other hand, private enterprises, which are substantially if not exclusively guided by profit motives, gear their trade activity primarily to economic considerations and are therefore basically internationally oriented" (Conference of the CESES 1971, Centro studie ricerche su problemi economico sociali, Stresa, Neue Zürcher Zeitung, October 6, 1971).

4) We may quote two authoritative Soviet authors on this point: "The Soviet Union and the other socialist countries have taken the form of trade developed by the bourgeois states under conditions of economic crises [bilateral clearing is meant] and given it a new content" (L. Frey, Mezhdunarodnye rashchety i finansirovanie vneshnei torgovli sotsialisticheskikh stran [International Accounting and Financing of Foreign Trade in the Socialist Countries], Moscow, 1960, p. 169). "Socialism has altered the character [of bilateral clearing] and adapted it to suit its own interests" (I. Zlobin, Mirovoi sotsialisticheskii rynok [The World Socialist Market], Moscow, 1963, p. 34).

5) See T. Scitovsky, Money and the Balance of Payments, London, 1969, p. 3.

6) Bertil Ohlin, "The Relations Between International Trade and International Movements of Capital and Labor," in Klaus Rose, ed., Theorie der internationalen Wirtschaftsbeziehungen, Cologne, 1966, p. 31.

7) See M. Senin, Sozialistische Integration, East Berlin, 1972, p. 11 (translated from the Russian); M. Guzek, Zasada kosztów komparatywnych a problemy RWPG [Comparative Cost Principles and the Problems of the CMEA], Warsaw, 1967, p. 11.

8) Professor Haberler observes that "in the international sphere [Marx's] labor theory could not be applied; this explains why the theory of comparative costs has stood up much better than other parts of the old classical theory" (see G. Haberler, A Survey of International Trade Theory, Princeton University Press, 1961, p. 1).

9) See Aussenhandel (Moscow), 1971, No. 2, p. 6.

10) The CPSU in Resolutions and Decisions of the Party Congresses, Conferences and Plenary Sessions of the Central Committee, 7th ed., 1954, Part II, p. 175.

11) See T. D. Zotschew, Die aussenwirtschaftlichen Verflechtungen der Sowjetunion, Tübingen, 1969, p. 18.

12) Aussenhandel (Moscow), 1970, No. 3.

13) Międzynarodowe stosunki ekonomiczne [International Economic Relations], Warsaw, 1964, p. 149.

14) The major legislative dispositions over the foreign exchange monopoly are taken from the Soviet textbook Denezhnoe obrashchenie i kredit SSSR [Cash Circulation and Credit in the USSR], 1970, pp. 363, 373.

15) On the basis of the Bucharest Resolution of the CMEA countries, June 24, 1963.

16) "Geld- und Kreditprobleme im Kampf zwischen den sozialistischen und kapitalistischen Industriestaaten," Wissenschaftliche Zeitschrift der Hochschule für Verkehrswesen "Friedrich List" (Dresden), 1968, Vol. 3, No. 15, p. 485.

17) Since these credits are seldom secured with a gold clause, any fluctuations in the corresponding currencies redound to the benefit of the socialist borrowers.

18) See W. Sztyber, "Theoretical Basis for the Reform of Sale Prices in Socialist Countries," Eastern European Economics, Winter 1970-1971, Vol. IX, No. 2, pp. 91-131 (translated from the Polish).

19) Ludwig von Mises long ago pointed out that the traditional economic concepts had become devoid of content in a planned economy: "Some of the terms of the capitalist market have been preserved, but they mean something entirely different from what they do in a true market economy" (Le gouvernement omnipotent, Paris, 1944, p. 90).

20) See Politická ekonomie, 1969, No. 6, p. 501.
21) See Finance a úvěr, 1970, No. 10, p. 40.
22) In some branches of industry, these should balance out the considerable differences between domestic and foreign prices. In 1968, subsidies were, on the average, 12.4 forints per dollar and 6.7 forints per ruble (see Wochenbericht des Deutschen Institutes für Wirtschaftsforschung, 1972, No. 35, p. 309).
23) See Jan M. Michal, "Price Structures and Implicit Dollar-Ruble Ratios in East European Trade," Weltwirtschaftliches Archiv, Vol. CVII, p. 179.
24) See P. Bozyk and B. Wojciechowski, Handel zagraniczny, 1971, p. 237.
25) See H. Kosk, "An Essay on the Comprehensive Accounting of the Profitability of Foreign Trade," Gospodarka planowa, 1972, No. 9, p. 26. After applying a price correction, the Institute for Business Trends of the Ministry of Foreign Trade obtained the following financial results for the total Polish exports:

	1965	1966	1967	1968	1969
Zloty/dollar	46.4	46.4	45.2	45.6	43.6

See Bozyk and Wojciechowski, op. cit., p. 237.
26) Bozyk and Wojciechowski, op. cit., p. 239.
27) Ibid., p. 226.
28) See H. Kosk, op. cit., p. 26.
29) See K. H. Nattland, Der Aussenhandel in der Wirtschaftreform der DDR, Berlin, 1971, p. 138. Nattland sets the conversion factor for trade with the West at 1 dollar = 7.28 marks, calculated at the official exchange rate, and at 1 transferable ruble = 6.07 marks, calculated at official rates for trade with the other CMEA countries.
30) J. Slama and H. Vogel, "The Level and History of the Kilogram Price in Soviet Foreign Trade with Machinery and Equipment," in Jahrbuch der Wirtschaft Osteuropas, Vol. 2, Munich, 1971, p. 450.
31) See Trybuna ludu, December 8, 1971.
32) Tourist trade, expenditures of diplomatic services,

transfers of emoluments, salaries, etc.

33) Wochenbericht des Deutschen Institutes für Wirtschaftsforschung, 1972, No. 50, p. 431.

34) See Polityka, June 1, 1972, p. 2.

35) In 1969, 20 percent of the population of Czechoslovakia traveled abroad, and 4.9 percent of these to the West. The corresponding figures for the other countries are: Hungary, 9.7 percent and 0.2 percent; Bulgaria, 3.3 percent and 0.5 percent; Poland, 2.5 percent and 0.3 percent; USSR, 0.6 percent and 0.2 percent (see Wochenbericht des Deutschen Institutes für Wirtschaftsforschung, 1971, No. 17, p. 119).

36) Ibid., 1972, No. 50, p. 431.

37) Ibid., 1971, No. 17, p. 120.

38) In Austria, this percentage is 32.9 percent.

39) Calculated from the Statistics Office of the Federal Republic of Germany. See Wochenbericht des Deutschen Institutes für Wirtschaftsforschung, 1969, No. 24, p. 151.

40) Since 1962, Albania has not participated actively in the CMEA, although it is still a member.

41) J. Konstantinov, "Currency and Financial Relations of the CMEA Countries," Aussenhandel (Moscow), 1972, No. 10, p. 6.

42) See O. Hoffmann, "Constitution and Foreign Trade Monopoly," Sozialistische Aussenhandelwirtschaft, 1968, No. 4, p. 2.

43) See Ivan Szász, Ungarns Rechtsnormen für den Aussenhandel, Budapest, 1970, p. 26.

44) Ibid.

45) See Wochenbericht des Deutschen Institutes für Wirtschaftsforschung, 1972, No. 35, p. 309.

46) See Marketing in Hungary (Budapest), 1971, No. 3, p. 23.

47) See Hoffmann, op. cit., p. 1.

48) See Nattland, op. cit., p. 61.

49) F. Kubiczek, "Modernization of the System of Foreign Trade Planning and Management," Aussenhandel (Warsaw), 1972, p. 81.

50) See V. Brzák and D. Maršiková, "New Methods of Management and Organization of Foreign Trade in Socialist

Countries (A Comparative Analysis)," Soviet and Eastern European Foreign Trade, Fall-Winter 1970, Vol. VI, No. 3-4, p. 261 (translated from the Czech).
51) Ibid., p. 263.
52) See Neuer Weg, March 19, 1971.
53) See Economic Bulletin for Europe, 1973, Vol. 24, No. 1, p. 37.
54) Ibid., p. 39.
55) See Marketing in Hungary, 1971, No. 3, p. 25.
56) Ibid.
57) See Szász, op. cit., p. 29.
58) See H. Weiss and D. Albrecht, "Foreign Trade in the Socialist Economic System," Sozialistiche Aussenwirtschaft, 1968, No. 1, p. 3.
59) See Nattland, op. cit., p. 66.
60) See J. Bohdanowicz, "New Organizational Forms in Polish Foreign Trade," Aussenhandel (Warsaw), 1971, p. 57.
61) See Życie gospodarcze, August 20, 1972, p. 4.
62) See Problemy handlu zagranicznego [Problems of Foreign Trade], Warsaw, 1971, p. 41.
63) See Kubiczek, op. cit., p. 80.
64) See Szász, op. cit., pp. 33-36.
65) See Bela Csikos-Nagy, "Effect of the Economic Reform on Hungarian Foreign Trade," Revue de l'est, 1970, No. 2, p. 12.
66) Szász, op. cit., p. 16.
67) Ibid., p. 77.
68) See Handbuch der Ungarischen Aussenwirtschaft, p. 17.
69) See Hospodárské noviny, December 21, 1969, No. 47, p. 4.
70) See Nattland, op. cit., p. 137.
71) See B. Wojciechowski, "Settlements Between Foreign Trade and Industry in the Process of Integration," in Integracja ekonomiczna krajów socjalistycznych, Warsaw, 1970, p. 378.
72) See U. Plowiec, "The System of Choice in Foreign Trade," Ekonomist, 1971, No. 5, p. 745.
73) Handel zagraniczny, 1972, p. 80.
74) Życie gospodarcze, August 20, 1972, p. 4.

75) Handbuch der Ungarischen Aussenwirtschaft, p. 20.

76) Quoted from Documents of the National Conference of the Romanian Communist Party, 19-21, 1972, Bucharest, Agerpress, p. 579.

77) Wissenschaftliche Zeitschrift der Hochschule für Verkehrswesen "Friedrich List," Department for Marxism-Leninism (Dresden), 1968, No. 15, p. 491.

3 | CMEA monetary institutions and steering instruments

1. From the Founding of the CMEA to the Comprehensive Program

1.1. The Specific Features of Economic Integration in Eastern Europe

Eastern Europe was already a tightly knit political and ideological bloc when the first institutions for economic cooperation among the Eastern European nations were created. Yet this circumstance could only work to the advantage of economic integration, which, indeed, fit right in with the overall design of one unified social order for all these countries. Integration also had better chances for success there than in Western Europe: a domestically oriented planned economy is not dependent on competition and the conquest of new markets. But economic integration still finds itself plagued by a wide range of difficulties stemming from conditions peculiar to each country and from various other factors, inherent to a planned economy, that tend to encourage autonomy.

In the CMEA, the Soviet Union is preeminent not only politically and militarily, but economically as well. It accounts for about 70 percent of the population (1), about 70 percent of the national product (2), and about 72 percent of industrial production (3) of the CMEA nations.

The Eastern bloc drew into its orbit a number of relatively small nations which, as a result, were forced to dissolve most of their traditional economic relations and seek new ones, principally with the Soviet Union. (Before World War II, the Soviet Union accounted for only 1 percent of the foreign trade of these countries; in 1972, this figure was 36 percent.) (4)

The Soviet Union has rich deposits of raw materials and energy sources as well as a diversified economic structure. All the other CMEA nations are to a large extent dependent on imports of raw materials and fuels from that country.

Before World War II, the theory and practice of socialist economic planning were geared to the specific economic structure of the USSR, which was richly endowed with raw materials and fuels and largely independent of the international division of labor. Questions concerning the regulation of economic relations between two or more planned economies did not even arise. In the Soviet system, which took shape under very special historical conditions, economic steering instruments were used very sparingly. After extensive debate and the practical experience of moneyless war communism and later the monetary relations under the NEP (which retained a number of market features), a centrally planned economy finally emerged in which the monetary system had important supervisory and administrative but no steering functions.

Planning in natura became the key focus, and some interesting methods were actually developed in this area. (The 1973 Nobel prize winner W. Leontief worked out his first input-output balances in the Soviet Union.) After several futile attempts during the immediate postwar years — hardly a normal period — to work out economic and political steering methods tailored specifically to the needs of each country, the Eastern European nations — some former monarchies with semifeudal structures, some already industrialized — ended up modeling their economies after the Soviet system as more in keeping with the new social order.

In their isolation from the world monetary system, the domestic monetary systems of the planned economies could provide no groundwork out of which multilateral economic relations could grow. This was not, however, seen as a serious drawback during the first years of the CMEA's existence. A single social system and a uniform model for growth, went the theory, would even out differences in development among all the member nations, and the socialist community as a whole would advance down the road of economic progress.

During this period, the international division of labor in the CMEA was cast in the same mold as CMEA foreign trade, which itself was scarcely more than an extension of the national plans for supplying domestic needs. It was structured in accordance with the economic growth model and gave a special and stable place to trade between the Soviet Union and the people's democracies. The Soviet Union, politically and economically the most powerful nation in the bloc, became, on the one hand, the chief supplier of raw materials and fuels, and, on the other, the principal market for the products of the processing industries of the smaller CMEA nations.

The economic and foreign trade policies followed at that time, although based on extensive growth factors, were able within a relatively short period to restore production capacity, which had been all but wiped out by the war, to industrialize and restructure the economies of the former agricultural countries, and to reduce the surplus population in the countryside.

It was inevitable, however, that the single broad model for economic growth and the concept of a uniform economic system should come up for criticism once they had exhausted their progressive features and begun to obstruct continued economic progress. New steering and growth models tailored to the particular needs of each individual nation were sought. The single road to a commonly shared goal was no longer viable. The CMEA division of labor, reproducing the formal features of foreign trade, now seemed inadequate to maintain the relationships — however underdeveloped — that had already been formed. (In 1953, intra-CMEA trade accounted for about 75 percent of the total foreign trade.) According to the new perspective, new forms of cooperation, international specialization, and coordination of the various national economic plans were to precede foreign trade agreements and establish the framework within which they were concluded.

The CMEA developed into an impressive information and research agency where important bilateral and even multilateral agreements on cooperation, specialization, and trade were concluded. A number of multilateral organizations — exerting quite an influence on economic development — were formed, among them, the oil pipeline system "Druzhba," the united energy system "Mir," a joint trucking depot, as well as useful coordinating centers such as Intermetall, Interchim, etc. The first two banks expanded their clearing and credit activities. The most important consequence of CMEA cooperation, however, has been the coordinated production and distribution of raw materials and fuels, and the autarky achieved in this area. For example, in 1971 the energy shortfall of four Eastern European countries (Bulgaria, 57 percent of total consumption; Hungary, 32 percent; German Democratic Republic, 22 percent; and Czechoslovakia, 15 percent), which amounted to 68 million tons of soft coal units (SCU) (5), was covered by surpluses in the other CMEA countries. The Soviet Union (138 million tons SCU surplus), Poland (20.6 million tons SCU surplus), and Romania (1.9 million tons SCU surplus) not only made up the deficits of these four countries but also shipped a portion of their energy resources to Western Europe. (6)

Yet in monetary and price matters, each nation continues to operate autonomously, and the steering functions of money and prices have developed more or less along separate lines in the various countries since the economic reforms.

For specialization projects, there exist no standard parameters for measuring the flow of goods and money (7) or established channels for effecting their transfer from country to country. This deficiency has been especially obstructive in the more advanced stages of integration, for example, in the construction of joint enterprises.

A supranational agency would have been even less capable of dealing with the divergent interests arising out of differences in economic structures and the uneven levels of development among the various countries. It was impossible not only to set a common plan target but also to meet such a target by means of administrative directives alone. (8)

Integration, conceived as the "unification of international economic relationships," is still in its infancy. (9)

The "Comprehensive Program for the Further Intensification and Improvement of Collaboration and the Development of Socialist Economic Integration of CMEA Member Nations," adopted at the Twenty-Fifth Session of the Council in Bucharest in July 1971, does not aim at the creation of an international economic system steered by one economic plan and administered by one supranational agency. It does, however, provide a realistic framework within which future CMEA cooperation will take place.

1.2. The Founding of the CMEA and Its Goals

The Council for Mutual Economic Assistance (CMEA) was founded on January 25, 1949. (10)

There were several reasons for its establishment, although the founding communiqué says only that the Eastern European nations felt slighted by the Marshall Plan, and that they had therefore resolved to set up their own economic bloc as an answer to the Western embargo. (11)

But the decision to form the CMEA was probably also influenced by Tito's resistance to Stalin's policies and Yugoslavia's expulsion from the Cominform (1948), as well as by the tendency of some of the smaller Eastern European countries (notably Romania and Bulgaria) to form groups of their own within the Eastern bloc. (12)

Initially, the general objectives of the CMEA were limited to the "exchange of practical experience, the tendering of mutual technical assistance, and reciprocity in the exchange of raw materials, foodstuffs, machines, and equipment." (13) At the time, the word "integration" was not even mentioned.

The goals of the CMEA were broadened or narrowed a number of times in the following years. Under Stalin, the activities of the CMEA were limited in scope. For a time, Khrushchev hoped to convert the CMEA into a central planning agency and ultimately into the central executive organ for the economy of the entire Eastern bloc. Pragmatists to the bone, the present

Organizational Chart of the Council for Mutual Economic Assistance, as of End of 1973

```
                                  SESSION OF THE COUNCIL
                                  Chair: alternating among the national
                                  representatives

                                  EXECUTIVE COMMITTEE
                                  Chairman: alternating

                                  SECRETARIAT OF THE COUNCIL
                                  Secretary: N. V. Faddeev
                                  Deputy Secretaries: Angelov-Todorov,
                                  Bulgaria; R. Görbing, German Democratic
                                  Republic; R. Szopa, Poland; V. Constanti-
                                  nescu, Romania; Z. Vadas, Hungary
```

COMMITTEE FOR COOPERATION IN PLANNING
Chairman: alternating

CMEA COMMITTEE FOR SCIENTIFIC-TECHNICAL COOPERATION (Moscow, 1971)
Chairman: alternating

CMEA Conferences

CONFERENCE OF HEADS OF SCIENTIFIC AGENCIES (1962)
Chairman: alternating

CONFERENCE OF REPRESENTATIVES OF THE OFFICES FOR LEGAL AFFAIRS OF CMEA MEMBER NATIONS (1969)
Chairman: alternating

CONFERENCE OF MINISTERS OF DOMESTIC TRADE OF CMEA MEMBER NATIONS (1972)
Chairman: alternating

Permanent Commissions

CONSTRUCTION INDUSTRY (Berlin, 1958)
Chairman: W. Junker, Minister of Construction of the GDR

LIGHT INDUSTRY (Prague, 1963)
Chairman: Ing. Jozef Kopča, Deputy Prime Minister of the Council of Ministers of Czechoslovakia

FOOD INDUSTRY (Sofia, 1963)
Chairman: G. Krstev, Minister of Agriculture of Bulgaria

ELECTRIC POWER INDUSTRY (Moscow, 1958)*
Chairman: N. S. Neporozhny, Minister for Energy and Electrification of the USSR

USE OF ATOMIC ENERGY FOR PEACEFUL PURPOSES (Moscow, 1960)
Chairman: A. M. Petrosyants, Chairman of the State Committee for the Use of Atomic Energy of the USSR

COAL INDUSTRY (Warsaw, 1956)
Chairman: J. Mitrega, Acting Minister-President of Poland

CMEA Institutes

INTERNATIONAL RESEARCH INSTITUTE FOR ECONOMIC PROBLEMS IN THE SOCIALIST COMMUNITY (Moscow, 1970)

Director: M. Senin

INSTITUTE FOR STANDARDIZATION (Moscow, 1962)

Director: L. Konorov

OIL AND GAS INDUSTRY (Bucharest, 1956)

Chairman: B. Almasan, Minister of Mining, Industry, and Geology of Romania

GEOLOGY (Ulan Bator, 1963)

Chairman: M. Pelzhee, Minister of the Fuel and Energy Industries and Geology of Mongolia

FERROUS METALLURGY (Moscow, 1958)

Chairman: I. Kazanets, Minister for Ferrous Metallurgy of the USSR

NONFERROUS METALLURGY (Budapest, 1956)

Chairman: D. Seker, Minister for Heavy Industry of Mongolia

MACHINE-TOOL INDUSTRY (Prague, 1956)

Chairman: Ing. Josef Simon, Minister for Metallurgy of Czechoslovakia

RADIO-TECHNICAL AND ELECTRONICS INDUSTRY (Budapest, 1963)

Chairman: G. Horgos, Minister of Metallurgy and the Machine Industry, Hungary

CHEMICAL INDUSTRY (Berlin, 1956)

Chairman: G. Wyschofsky, Minister of the Chemical Industry of the GDR

AGRICULTURE (Sofia, 1958)

Chairman: G. Krstev, Minister of Agriculture of Bulgaria

FOREIGN TRADE (Moscow, 1956)

Chairman: N. Patolichev, Minister of Foreign Trade of the USSR

CURRENCY AND FINANCE (Moscow, 1962)

Chairman: V. F. Garbuzov, Minister of Finance of the USSR

STATISTICS (Moscow, 1962)

Chairman: V. N. Starovsky, Director of the Central Statistical Administration of the USSR

STANDARDIZATION (Berlin, 1962)

Chairman: H. Emmerich, Director of the Bureau of Standards of the GDR

TRANSPORT (Warsaw, 1958)

Chairman: M. Zaifrid, Minister of Transport of Poland

TELECOMMUNICATIONS AND POSTAL AFFAIRS (Moscow, 1971)

Chairman: N. Psurtsev, Minister of Postal Affairs of the USSR

* Founding date.

leadership of the Soviet Union sees the CMEA as an agency for introducing scientific and technical ideas into the Eastern bloc economy, for keeping tabs on the development of the member nations, for furthering specialization in production, especially in the machine-tool industry, and for coordinating important sectors of the economy.

1.3. The Goals of the CMEA

Under Stalin, the CMEA played a minor role. Council meetings were rare occurrences, and the important decisions were made elsewhere. For example, the decision to adjust the five-year plans to the needs of the Korean War by expanding the armaments industry at the expense of consumer goods production was made not in the CMEA, but at a conference of top-level officials of the Eastern European communist parties in Holohasa, Hungary (1951).

The rechanneling of the foreign trade of the Eastern European countries away from their traditional markets in the West and toward the Soviet Union was accomplished through various devices independent of the CMEA. In the first place, the postwar reparation debts the Soviet Union imposed on some Eastern European countries paved the way for the establishment of closer relations between the Eastern European economies and the Soviet Union. Joint associations, such as the Soviet-German Association (SGA) and the Soviet-Romanian Society (SOVROMS) also tended to promote close ties. The construction of giant steel and iron works in a number of Eastern European countries, such as Stalinvaros in Hungary and the Lenin Steel Mill in Poland, furthered foreign trade relations. These projects intensified the dependence of the Eastern European countries on the Soviet Union, since at that time only the latter was in a position to supply the raw materials and fuels necessary to heavy industry.

The Western embargo also did its share to hasten the establishment of close economic ties among the Eastern European countries. During the cold war era, trade and credit relations between East and West dwindled to almost nothing. For example, from 1948 to 1953, the share of intrabloc trade in total foreign trade activity rose from 46 percent to 70 percent in Poland, from 33 percent to 78 percent in Czechoslovakia, and from 34 percent to 76 percent in Hungary. (14)

Under Stalin, the CMEA was able to perform its minor functions with a modest administrative apparatus that consisted of the Council and a small bureau sustained by the official representatives of the member nations and the Council Secretary.

During this period, in which the economies of the individual Eastern European nations were steered primarily by means of directives issued by the central planning authorities, money played only a minor role, even in domestic transactions. At that time, it was quite impossible for effective monetary relations capable of undermining the system of bilateral clearing to develop in intrabloc trade.

1.4. Upswing of the CMEA

Stalin's death in March 1953 was followed by a period of political uncertainty in the Soviet Union which lasted until Khrushchev was able to consolidate his leadership. After some time had passed, it became possible to criticize some of the weaknesses in earlier economic policies, such as parallel investment projects, high costs, low productivity, the obstruction of technical progress, etc.

As a result of the one-sided emphasis on investments (25 to 30 percent of the national income), especially in the capital goods industry, and the broad neglect of the consumer goods industries and agriculture, the population long had to endure inadequate supplies of even the most necessary consumer goods. The situation was especially serious in agriculture. Agricultural production was less in 1953 than in 1913 in the Soviet Union, and the situation was not much better, if at all, in Poland and Czechoslovakia. In Hungary, real wages fell by 20 percent between 1949 and 1953. (15)

The international situation following the Korean War also demanded reforms of earlier economic policies. The West retreated from its embargo against the Eastern European nations and began to liberalize its foreign trade and make its foreign currencies convertible. In the West, 1953 marked the beginning of a period of long, sustained economic growth that exceeded all expectations, despite occasional recessions and a currency crisis that has recently threatened to become chronic. In the East, economic growth was even more rapid than in the West, although there it was primarily due to extensive factors whose impetus gradually waned without there having been brought about a corresponding increase in economic productivity through technical progress and improved operating methods.

In the Soviet Union, a gradual realization occurred that the political and ideological union of socialist states could achieve a lasting stability only if it were ultimately rooted in the firm soil of economic cooperation. (16) The need for closer cooperation was felt even more keenly in the people's democracies than in the Soviet Union; their ties with the world market had been severely curtailed, and the founding of the Common Market threatened to hamper their foreign trade even further. Above all, they hoped that in the CMEA they would be able to apply the achievements of technical progress on a broader and more efficient basis than if they had been forced to go it alone.

The basic outlines of economic cooperation among the CMEA countries were drawn up in the Sixth, Seventh, and Ninth Council meetings (December 1955, May 1956, and April 1958). (17) Each Eastern European country was to specialize in those branches of the economy and in those products with which it was best equipped to deal. The national economic plans of the CMEA nations were to be coordinated internationally on both a short-term and long-term basis. The closing communiqué of the Seventh Council meeting reads: "For the first time in history, the coordination of the economic plans of the individual countries becomes a practicable objective." (18) At the Seventh Council meeting, concrete resolutions were drawn up concerning important specialization projects — for example, in the machine-tool industry, in chemistry, and in ferrous and nonferrous metallurgy — for the years 1956 through 1960. These specialization projects were to be backed up by adequate supplies of raw materials and energy. The first draft of an extensive power grid was also approved at this meeting. At the Ninth Session of the Council, a joint plan extending over a ten- to fifteen-year period was drawn up for the entire CMEA area.

Whereas Western Europe elected to promote economic integration by creating a common market, Eastern Europe sought to achieve the same goal by means of coordinated economic plans. [19] Article I of the CMEA statutes, which were adopted at the Twelfth Session of the Council (December 1959), sets forth the goals and principles of the CMEA (1962 version):

>   1. The Council for Mutual Economic Assistance has as its goal to promote the planned development of the national economies, to accelerate the economic and technical progress of its member nations, to step up industrialization in those countries with an underdeveloped industry, and to raise steadily the productivity of labor and the standard of living of CMEA nations through joint and coordinated efforts.
>
>   2. The Council for Mutual Economic Assistance is based on the recognition of the equality and sovereignty of all its member nations. Scientific and technical and economic cooperation among CMEA member nations must take place in a manner consistent with the principles of full equality of rights, respect of national sovereignty and national interests, mutual advantage, and comradely mutual assistance. [20]

The statutes of the CMEA do not explicitly mention the governing principle of relations among socialist countries, namely, socialist internationalism. In the official interpretations, the general democratic principles of the CMEA (equality, sovereignty, etc.) seem to be corollaries of the more general principle of socialist internationalism. [21]

The fundamental principles of the international socialist division of labor were approved at the Fifteenth Session of the Council (December 1961). Coordination of the national economic plans is the "principal method to be used for methodically expanding the international division of labor and for achieving the ultimate unification of the productive efforts of the socialist countries in the present stage." [22]

Khrushchev believed that Eastern Europe could develop an integral and coherent planned economy by relying basically on administrative steering methods. He therefore placed great stock in the expansion of the administrative apparatus of the CMEA. Only later was it perceived that monetary steering instruments were as indispensable to comprehensive planning for the CMEA territory as a whole as they were to the individual national planned economies. But by the time this was fully realized, the national economies had progressed so far along divergent paths that it was no longer a simple task to coordinate the various national economic policies. In particular, multi-lateralization of CMEA economic relations encountered insuperable difficulties on account of the underdeveloped monetary and credit systems.

The "Agreement Concerning Multilateral Settlements in Transferable Rubles and the Organization of the International Bank for Economic Cooperation" (October 22, 1963) took place while Khrushchev was still in power. At that time, however, given the existing conditions, the objectives spelled out in the agreement were unattainable.

1.5. Difficulties During the Period of Growth

The growth rates in the Eastern bloc, 7-12 percent in the 1950s and 6-7 percent in the 1960s, were higher than those of the Western economies. However, the CMEA did not really have much to do with this impressive growth. The two primary objectives — the development of a comprehensive plan for all the national economies of the CMEA and the creation of central steering agencies — remained unachieved; the necessary preconditions simply did not exist. The CMEA suffers from a fundamental contradiction: it must work toward the integration of the Eastern European economies without infringing on the autonomy of its member nations in matters of economic policy.

Although under Khrushchev each of the individual countries was permitted to adapt the Soviet model, intended originally as a universal standard, to its particular situation, the net long-

National Income of the CMEA Countries and Their Industrial
and Agricultural Gross Product per Capita

	Year	Bulgaria	Czechoslovakia	Hungary	GDR	Poland	Romania	USSR
National income	1950	0.6	1.6	1.2	1.5	1.1	0.5	1.0
	1970	0.8	1.2	0.9	1.3	0.8	0.8	1.0
Industrial production	1950	0.4	1.5	0.8	1.5	0.7	0.3	1.0
	1970	0.8	1.3	0.8	1.5	0.8	0.6	1.0
Agricultural production	1950	0.8	1.2	1.6	0.8	1.7	0.8	1.0
	1970	1.1	1.0	1.3	1.1	1.2	0.8	1.0

Source: Vneshniaia torgovlia, 1972, No. 4, p. 7.

term effect of such a policy was necessarily a disintegrating one.

The goal of the CMEA — the gradual achievement of a uniform level of production in all the member countries — still remained largely unattained after a quarter of a century. The reasons for this are not hard to find. Between 1950 and 1970, the less developed countries, such as Bulgaria and Romania, reduced their backwardness relative to the Soviet Union from 40-50 percent to 20-30 percent, measured in terms of the social product per capita of population. Czechoslovakia's lead over the Soviet Union diminished from 60 to 20 percent within that same period. Poland and Hungary, which in 1950 were 10 percent and 20 percent ahead of the Soviet Union, respectively, had fallen 20 percent and 15 percent behind the USSR by 1970. Only the German Democratic Republic was able to maintain its advantage of 30 percent over the Soviet Union. A spread of

50 percent still separates the German Democratic Republic, economically the most developed, and Romania, the least developed country in the CMEA. (23)

Because of these appreciable differences in development, each of the individual CMEA nations has had to define the goals of its economic policies differently. Each country developed its own price and wage structure and worked out its monetary, credit, and fiscal policies autonomously.

Under these circumstances, the CMEA is hardly amenable to being steered by a central authority, either as a market economy or by planning methods.

The "intrinsic" price basis (i.e., prices for intra-CMEA trade alone), discussed since 1959, has remained only an idea, while the first CMEA bank, founded in 1964, has since limited its activities essentially to settling bilateral trade under strict quotas.

In Western Europe, the chief instruments for achieving economic integration have been a liberalized foreign trade and the free movement of capital and labor, with the various firms then competing on the open market. In Eastern Europe, where factors inherent to the system impede the mobility of production factors, the international division of labor is seen as a goal to be achieved through agreements on specialization in production and cooperation. The central planning authorities then undertake the implementation of these agreements through the issuance of practical directives, although they have no price system of their own to which they may refer. So far, this gargantuan task has remained unfulfilled, even though the various agencies of the CMEA, especially the Secretariat, have been considerably expanded. (The number of experts in the Secretariat was increased tenfold during the Khrushchev era.)

The further extension of the international division of labor and the furtherance of technical progress — objectives shared by all the member nations — have so far been pursued but very imperfectly. Since objective criteria were lacking, the needs of the individual countries could not be coordinated with one another. For example, Bulgaria and Romania, which hope to overcome their backwardness through specialization, would understandably like to increase their share in the machine-tool industry in the CMEA, while countries with a highly developed machine-tool industry, such as the German Democratic Republic and Czechoslovakia, want to maintain their dominant position in this area. The latter have argued cogently that labor productivity in their machine-tool industry is 20-30 percent higher than in those countries who wish to enter that field for the first time. (24) It was, and continues to be, even more difficult to achieve a consensus between the Soviet Union, which is practically autarkic, and the smaller CMEA countries, which are highly dependent on foreign trade; the objective criteria for selecting objects suitable for specialization simply do not exist.

Specialization agreements among the CMEA countries have had a relatively minor role to play. In the machine-tool industry, where specialization is especially useful, only 2 to 6 percent of the total production had been covered by specialization agreements by the end of the sixties. (25) The quality of the machines built in the CMEA countries frequently does not reflect the most up-to-date technology. Therefore, high-quality machines are among the most coveted imports from the West.

Specialization in production was supposed to set the stage for the development of joint enterprises, joint research, reciprocity in capital investment, etc., the objective in all cases being a higher level of economic integration. So far, however, the practical results have not been very encouraging. The joint Polish-Hungarian enterprise "Haldex," to mention one, which began operations in 1959 in Katowice, has found very few imitators; the cost and price calculations proved to be extremely complicated, while profits are transferable only under certain conditions. (26)

There are essential differences between the Eastern and Western approaches to economic integration. For example, foreign trade connections among the Eastern European nations are much more extensive than among the Western European countries. Even in 1953, intra-CMEA trade accounted for 75 percent of the total foreign trade of the CMEA members, although it had diminished to 60 percent in 1972. (27)

Trade among the Common Market members, on the other

hand, did not reach 34 percent until 1960 (a few years after the Rome conventions became effective) but had risen to 50 percent by 1972. (28) Intra-EFTA trade developed along the same lines as intra-EEC trade.

In the areas of production, tourism, establishment of branches abroad, capital and credit flow, and the labor force, economic integration has proceeded at a much greater pace in the West than in the East. (29)

As has always been the case, foreign investments in the CMEA are possible only through the utilization of long-term credits, and these are generally credits granted for opening new raw material and fuel deposits in the CMEA territory, principally in the Soviet Union. Such credits are granted in kind (usually in the form of machinery and equipment) and paid back the same way (mainly in raw materials and energy). Bilateral credits among CMEA countries usually yield 2 percent (30), a rate which is much lower than the rate of profit used for cost accounting in the CMEA. Nevertheless, this low interest rate was accepted by the people's democracies because, given the lack of freely convertible foreign exchange, it was the only means whereby they could insure themselves of a steady supply of necessary raw materials and fuels. (31)

The relatively low volume of foreign trade in the CMEA is a direct indication that the Eastern European countries are not using the international division of labor to the fullest advantage. In 1971, the CMEA countries accounted for about one-fourth of the total world industrial production (about 9 percent without the Soviet Union), but only 9.4 percent of world trade (5.5 percent without the Soviet Union). Moreover, the share of the CMEA countries in total world trade has decreased by 1.5 percent over the last ten years. (32)

The trend was quite different in Western Europe. In 1971, the EEC "Nine" accounted for 18 percent of total industrial production but for 36 percent of world trade (33); these figures have undergone a 2 percent increase over the last decade. (34)

Although in the 1960s the economic growth rate was greater in the East than in the West, the CMEA nations found themselves forced increasingly to turn to the West for high-quality machinery, licenses for modern products, and technical expertise. Distinguished Eastern European economists attributed this unsatisfactory situation to functional flaws in the economic planning and steering systems in the CMEA, and the whole conception of the relationship between plan and market was rethought. Some CMEA members urged a restructuring of intra-CMEA trade relations along more efficient lines by incorporating certain elements of a market economy into the steering mechanism of an integrated CMEA. Others wanted only to improve the existing traditional steering mechanisms. A variety of solutions was proposed. Poland favored a collective CMEA currency that would be made convertible within the near future and saw this as an indispensable condition for the multilateralization of economic relations within the CMEA. Hungary and, with a few qualifications, Czechoslovakia represented a similar view. Romania, as usual, preferred the status quo, and the German Democratic Republic was also uninterested in any radical changes in the existing CMEA policies. As on earlier occasions, Bulgaria pointed out that the current CMEA agricultural prices discriminated against it, and called attention to the original goal of the CMEA, which was to achieve a uniform level of production throughout the member nations. Finally, the Soviet Union focused on the problem of raw materials and fuels, and urged the other member nations to participate in the tapping of new deposits. Neither the Soviet Union, Bulgaria, the German Democratic Republic, or Romania were interested in any fundamental changes in the existing foreign trade and clearing system of the CMEA.

The events in Czechoslovakia in 1968 prevented any more substantial development of reforms in the direction of a market economy. In the aftermath of these events, the Twenty-Third Special Session of the Council (April 1969) resolved to work out a long-term program for the further development of the CMEA, and the basic guidelines for the future comprehensive program were laid down at this time, with explicit emphasis placed on the planning principle in the management of the national economies.

1.6. The Comprehensive Program

"The Comprehensive Program for the Further Intensification and Improvement of Collaboration and the Development of Socialist Economic Integration of CMEA Member Nations," adopted by the Twenty-Fifth Session of the Council, July 27-29, 1971, in Bucharest, represents a realistic assessment of the limited possibilities that exist for the economic integration of the CMEA countries and defines the direction and goals of the development of the CMEA for the next fifteen to twenty years. At the same time, the Comprehensive Program provides for a long period of cooperation with the West.

Closer collaboration among the CMEA countries is being encouraged by increasing bilateral relations both in intra-CMEA trade and in specialization and cooperation.

Although the Comprehensive Program places a premium on planning as the sovereign principle in the steering of the national economies, it provides no economic plan for the CMEA territory as a whole. It does, however, recommend that the member nations work out long-term forecasts in the areas of economics, science, and technology, and that they undertake, wherever expedient, the joint planning of specific branches of industry and particular projects. Bilateralism is the explicit watchword of foreign trade: "Intra-CMEA trade relations will continue to be the monopoly of the respective states, even as planning becomes more and more a factor in the economy" (35); i.e., goods and services will continue to be exchanged bilaterally on the basis of preset quotas expressed in terms of quantity or value. Poland's proposal (which Hungary supported) that the exchange of industrial consumer goods be liberalized was rejected. Free exchange of goods is possible only within very circumscribed limits, for deliveries beyond the scope of plan targets. The comment in the Comprehensive Program that "the mutual exchange of nonquota commodities need not unconditionally be balanced out bilaterally" (36) is an indication that bilateral clearing will continue to be the rule in intra-CMEA trade. Under these conditions, the CMEA should be able to do without a convertible currency for at least fifteen to twenty years.

Section 7 of the Comprehensive Program, which deals with ways to improve foreign exchange and finance relations among the CMEA countries, contains vague allusions to the possible future role of the transferable ruble as a collective currency in world trade as well. Nevertheless, for the present, the transferable ruble is not even partially convertible into Western currencies, as Poland and Hungary had wanted.

For certain transactions, which have not yet been specified, the national CMEA currencies are supposed to be convertible against one another and against the transferable ruble. "A decision on the establishment of standard exchange rates for the national currencies and the date for their introduction will be reached in 1980." (37)

The Comprehensive Program also fails to provide a solution to the paradoxical price situation in intra-CMEA trade. The member nations "will in the immediate future continue to set prices in intra-CMEA trade in the same way as they now do." (38)

The idea of a supranational CMEA organ was dismissed with the following words: "Socialist economic integration will be pursued on a completely voluntary basis and in no way involves the creation of supranational agencies. It has nothing to do with the problems of domestic planning, financial operations, and the activity of organizations in the area of economic management." (39)

Although the Comprehensive Program left important economic problems unsolved, or set them aside to some remote future date (as, for example, the gradual development of a standard costs and price structure for the entire CMEA territory linked to the world market through convertible CMEA currencies, thus setting the stage for a better utilization of the advantages of the international division of labor) it still represents a major step forward insofar as it is a conscious attempt to explore and put to use all possible ways to increase the efficiency of the CMEA economies within the framework of the existing economic and social order and, moreover, sets cooperation with the Western nations as one of its goals.

At the Council session of the CMEA in June 1973 in Prague,

the problems of fuel and energy supplies, joint industrial projects, and scientific and technological cooperation were discussed in the context of the Comprehensive Program, and long-term perspectives were outlined for the planning period 1976-1980. Contacts with the EEC and EFTA were also sounded out at this time.

2. Clearing in Intra-CMEA Trade and the IBEC

2.1. From Bilateral to Multilateral Clearing

Bilateral clearing was universal immediately after World War II. However, the socialist nations adopted this method of settlement as structurally appropriate to a planned economy and modified it as required. The initial unit of settlement was the clearing ruble, but like the transferable ruble today, the only thing it had in common with the Soviet ruble was its gold content. "The clearing ruble was used in a closed system of mutual settlement between two partners." (40)

There was no connection between the unit of settlement of the Eastern bloc and the internationally accepted currencies. Terms of payment contained no gold or dollar clause in the event a stipulated swing in intra-CMEA bilateral trade was exceeded. During the period from 1955 to 1968, settlement procedures were steadily improved (e.g., the practice of "immediate payment" upon submission of clearing documents was introduced) so that it was no longer necessary to use credits to bridge gaps in clearing. Credits were henceforth necessary only if the conditions of delivery were not met.

Such a clearing system, considered appropriate for a planned economy, can only be justified within the framework of the former foreign trade model, in which it fulfilled a stopgap function. For intra-CMEA trade, on the other hand, it created tremendous problems from the very outset. While it did permit exchange without currency and extended the clearing function beyond the national territory covered by the plan, it also retained the traditional shortcomings of this form of settlement: exchange had to be kept within the capacities of the weaker partner to pay; the choice of trading partner was limited; and the relatively liberal settlement terms — i.e., the allowance of an unlimited swing without a gold clause (initially even without interest) — gave rise to a number of undesirable side effects, not the least of which was a remissness in meeting delivery dates. (41) It therefore soon became a general desire to go beyond the narrow limits of bilateral clearing. Although official theory still continued to issue pronouncements on the superiority of bilateral clearing for a few years, on January 29, 1948, the Soviet Union and Poland signed an agreement that enabled balances from bilateral settlements to be transferred to a third party — provided, of course, the latter was in agreement. Similar agreements were concluded between other CMEA countries. (42)

Multilateral trade was relatively slight, however. Even in Western Europe, multilateralization of foreign trade payments flows had not progressed very far in the early fifties.

Only a few of the reasons for the failures of the first multilateralization attempts were the same in Eastern and Western Europe. During the immediate postwar period, neither Western nor Eastern Europe could offer a broad range of goods, and neither possessed sufficient currency reserves — although both of these conditions are indispensable for any multilateral trade activity to take place.

As the two economic systems developed, however, multilateral trade proved to be especially suited to a market economy, and particularly unsuited to a planned economy, at least as the latter was then conceived. (43)

In January 1957, a second, much more broadly conceived attempt at multilateralization was undertaken in the CMEA. Pursuant to the resolution of the Eighth Session of the CMEA, the "Agreement on Multilateral Clearing Between CMEA Member Nations" was signed on June 20, 1957, and a central clearing office was established with the State Bank of the Soviet Union. The terms of this agreement were fashioned after the multilateral agreements concluded in Western Europe between 1947 and 1950. Trade was still to be pursued on the basis of planned quotas and bilateral clearing. Only the net results were to be cleared multilaterally. Even this, however, was not to ensue automatically nor in all cases; a prerequisite was that the parties to a bilateral settlement had to be in agreement on a suitable third party. Neither at that time nor at any later date was there any notable willingness to permit departures from the bilaterally set quotas that had been firmly established in input-output plans.

Chief emphasis, therefore, was not on the settlement of outstanding balances remaining from a bilateral clearing, but on the direct settlement of nonquota deliveries not provided for in the plan. However, these consisted only of excess goods that could not be disposed of domestically. Bilateral balancing of reciprocated orders was not obligatory in this case. Any goods exported by a country in addition to the amounts stipulated in the basic bilateral agreement during a calendar year were to equal the excess deliveries of all the other parties to the agreement.

The clearing office had no funds in gold or convertible currency at its disposal. The agreement was accompanied by a list of "hard" goods that could be used as a means of settlement in the event of long-standing debts. The list was never used, however. The trade that actually took place under the terms of this agreement was very slight. Multilateral cleared balances amounted, on the average, to scarcely 1.5 percent of the total intra-CMEA trade (in 1961, they accounted for only 0.5 percent — 38 million rubles — of the total turnover). (44)

The extremely modest turnover of the Moscow clearing office was no accident. Foreign trade continued to be pursued bilaterally on the basis of preset quotas. Balance settlements with third-party nations were used only in the case of consumer goods excesses, and these were never inordinately large.

Throughout the entire period from 1957 to 1963, the conditions necessary for the development of multilateral trade remained largely unmet, and the turnover volume of the clearing office continued to decline. Not even the slightest attempt was made to give the CMEA unit of settlement some of the features of a hard currency.

2.2. The International Bank for Economic Cooperation (IBEC)

2.2.1. Goals and Responsibilities of the IBEC

After Western Europe's first unsuccessful attempts to multilateralize foreign trade, the European Payments Union (EPU) was founded in 1950. The unsatisfactory results of multilateral clearing (through the Moscow clearing office) induced the CMEA to create the International Bank for Economic Cooperation (IBEC) along the same lines as the EPU. The bank was founded with the agreement of October 22, 1963, and began operations on January 1, 1964. Two principal objectives were thus served: (a) the elimination of the limits imposed by bilateral clearing; (b) the creation of a collective currency, the transferable ruble, which was to facilitate the financing of large-scale investment projects in the pursuit of ambitious specialization goals.

Accordingly, the first two articles of the agreement state: "Each member country of the Bank entering into trade agreements shall insure the balance of collections and payments in transferable rubles with all other member countries of the Bank as a whole, within the calendar year (or any other period agreed upon by member countries of the Bank).

"The Bank, by order of interested countries, can effect financing and crediting of operational exploitation of working joint industrial enterprises and other undertakings from funds allocated by these countries." (45)

The organizational structure and operations of the IBEC were much more broadly conceived than those of the Moscow Clearing Office. Not only the net excesses of bilateral agreements and uncontemplated deliveries but all intra-CMEA trade, both projected and supplementary, were to be cleared through the IBEC. Multilateral settlement was to take place automatically without the assent of the countries involved. No other method of settlement was to be permitted.

Like any other banking institution, the IBEC was also to have capital at its disposal, grant credits (both short- and medium-term), accept deposits, charge interest, and make a profit from its operations.

The IBEC was conceived as an open organization, i.e., its operations were not to be restricted to the CMEA countries. (46) Other nations could also become affiliated with the bank as long as they accepted its objectives and fulfilled their statutory obligations (Article XIII). So far, however, only CMEA nations have joined the IBEC. (47)

From a technical and structural standpoint, the agreement was doubtless a significant event. The concentration of all settlements involving the movement of goods in the hands of one central office makes it possible to maintain a steady watch over plan fulfillment, to take appropriate steps in the event of delivery lags, and to provide financial assistance on a collective basis to any country that might find itself in difficulties. In addition, joint CMEA trade policy would have been feasible, given the right conditions. But factors other than those of a purely technical and structural nature were crucial to the decision to establish the IBEC. What was really needed was a bank which would be instrumental in carrying out fundamental decisions bearing on integration.

In a general way, the IBEC was a component part of the overall integration plan. Banking operations had, of course, to be adjusted to the practical possibilities of integration, although it must be said that quite a gap still existed between what was contemplated and what was feasible. Both the agreement and the bank's statutes, therefore, contain provisions that give some ground to the proposal, advocated mainly by Poland and Hungary, that all banking functions be transferred to the IBEC, as well as to the designs of Romania and the Soviet Union, which attempted to block the efforts of the maximalists and limit the function of the bank to that of a clearing office.

The general concept of the bank and its founding documents enable the IBEC to function as an active bank or as a mere clearing office, or as both. The manner in which foreign trade transactions are implemented remains the crucial factor determining the nature of the bank's activities. The foreign trade managers insisted from the outset, however, that they were neither willing nor able to alter current foreign trade practices in any way, so that the IBEC became essentially a clearing office — a well-run one, to be sure — and nothing more.

Its clearing procedures were modeled after those of the EPU, which had contributed to the multilateralization of foreign trade in Western Europe by a judicious combination of liberalized foreign trade (48) and constantly improving clearing procedures. (49) In contrast, the CMEA found itself unable either to eliminate the quota system from foreign trade or to create a more functional currency.

The contradiction between the optimum design and the limited methods available for implementing it was nowhere more evident than in the way the collective currency functioned.

2.2.2. The IBEC as a Clearing Office; the Transferable Ruble as a Clearing Currency

From a technical and structural standpoint, there was nothing to hinder the free circulation of the transferable ruble. The bank's members did not abandon bilateral balancing of deliveries, however. Currently, money, as a medium of exchange, is actually transferred in the barest minimum of multilateral transactions (50), and the total amount transferred is nowhere allowed to exceed the prior limits set by the Moscow clearing office for multilaterally cleared balances, namely, 1-2 percent of a country's total turnover. The volume of collective CMEA currency in circulation is determined by the time lags in delivery flows. However, settlement of outstanding balances does not mean the final adjustment of mutual claims and obligations; these are ultimately covered by commodities specified in the agreement. The transferable ruble is, in the economic meaning of the term, nontransferable. (51)

Yet clearing procedures have improved considerably since the transferable ruble was made the clearing unit of the IBEC. Settlements take place smoothly. A member now has a net positive or negative balance with the IBEC instead of a clearing balance with each of its trading partners. Nevertheless, it is the specific technical and organizational achievements of the transferable ruble, rather than its economic function, which stand out and which, moreover, have had a considerable influence on IBEC operations.

2.2.3. The Credit Operations of the IBEC

The October 22, 1963, agreement establishing the IBEC provided for six types of credit to member banks (Article VI):
1) settlement credits;
2) seasonal credits to cover seasonal negative balances;
3) credits to be extended in the event that commodity exchange exceeds planned volume;
4) supplementary credits not covered in the plan;
5) credits for squaring the balance of payments;
6) credits from the funds of countries interested in joint investments.

Foreign trade transactions carried out on the basis of bilaterally balanced delivery quotas showed no major departures from the plan. If one were to judge only from the results of the first two years of banking operations, it would appear that Bulgaria, Mongolia, and Romania were chronic debtors of the IBEC. However, in the following years, the situation changed. Czechoslovakia, which at the outset had been a consistent creditor of the IBEC, showed a negative balance of 170 million transferable rubles in July 1967, and 270 million transferable rubles by the second half of 1969. (52) All the other member nations have had payment difficulties from time to time, though none has become a chronic debtor.

The totals for credits granted during a calendar year, as well as their share in the total volume of settlements, gives some idea of the magnitude of deliveries still outstanding at any given time:

	1964	1965	1966	1967	1968	1969	1970	1971
Total credits granted (in billions of transferable rubles)	1.5	1.8	1.6	1.9	2.0	1.6	2.0	2.8
Share of credits in total clearing activities	10.0	13.0	12.0	12.0	12.0	—	10.1	12.6

Source: Annual reports of the IBEC.

The share of credits in the total clearing activities of the IBEC was greatest in 1965 and 1971, but it never exceeded 13 percent. Payments, surpluses, and deficits are smaller in the IBEC than they were in the EPU. (53)

Whatever one calls them, credits ultimately have one function, namely, to bridge lags in deliveries in planned trade. Credits must be granted so as not to impede the smooth flow of clearing activities. Credit is extended automatically.

Settlement credits account for the lion's share of total credits extended, and have never been less than 80 percent. (54)

The bank president, K. Nasarkin, put his finger on the crux of the problem: "If credit is extended to pay for imports that exceed in value the proceeds from exported goods within a given period, there is no way to determine for what reason the member bank needs a credit — whether it is required because of the effects of seasonal fluctuations in production on exports or because of a lag in the fulfillment of export obligations, or whether this need for credit has arisen out of a short-term discrepancy between receipts and payments that is usually covered by settlement credits." (55)

The volume of credits extended to CMEA nations has increased steadily from year to year. However, the wide range of different types of credits provided for by the agreement has been the target of growing criticism from the bank members. In multilateral clearing, any credit, regardless of its form, will have the technical function of a settlement credit, and it will be impossible to determine the reason the credit was needed. At the end of 1970, the member nations agreed to a radical simplification of the existing practices.

Two types of credit were agreed upon:

a) Settlement credit — to cover the needs of the authorized banks for funds during short-term excesses in payments over collections. This is revolving credit; when necessary, it is granted immediately within limits set by the Bank Council, without stipulation of the period of repayment.

b) Term credit — to cover the needs of the authorized banks for funds over longer periods of time. This type of credit is extended for arrangements relating to specialization and cooperation in production, for the expansion of trade turnover, for squaring the balance of payment, for seasonal needs, etc. The bank advances this credit on the basis of well-grounded applications of the authorized banks for fixed terms of up to one year or, in certain instances, for a period of up to two or three years by special order of the Bank Council. (56)

The credit machinery of the IBEC is doubtless an improvement over the system of bilateral clearing. Trading partners are not bound by mutual obligations in this system. The IBEC is the collective creditor and debtor of each country.

The credit volume has been reduced to half the volume extended when bilateral clearing was in effect. Credit has fewer functions in trade among the planned economies than in trade among the market economies. In the former, credit does not help improve economic efficiency. For instance, the 1971 figures for total credits, position at year's end, and share of credits in total turnover showed increases of 42.1 percent, 34.3 percent, and 24.7 percent, respectively, over the preceding year; yet no positive implications can be drawn from these figures. The only certain conclusion one can draw from such data is that in 1971 the trading partners were less disciplined than in the preceding years and caused the creditors greater losses (through delivery delays).

2.2.4. Deposits in the IBEC

In accordance with Article XI of the bank statutes, authorized banks that have funds in transferable rubles in accounts with the IBEC have free access to the use of these funds for settlements in transferable rubles.

These accounts, which are either sight or time deposits, are balances left over from the multilateral settlements of the member nations and are charged interest in proportion to the time for which they are tied up. This is intended to provide an incentive to exports and to encourage the overfulfillment of plan targets. In practice, however, deposits with the IBEC can be used neither on the CMEA market nor elsewhere for the purchase of any unspecified goods. They are not employed by the authorized banks to pay for additional goods, nor are they used by the IBEC as funds for credits. (57)

In the IBEC's clearing system, the setting up of deposits is not a precondition for credit transactions.

The automatic settlements give rise to positive and negative residual balances — "credits" and "deposits," in traditional banking terminology, although these terms are strictly applicable only in the technical, not the economic, sense. Accordingly, a depositor may not have free access to the money, while credits may contribute nothing to the economic growth of the borrower. (58)

In a quantity-based planned economy, there is only one way to liquidate these deposits, namely, by delivering the planned quotas of goods for the planned volume of production. (59)

2.2.5. Foreign Exchange Transactions

The IBEC has also carried out transactions in convertible currencies since February 1964, and especially since 1966, when contacts with correspondent banks in the West were expanded and some of the founding capital had been raised in convertible currency.

The IBEC raises freely moving funds on the international markets, as well as from the banks of the CMEA nations, and places these funds at the disposal of its member banks and, in some cases, the banks of other countries. Deposits are mostly accepted for three and six months. Conversion transactions, as well as the purchase and sale of foreign currencies with varying periods of repayment, are also part of the bank's activities.

The IBEC assumes short-term (up to one year) and medium-term credits and participates jointly with the large Western banks in loans to CMEA countries.

The total volume of IBEC transactions in convertible currency increased from 900 million transferable rubles in 1964 to 27.2 million transferable rubles in 1972. (60)

2.2.6. The Bank Interest Rates

"The Bank Council sets the interest rates for credits and

deposits with a view toward stimulating economical use of funds and insuring the profitability of the bank" (Article VI of the agreement). In a planned economy, where the function of money is subordinate to quantity planning and prices play no important role in determining the allocation of resources, interest cannot and should not exercise the function of the price of money.

Since credits and bank deposits are created automatically anytime the mutual exchange of goods diverges from the planned volume, the interest rate will influence the volume of credits and deposits only very slightly.

Those IBEC members that had envisioned an active bank wanted to make the interest rate and the partial convertibility of the transferable ruble into gold and into freely convertible currencies the most important instruments of the IBEC.

The other countries, which were interested only in improving clearing procedures, saw no value in covering a part of their negative clearing balances with gold or freely convertible currencies, nor were they inclined to accept an excessively high interest rate for credits, whose function as a technical stopgap measure they wished to see retained. In their proposal, the effectively compounded interest was not to be much larger than the interest rate in bilateral clearing. These countries achieved their aim insofar as the agreement of October 22, 1963, provided for interest-free credits of up to 3 percent of the annual volume of trade of each member nation with the other IBEC nations. The second meeting of the Bank Council yielded to pressure from those who advocated an effective, active bank and set the limit for interest-free credit at 2.5 percent of the annual trade volume. Credits in excess of this limit were charged with 1.5 percent to 3 percent interest. In 1969, the average interest on total credit was no more than 0.81 percent, varying from 0.44 percent to 1.03 percent in the individual case. But only one year later, after the borrowers had unearthed the loopholes and weak points of the agreement (the seasonal credits, which enjoyed favorable interest rates, were especially popular), the average interest fell to 0.64 percent. (61) At the same time, more creditors began to convert their clearing balances into time deposits. The average interest on deposits rose from 0.55 percent to 0.64 percent. The difference between the deposit interest rate and the credit interest rate narrowed, with the consequent risk that the IBEC would no longer be able to cover its operating costs (about 1 million rubles annually). Under these circumstances, the controversy among the proponents of various theories of the IBEC activity sharpened.

The Soviet Union vigorously opposed attempts to tie the collective CMEA currency to gold or foreign exchange. However, to strengthen delivery discipline, it supported those who favored an increase in interest rates. The Twelfth Session of the Bank Council (July 1966) resolved to offer only half of the credits interest free, but with the proviso that the total sum of interest-free credit not exceed 2.5 percent of a given member's trade with all the other member nations. In the wake of this resolution, the average interest rose to 0.79 percent in 1966 and to 0.84 percent in 1967. (62) In this way, the IBEC was able to avoid losses, but it was unable to improve delivery discipline.

Those member nations advocating an active credit policy applied increased pressure, and, as a result, it was decided late in the second half of 1967 to scale interest rates to the term of repayment: 2 percent for clearing credits up to three months, 2.5 percent for up to six months, 2.75 percent for up to nine months, and 3 percent for credits longer than nine months. For credits to be used to promote foreign trade, the interest rate was raised to 2 percent or 2.5 percent, depending on the term of repayment (i.e., less than or more than one year, respectively). For unplanned and overdue credits, the rate was raised from 3 percent to 4 percent. (63)

The resistance of Bulgaria, Romania, and Mongolia prevented the complete abolition of interest-free credits at this time. Although the average interest rose to 1.16 percent in 1968 and 1.52 percent in 1969 (64), it still remained much lower than the lowest interest rate (2.0 percent).

No radical improvement was instituted in interest policy until the passage of the resolution of the Twenty-Fourth Session of the CMEA (May 1970) entitled "On the Improvement and Expansion of the Operations of the IBEC," and the later passage of a second resolution at the Twenty-Eighth Session of the Bank Council (July 1970). Interest-free credit was abolished, and the interest rates for credits and deposits were raised. A clear distinction was drawn between the two types of credit specified in the July decision of the Bank Council, i.e., settlement credits and fixed-term credits. Fixed-term credits would be granted where the limit of the clearing credit, 2 percent of the total intra-CMEA trade of the member, was exceeded. This measure, and the abolition of interest-free credit, produced a marked increase in the average annual interest (from 1.52 percent in 1969 to 3.77 percent in 1971). (65)

In 1971, deposit interest rates were adjusted more closely than previously to the term for which they were tied up, i.e., 1.5 percent for deposits with a fixed period of one month, 1.75 percent to 2.5 percent for two to four months, and 3.5 percent for over six months. The average interest on deposits rose from 0.55 percent in 1964 to 1.15 percent in 1968 and 2.70 percent in 1971. (66) Current credit and deposit interest rates for transactions in transferable rubles are still much lower than the interest rates for credits in foreign exchange. Under the given conditions, the CMEA could not create an internal capital market or introduce a corresponding market interest rate for bank transactions in transferable rubles, nor did it need to do so. However, when credit terms were tightened, bank interest became a more effective instrument for regulating intra-CMEA trade than before. As long as foreign trade continues to be based ultimately on the bilateral balancing of specified volumes of delivered goods, the growth in interest on deposits and credits may be an indication of the nonfulfillment of delivery contracts, but it will not be a measure of the efficacy of the recently improved banking instruments, which is more accurately reflected in the reduction of the average annual interest yield on both deposits and credits.

2.2.7. The Founding Capital of the IBEC

The bank statutes provide for a founding capital, or capital

Apportionment of the Founding Capital of the IBEC

	Share of founding capital	
Member	In millions of transferable rubles	In %
1. Bulgaria	17	6
2. Czechoslovakia	45	15
3. GDR	55	18
4. Hungary	21	7
5. Mongolia	3	1
6. Poland	27	9
7. Romania	16	5
8. Soviet Union	116	39
Total	300	100

stock, of 300 million transferable rubles. This sum was apportioned among the member nations in accordance with their respective shares in total intra-CMEA exports in 1960, and the distribution has remained unchanged to the present. All members have an equal voice regardless of their share in the founding capital.

As a pure clearing currency, the transferable ruble is not suited for capital formation. For this reason, those countries that had been in favor of an active bank succeeded in pushing through the following wording for Article II of the agreement (October 1963 version): "After the lapse of one year, the Bank Council will explore the possibility of raising a portion of the capital stock in gold and freely convertible currency."

On the other side, the members placing primary stress on the clearing function of the IBEC, knowing that a clearing office needs no capital, got through the following amendment to Article III of the agreement: "A nation's share in the bank's capital stock (in transferable rubles) can also be raised in freely convertible currency or in gold if that country so wishes."

Without waiting to see how the IBEC would shape up, payment during the first year of the bank's operations was set at 20 percent of the total sum. However, the IBEC has become merely a clearing office, and the transferable ruble merely a clearing unit.

That the transferable ruble is not suited for capital formation became abundantly clear when actual attempts were made to raise the capital stock. (67)

The payment of 20 percent of the capital stock was effected in a technical manner by granting larger credits to debtors and by reducing the deposits of creditors. However, the ensuing years have demonstrated that no use could be made of this capital. In a closed clearing system, the positive balances are equal to the negative balances by definition, and credits granted are automatically equal to deposits, which are formed at the same time.

Thereafter, no further capital deposits in transferable rubles were demanded.

In 1966, the IBEC members raised capital amounting to 30 million transferable rubles in gold and convertible currencies. In 1971, the portion of these media in the capital stock was doubled. This capital was used not for settlement purposes in intra-CMEA trade, however, but to alleviate payments difficulties in trade with the West.

2.2.8. Banking Operations from 1964 to 1971

Contrary to the hopes of Poland and Hungary, the IBEC was not able to develop into an effective banking institution with a currency that was at least partially convertible and with a traditional credit system for the promotion of foreign trade. But clearing operations continue to proceed smoothly, while volume steadily increases. In contrast to the experiences of the EPU, chronic debtors and creditors have been avoided in the clearing operations of the IBEC. The IBEC has also been successful in procuring and making available freely convertible currencies. The accompanying table, which gives a review of bank balance sheets for a few typical years between 1964 and 1972, brings this out clearly.

The balance sheets of the IBEC are highly aggregated. They

IBEC Balance Sheets for the Period 1964-1972
(millions of transferable rubles)

	1964	1966	1968	1971	1972
Assets					
1. Deposits					
Cash holdings with credit institutes*	0.7	5.3	11.6	11.0	9.5
Other deposits	42.7	123.2	303.7	512.7	1,150.4
2. Office equipment	0.1	0.1	0.1	0.2	0.2
3. Credits to banks of member nations	125.8	248.8	351.4	741.7	1,079.5
4. Other assets	–	6.1	3.1	1.7	6.4
Total assets	169.3	383.5	669.9	1,267.3	2,246.0
Liabilities					
1. Own capital					
Capital stock, paid-in capital (300.0)	59.7	89.7	89.7	104.7	119.7
Reserve funds	–	0.9	1.6	9.2	16.8
2. Deposits					
Sight deposits	43.9	111.9	121.1	91.7	225.7
Time deposits	65.1	173.4	452.6	958.0	1,659.4
3. Credit received				84.4	194.6
4. Other liabilities	–	6.3	3.3	7.3	15.9
5. Net profit	0.6	1.3	1.6	12.0	13.9
Total liabilities	169.3	383.5	669.9	1,267.3	2,246.0

*Including deposits payable on demand.
Source: Annual reports of the IBEC.

contained data neither on the type of credits granted nor on the respective percentages of transactions in transferable rubles and in freely convertible currencies. All bank transactions are carried out in transferable rubles at the official exchange rate

Breakdown of Balance Sheet as of the End of 1971 by
Transferable Rubles and Convertible Currencies (in millions)

	Transferable rubles	Convertible currencies	Total
Assets			
1. Deposits payable on demand at credit institutions	–	523.7	523.7
2. Credits to banks of member nations	612.3	129.4	741.7
3. Other assets	1.9	–	1.9
Total assets	614.2	653.1	1,267.3
Liabilities			
1. Subscription capital	59.7	45.0	104.7
2. Repayments	9.2	–	9.2
3. Credits obtained	–	84.4	84.4
4. Deposits	526.0	523.7	1,049.7
5. Other liabilities	19.3	–	19.3
Total liabilities	614.2	653.1	1,267.3

(1 transferable ruble = 1.11 dollars before the realignment of December 1971).

The table above is a breakdown of the balance sheet items at the end of 1971 into transferable rubles and freely convertible currencies.

This breakdown of the balances was done on the basis of the following supporting data. Assets column: The figures for total credit at the end of 1971 in transferable rubles are to be found in Russian sources (68); the deposits with credit institutions (523.7 million) consist wholly of short-term money in freely convertible currency deposited with Western banks. Liabilities column: A fraction of the capital stock in transferable rubles (59.7 million) was paid in 1964; further payments were suspended.

Credits Granted in 1970-1971 (at year-end, in millions of transferable rubles)

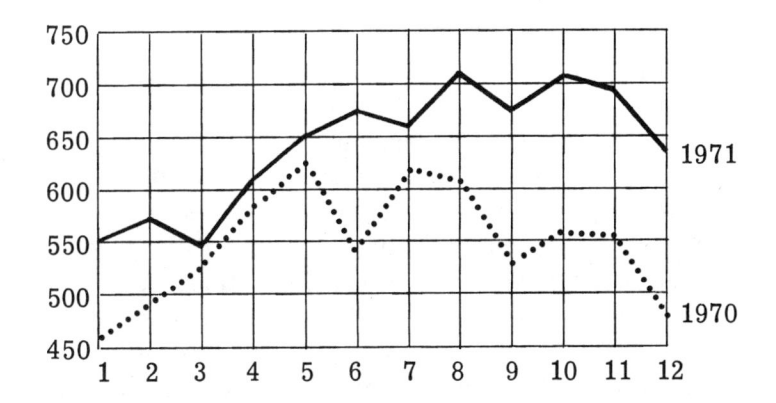

The capital in convertible currency is composed of the first payment portion from 1966 (30 million transferable rubles) and the second portion from 1971 (15 million rubles) (pursuant to the decision of the Twenty-Eighth Session of the Bank Council to augment the convertible currency portion of the capital stock by another 30 million). To arrive at the sum of deposits in transferable rubles, we subtracted the sum on the asset side, which was known, from the total sum of deposits with credit institutions in convertible currencies (523.7 million transferable rubles).

Credits received (84.4 million transferable rubles) consist wholly of credits advanced by Western banks in convertible currencies.

The IBEC's credit business fluctuates over the course of a year. As a rule, it increases steadily during the first eight months of the year and then declines steadily in the last months as delivery gaps grow narrower. The chart above shows this clearly.

The scope of the IBEC's activity is defined by the volume of settlements. Transactions cleared through the bank rose from 22,900 million transferable rubles in 1964 to 23,900 million transferable rubles in 1966, 29,400 million transferable rubles in 1968, and 43,300 million transferable rubles in 1972.

3. Investment Credits and the International Investment Bank (IIB)

3.1. Investment Credits Before the Founding of the IIB

As long as commodity exchange depends on a quota system, credits for capital development can be extended only in the form of goods. Investment credits were granted in the form of machinery and equipment and paid back as well in goods agreed upon beforehand (copper, sulfur, coal, fertilizers). "Thus credits are not only tied loans, they are also tied debts." (69)

From 1957 through 1962, sixteen credit agreements were concluded in the CMEA; these included commitments to finance the construction of five industrial projects in Poland and four in the USSR. Czechoslovakia granted 60 percent and the German Democratic Republic 20 percent of the credits. (70) Jozef M. van Brabant, whose studies cover a longer period from 1955 to 1971, estimates the total sum of the major investment credits to be 1,658.5 million transferable rubles. (71) In this survey, Czechoslovakia (74.1 percent of the total sum) and the German Democratic Republic (20.7 percent) emerge as the principal creditors and the Soviet Union (54.6 percent), Poland (30 percent), and Romania (12.3 percent) as the principal debtors. The most important projects were financed by Czechoslovakia: in the USSR, help in opening up deposits of ore (288 million transferable rubles) and crude oil (500 million transferable rubles) and, in Poland, the construction of copper plants (123 million transferable rubles) and the expansion of the coal industry (56 million transferable rubles). The German Democratic Republic helped substantially to increase the output of soft coal (90 million transferable rubles) and sulfur (90 million transferable rubles) in Poland and to finance construction of a cellulose and paper factory in Romania (110 million transferable rubles). Czechoslovakia and Poland were also involved in the Romanian cellulose factory, with credits of 30 million and 10 million transferable rubles, respectively.

The increasing costs connected with the progressive

specialization of major branches of industry in the CMEA nations and the tapping of new deposits of raw materials and fuels placed the problem of multilateralization of investment credit at the top of the CMEA agenda. The International Investment Bank (IIB) was created to solve this problem.

3.2. The Tasks of the International Investment Bank

The Twenty-Third Special Session of the CMEA (April 1969) hosted a discussion of memoranda from member nations seeking new ways to pursue the goal of economic integration in the Eastern bloc. It was decided to "prepare a comprehensive prospective program on the broadening of cooperation and the development of socialist economic integration." The Twenty-Fourth Session approved the draft outline, the structure, and the provisional content of this program. These two sessions also formulated the resolution establishing the IIB (Twenty-Third Session) and approved the general outline of its activities (Twenty-Fourth Session).

Article III of the agreement reads: "The principal function of the bank is the granting of long- and medium-term credits, primarily for the execution of projects in connection with the international socialist division of labor, specialization and cooperation in production, and expenditures for the expansion of raw material and fuel reserves in the common interest; for the construction of projects in other sectors of the economy that are of common interest for the economic growth of the bank's member nations; for the construction of projects to further economic growth of the national economies of the respective countries; and for other purposes...." (72)

"The activities of the bank should be organically connected with practical programs promoting socialist economic cooperation, and working toward the achievement of a uniform level of development in all the member nations...." (73)

The IIB is primarily involved in the financing of projects of common interest for the promotion of international specialization. The bank is to encourage the multilateralization of economic relations and make available the multilateral funds required for that purpose. In the integration plan of the CMEA, the "founding of the International Investment Bank was a comprehensive measure that paved the way for the systematic and deliberate international utilization and concentration of investments in the pursuit of solutions to current international and national economic problems." (74)

The IIB was charged with a qualitatively new task: to put an end to the current practice of extending credits in commodity form for investment purposes and to create a new, progressive form of multilateral bank credit.

The investment bank assumed a task much more complicated than that of the IBEC. It was to create a joint fund of capital and dispense it in the form of credits. The founding of the bank marked the beginning of a new stage in which special emphasis was given to cooperation in currency matters. (75) An investment bank, however, has more need of a viable currency than does a clearing bank.

It should be pointed out that the European Investment Bank was founded before, not after, the postwar currency crisis had passed. It was not established at the same time as that clearing institution par excellence, the EPU, but only after convertible currencies were restored in Western Europe, i.e., when the EPU had already been in operation for seven years.

The CMEA investment bank, however, was founded when it was realized that the IBEC would be obliged to continue functioning as a clearing office because the necessary preconditions for abolishing bilateralism in the CMEA did not exist. The Investment Bank was unable to inaugurate a new system of monetary relations, and it had perforce to adapt itself to the existing one.

3.3. The Capital Stock of the IIB

The capital stock of the IIB was set at one billion transferable rubles, of which 70 percent was to be raised in transferable rubles and 30 percent in freely convertible currencies or gold. (76) In accordance with Article III of the agreement founding the IIB, the first payment (175 million transferable rubles) was to be made at the time the bank was founded, with the second (in the same amount) to follow some time during the second year. The remainder was to be paid "with due consideration as to how the operations of the bank had progressed and to its needs for funds in accordance with the conditions and terms laid down by the Bank Council." (77)

Later, when Romania became a member, the founding capital was increased to 52 million transferable rubles. By the end of 1972, 368 million transferable rubles had been paid into the capital stock. In the preliminary discussions, the possibility of setting the capital stock subscription quota of the individual countries on the basis of their share in the aggregate national income of all CMEA countries was considered. (78) Although promoting and transacting foreign trade is not the main focus of the IIB's activities, it was decided that subscription quotas should be made proportional to the export volume of the particular member nation. This would give countries with low export volume an advantage. The differences in the subscription quotas assigned by these two distinct criteria may be seen in the following table:

	On the basis of share in total national income	On the basis of share in CMEA exports
	(millions of transferable rubles)	
Bulgaria	21	85.1
Czechoslovakia	52	129.9
GDR	71	176.1
Hungary	26	83.7
Poland	85	121.4
USSR	704	399.3

The greatest problem, however, was the formation of capital stock quotas from the transferable rubles issued by the IBEC, since this was only a settlement currency and could not be used as capital for the financing of capital projects.

Directly after signing the agreement establishing the IBEC,

L. Siemiatkowski, then president of the Polish National Bank, observed: "I can state with full confidence that the need to create a real basis for capital payments constituted the chief problem of the preliminary deliberations, since only if that problem were solved could the bank fulfill the functions defined for it in the statutes." (79) Yet the problem remained unsolved. A half-year later, his representative, Professor Fedorowicz, was able to bring some insight to the problem: "Since the transferable ruble is a clearing unit, not a unit of currency, subscription quotas to the capital stock will entail the obligation to deliver capital or other goods stipulated by borrowers determined by the investment bank over and above quotas set in the trade agreement." (80)

Both the payment of capital stock and the granting of credits were carried out in the form of goods (except where convertible currencies were involved). Since monetary relations in the CMEA had not notably progressed at the time the IIB was founded, no other solution was available.

The portion of the founding capital that was raised in convertible currencies is the only universally available capital of the IIB. A borrower has free use of funds granted in convertible currencies, which are then used exclusively for the purchase of capital goods in the West.

The intended function of the foreign exchange portion of the founding capital was to insure that capital investment projects financed with credits meet the highest scientific and technical standards and that manufactured goods are of the highest quality. (81) A discrepancy may arise between the composition of the founding capital and the specific amount of foreign exchange needed. (82) The foreign exchange portion of the bank capital is determined by the shortage of foreign exchange, not by actual need: "The transfer of such a considerable sum to the new CMEA institution by the founding countries doubtless places a major burden on the member countries, and that burden is really the upper limit." (83)

3.4. Other Bank Resources of the IIB

The founding capital was not meant to be the IIB's only source of funds. (84) Article VI of the agreement states: "The bank can mobilize funds in the collective currency (transferable ruble), in the national currencies of the countries involved, and in freely convertible currencies by accepting government and bank credits, through loans, through the acceptance of middle-term and long-term deposits, and in other ways. The Bank Council can pass resolutions on the issuance of interest-bearing bonds for circulation on the international capital markets." (85)

In contrast to the EIB, however, which has 70 percent of its bonded loans (1,014 accounting units) in the currencies of the Common Market nations (86), the CMEA bank can count neither on the money and capital markets of its members nor on those of the CMEA. They simply do not exist. Like the IBEC, which does a thriving business in convertible currencies, the IIB establishes connections with the capital markets of the West, where its efforts are concentrated especially on the procurement of long-term capital, which is not so easy to obtain on the Western markets. (87) One may therefore concur with the deputy president of the Czechoslovakian State Bank in his statement that "the bank will have to employ unconventional methods during the first stages of its operations in order to be able to provide its debtors with funds for obtaining the capital goods necessary to insure a high technical standard for their planned projects; its job will not be easy"; and that "for this bank to be able to realize its full potential, its financial resources must be universally utilizable...." (88)

3.5. Banking Operations

During the first two years of its existence (1971-1972), the investment bank operated solely with the founding capital on hand. It had on hand 368 million transferable rubles; since beginning operations, it had accepted credit applications amounting to 340 million transferable rubles; 279 million rubles in credits had been granted by the end of 1972. (89) A credit application must be accompanied by a list of specific equipment required for the project for which the credit is intended. The possibilities of the party granting capital to deliver are then

Member	Capital paid in (35% of total sum) (in millions of transferable rubles)	Number of credits obtained	Credit sum (in millions of transferable rubles)	Maturity
Bulgaria	29.8	6	14.5	6-7 years
Czechoslovakia	45.5	1	77.5	11 years
GDR	61.2	2	25.1	6-9 years
Hungary	29.3	3	47.6	8-10 years
Mongolia	1.4	—	—	—
Poland	42.5	8	35.2	3.3-7 years
Romania	18.2	8	78.8	8-11 years
Soviet Union	139.8	—	—	—

Source: Die Wirtschaft (East Berlin), October 11, 1972, and Aussenhandel (Moscow), 1973, No. 8.

coordinated with the requirements of the borrower. A breakdown of credits lent out in 1971 and 1972 is given in the table above. (90)

Thus, we see that the sum of the credits received by Romania, Czechoslovakia, and Hungary exceeded the amount of founding capital paid in by these countries, while with Poland and the German Democratic Republic, the opposite was the case. Pursuant to Article XV of the bank statutes, the aforementioned credits are granted on the condition that the borrower also participate in financing the given project with its own funds. Self-participation varies from 43 percent to 89 percent depending on the project. (91)

By the end of October 1973, the total sum of credits granted by the IIB had reached 483 million transferable rubles. The overall value of investments made possible by bank credits had reached about one billion transferable rubles for the first time. (92) In 1973, the IIB approved credits to the Soviet Union for the expansion of foundry and mining works.

In the financing of investment projects from its founding capital stocks, the bank has functioned as a simple intermediary between creditor and debtor nations.

The founding capital has been paid and credits have been granted in the form of goods, not money, as Professor Fedorowicz has described. For example, the Soviet Union delivered seventy diesel locomotives to Hungary as part of its capital subscription quota (amounting to a credit claim of 20.5 million transferable rubles). Czechoslovakia as well has delivered to Hungary spinning machines valued at 14.4 million transferable rubles, also nonrepayable, for the modernization of a cotton plant. The German Democratic Republic, Poland, and the Soviet Union have also agreed to deliver 7.95 million transferable rubles' worth of machinery and equipment to Czechoslovakia for the modernization of the Tatra automobile plant. (93)

3.6. The Investment Bank and the Evolution of Investment Credits

If the investment bank were the only institution in the CMEA that granted credit, one might conclude from the above data that the availability of such credits has lessened over the last two years. That would be incorrect, however. The principal demand for investment credits is still met outside the IIB. It is not projects of common interest but primarily those in which only particular member nations have an interest that are generally financed with IIB credits. According to the resolutions of the policy-setting Twenty-Fifth Session of the CMEA, the main focus of CMEA operations was to be financing the expansion of existing reserves of raw materials and the tapping of new deposits of raw materials and fuels. (94)

The Comprehensive Program has declared the financial participation of the individual CMEA nations in the tapping of new deposits to be the most important task of the next fifteen to twenty years. This participation will have to be on a broader scale than in preceding years. It will cover such ambitious projects as the construction of the mammoth cellulose plant on the Angara River, the construction of an asbestos combine (annual output 500 thousand tons), an iron and steel works to process the iron ore from the Kursk Region (annual output 12 million tons), etc. (95)

The construction of these industrial giants is expensive, and the costs are far in excess of existing IIB funds (the construction costs of the cellulose combine alone have been estimated at 800 million transferable rubles).

These mammoth plants were declared to be projects of common interest in accordance with the resolution of the Twenty-Sixth Session of the Council, although the participatory credits were granted directly to the Soviet Union by the bank's members. But this practice is in no sense a breach of the agreement founding the IIB. Article XII makes it clear that "bank membership and the bank's operations shall not hinder the bank's members from entering into direct financial or other business relations with one another, with other countries, and with international financial organizations and banks." (96)

The IIB and its credit policy are an integral part of the overall activity of the CMEA. It is not the bank's credit policy or its credit transactions undertaken outside the bank that have come under attack; rather, it is the fact that some countries have been condemned to the role of borrowers and others to the role of lenders that has been criticized. The essence of the controversy has been described rather well by the respected Polish journal Polityka: "Participation in the financing of investment projects in other countries through the extension of credits cannot be accepted as a general principle.... If this practice were to be the rule, specialization would lose all meaning." The author criticizes this practice not only because it is contrary to the objectives of specialization, but also because it appropriates credit funds which are not directly connected with the project. "It is unacceptable that all subsidiary costs, including those associated with the infrastructure, should be allowed to burden the investment project and enlarge the amount of credit." (97)

Criticism has also been directed against the credit terms, which are much more favorable in bilateral agreements than with IIB credits. In the IIB, the interest rates for credits in transferable rubles vary between 4 and 6 percent, depending on the maturity, while for credits in convertible currencies, they are determined by conditions prevailing on the international markets. (98)

In direct credit relations between countries, the interest rate never exceeds 2 percent annually. In this connection, the Polish journal has called attention to the double burden imposed on the lender: "If one takes into consideration the tendency for the prices of raw materials and fuels to rise, the purchaser overpays for these goods twice — namely, through low interest rates and through high prices."

There still does not exist even the most rudimentary basis for the development of a capital market. The IIB has been unable to alleviate the acute shortage of capital in the CMEA countries. The modest capital stocks of the IIB have been the principal source for credit grants. Under the existing conditions, the IIB has not been able to fulfill the function for which it was intended, namely, to finance major projects of common interest. Financial participation in the tapping of new raw materials deposits was made the chief objective of investment credits in the CMEA; however, this participation is effected independently of the IIB.

As long as the IIB capital stock remains the sole or principal source of credit funds, the potential of the investment bank will remain limited, especially if one considers that bank credits are granted over the long term, as the following table shows. (99)

5 years or less	10 million transferable rubles	2 projects
5-10 years	154 million transferable rubles	18 projects
10-15 years	115 million transferable rubles	6 projects

If the sum of credits granted equals the amount of capital paid in, the bank must postpone the advancing of additional credits until either a new share of capital has been paid in or the debts outstanding have been paid off. This limitation could be eliminated (apart from recourse to the Western money markets) if the CMEA developed its own internal capital market. However, that would be contingent upon how the economic system as a whole develops and, particularly, on the creation of a functional currency resting on a uniform price basis.

4. The Price System in Intra-CMEA Trade

4.1. Derivative World Market Prices as a Price Basis in CMEA Trade

Since no economic relationship existed between the national currencies and prices of the planned economies among themselves and between these and the Western currencies and prices, foreign standards had to be employed in both intra-CMEA and East-West trade.

During the first years after World War II, the people's democracies used the unmodified world market prices in trade relations with the USSR as well as among themselves. When the Korean War brought about a sharp rise in world market prices, the socialist nations agreed to allow the 1950 prices to remain in force. These remained the standard until 1957, when modified world market prices became the price basis in intra-CMEA trade. This was at least a pragmatic solution, although it did have some theoretical justification. According to Marx, the value of a commodity is determined by the average socially necessary labor expended to produce it. Thus, the international as well as the national value of a commodity is derived from the average amount of labor expended. In the CMEA there exists the opinion that the world market prices express this average socially necessary labor more accurately than any other standard of value.

Nevertheless, this theoretical argument is open to the objection that the gap between the developed countries and the developing countries — that is, the scissors trend between the prices of finished products and the prices of raw materials — and the increasing monopolization of various areas of production brought about by the growth of international firms and cartels, all serve to distort the world market prices.

In foreign trade between two member nations, the contract price consists of the base price plus transport and insurance costs. Since there are no uniform CMEA prices, the same goods do not always have the same price. Price formation is an extremely complicated process. Adjusted world market prices serve as the base price. "Adjusted," in this case, means that the influence of cyclic, seasonal, and speculative factors have been eliminated from world market prices (which themselves, in a certain sense, have already been selected) by computing an average over a relatively extended period. Moreover, the base price is held fixed for the duration of a five-year plan, since the quantity-based foreign trade can be planned more easily if the prices in a given period are stable. Thus, the base prices for the 1966-1970 period were computed from the average world market prices for 1960-1964, while those in effect for the period 1965-1969 were used as the base prices for the 1971-1975 five-year planning period. CMEA foreign trade prices are therefore derived from world market prices that are six to ten years old.

The world market prices are adjusted in several steps, the first of which is the selection of Western markets for specific goods. This is in itself an important negotiating point in foreign trade relations. The criteria for selection are: (1) commercially normal commodity turnover in large quantities; (2) a favorable geographic location in relation to the CMEA countries; and (3) commodity turnover in freely convertible currencies. (100) Then comes the selection and evaluation of documented information on the prices on these markets from the following sources: stock market prices, auction prices, contractual prices, with consideration given to goods actually delivered, periodically published catalog prices, prices from foreign trade statistics, domestic market prices in Western countries, and, finally, the prices of socialist countries in their trade with the West. (101)

This price information is then adjusted to exclude influences from cyclic, seasonal, speculative, and noneconomic factors. Finally, prices are also adjusted to take account of differences in quality.

After these adjustments have been made, the world market prices are expressed in a convertible Western currency and converted into Eastern currency equivalents, using the ruble-dollar exchange rate.

Since the collective CMEA currency, the transferable ruble, and the Soviet domestic ruble have the same gold content, a common denominator is obtained for the CMEA base price.

Thus, any connection that may have existed between the base prices used in intra-CMEA trade and actual world market prices has been eliminated by the various adjustments and by the arbitrary and unrealistic exchange rate; moreover, the world market prices used are already obsolete.

The price problem was on the agenda at the Conference of Party Chiefs of the Member Nations in May 1958, and at the Ninth Session of the Council in June 1958, where it was decided to find the most immediately practicable solution and to work out a theoretically sound intrinsic price base. The current price base derived from world market prices was to be improved, but, at the same time, the possibility of creating a price base rooted in internal production and sales conditions was to be explored. How the world market prices were to be modified to meet the requirements of the CMEA market was defined: "The price basis should be those prices that have stabilized over a period of years in trade among the socialist countries, on the ultimate basis of the world market prices after appropriate adjustments have been made to eliminate the influence of cyclic factors in the capitalist market." (102) The principle of "equal prices for equal goods" and the freezing of prices for the duration of a multiyear trade agreement were to be important preconditions for the multilateralization of intra-CMEA trade.

The studies of the committee formed to draw up pertinent proposals for the price base for 1966-1970 covered 35.6 percent of all machinery sold in the CMEA, 69.9 percent of all raw materials, and 41.3 percent of all agricultural products. (103) Negotiations among the CMEA countries lasted about three years. Yet, eight years after the passage of the resolution by the Ninth Session of the CMEA, the modified average world market prices of 1957 were still in use. In 1965, an agreement was finally reached to use the average world market prices for the years 1960 through 1964, and, accordingly, these were gradually introduced over the next two years. However, the prices finally agreed upon were for the most part compromises between the trading partners. As the commodity structure of intrabloc trade changed, the prices, set several years earlier, moved further and further from reality.

4.2. The Discussion of an Independent Price Base for the CMEA

It has long been disputed whether the CMEA should adhere to prices derived from the capitalist world market prices, or whether it would be more expedient for the CMEA to create its own price base. The present price base is dissociated from both the actual world market prices and the national prices of the CMEA countries. Goods are exchanged in the CMEA without regard for national production costs. If the CMEA had its own price base, the discrepancy between prices in intra-CMEA trade and national production costs could be eliminated, or at least reduced. In terms of the Marxist theory of value, value would then be determined not by the socially necessary labor on a worldwide scale, but by the socially necessary production costs within the CMEA area.

The push for a uniform price base first took on overt form at the end of the fifties, when efforts were mounted to multilateralize CMEA foreign trade. At the same time as the procedure for determining a price base for the coming five-year period was improved, preliminary studies to explore the feasibility of creating an intra-CMEA price base rooted in internal CMEA production and sales conditions were begun. The idea of an intra-CMEA price base fits in well with the drive toward integration. Moreover, it should also contribute toward the solution of a major CMEA problem: the multilateralization of trade relations and the promotion of specialization. The lack of a uniform price base linked to production conditions in the CMEA countries is regarded as a major obstacle to making the collective CMEA currency effectively transferable and able to function as a uniform standard of value.

The discussion on an independent CMEA price base is still in progress. When the various differences of opinion finally crystallized around the alternative of the CMEA average of sales prices versus the average of the adjusted actual costs with an agreed-upon pure profit margin, the last phase of the discussion moved to the general concept of an "independent price base."

The divergent views were brought out most clearly at the Budapest Conference of the CMEA nations (April 1967). An independent price base was advocated only by the Soviet and Bulgarian delegations. The Soviet Union had a vested interest in an independent price base, since, as an exporter of raw materials, it found itself faced with steadily growing costs. (104) It would have liked to have reached the same level of efficiency in this area as in other areas of its economy. "The producing countries, however, are entitled to propose a price that corresponds to their national efficiency norms." (105) The Bulgarians, on the other hand, saw an independent price base as a means to effect a 40 percent price increase for their agricultural products. (106)

But the member nations that imported both raw materials and agricultural products had no desire to pay excessively high prices and therefore advocated the world market prices as the base for intra-CMEA trade. The motives were not the same in all cases, however. Romania wanted the world market price as a base because "the autarkic tendencies in the two world systems...are as absurd as the tendencies toward autarkic development in the individual countries." (107) The representatives from the German Democratic Republic advanced similar arguments. For both the German Democratic Republic and Romania, the world market prices are only a standard for assessing value, but they are still a heteronomic category imported from without.

The other countries wanted the world market prices to function in CMEA trade in the same way that they do in market economies — in a dynamic interaction with the convertible currencies and rates of exchange. This position was stated most clearly by J. Petrivalsky, the Czech representative: "What is meant here is not the use of world market prices in trade between CMEA countries but the forming of world market prices in the market of the CMEA countries." (108) The Hungarian expert Csikos-Nagy noted that "the immediate objective should not be the creation of a common price basis but the formation of a common market. This again assumes the solution of the currency problem, of convertibility." (109)

Thus, no independent price base was created, and the problem was struck from the agenda of the CMEA.

The 1971 Comprehensive Program of the CMEA makes no further mention of the idea of an independent price base. Rather, it states: "CMEA member nations will, for the time being, base their reciprocal trade on the price-forming principles currently in force, i.e., prices will be set on the basis of world market prices, after appropriate adjustments to eliminate the negative influence of the cyclic factors of the capitalist market." (110)

With the abrupt rise in the price of raw materials, the CMEA focused anew on the world market. While the Soviet Union insists on an immediate adjustment of the raw materials prices set for the planning period 1971-1975, the other CMEA nations demand adherence to the price-formation guidelines established at the Ninth Session of the Council.

Notes

1) Statisticheskii ezhegodnik stran-chlenov SEV [Statistical Yearbook of the Member Nations of the CMEA], 1972, p. 5.

2) Economic Survey of Europe, 1969, Pt. II, United Nations, p. 1.

3) Economic Survey of Europe, 1971, Pt. II, United Nations, p. 67.

4) See Chapter 2 of this study.

5) United Nations Yearbook, 1972, pp. 345 ff.

6) In 1972, the Soviet Union delivered 62 million tons of crude oil to the CMEA countries and 45 million tons to Western nations (see Kurier [Vienna], December 22, 1973).

7) On this point, the director of the Research Institute of the Polish Ministry of Foreign Trade, L. Ciamaga, observes: "We are not able to determine costs satisfactorily and agree on prices. If we use the world price as a criterion, we lose sight of comparative cost differences. If we use our own cost prices, then we cannot decide which currency exchange rate should be

used" (see Życie gospodarcze, July 10, 1973).

8) Thus, the Hungarian expert S. Ausch observed: "in the presence of diverging national interests, it is not possible to control reproduction on an international scale by means of direct instructions" (Theory and Practice of CMEA Cooperation, Budapest, 1972, p. 67).

9) Poland's permanent representative to the CMEA, M. Jagielski, commented in his statement before the Polish parliament: "Our results so far represent the introductory phase of socialist economic integration" (Życie gospodarcze, July 10, 1973, p. 3).

10) The founding nations were the Soviet Union, Bulgaria, Poland, Romania, Czechoslovakia, and Hungary. Albania joined the CMEA in February 1949 but has not been active since 1961. The German Democratic Republic followed in September 1950, the Mongolian People's Republic in June 1962, and Cuba in July 1972. Yugoslavia has been active in some CMEA agencies since 1964 without being a member. In May 1973, Finland concluded an agreement on cooperation with the CMEA, becoming the first market economy to do so.

11) See Pravda, January 25, 1949.

12) On the occasion of the Romanian-Bulgarian agreement in 1948, Bulgaria's top leader, Dimitrov, alluded to the possibility of a customs union or federation between the two countries. This prospect was decisively rebuffed by the Soviet Union. See Pravda, January 13, 1948.

13) See the Founding Communiqué of the CMEA, Pravda, January 25, 1949.

14) See B. Kiesewetter, Der Ostblock, Berlin, 1960, p. 36.

15) See L. Berend, "Eastern European Economic Integration," in Foreign Trade in a Planned Economy, Imre Vajda and M. Simai, eds., Cambridge, 1971, p. 20.

16) See M. Senin, Sozialistische Integration, East Berlin, Verlag Dietz, 1972, p. 334 (translated from the Russian).

17) The Eighth Session of the Council (July 1957) did not take up the question of the CMEA; it dealt instead with rectifying the damage caused by the revolt in Hungary in October 1956.

18) See Pravda, May 25, 1956.

19) On this point see P. Wiles: "Two countries are said to be fully integrated if they are subject without artificial distinction or barrier to one market or one planner" (Communist International Economics, Oxford, 1968, pp. 306-307); and the Hungarian expert I. Vajda: "it [CMEA integration] is not built on the integration of the market but on the coordination of plans" ("Integration, Economic Union and the National State," in Vajda and Simai, op. cit., 1971, p. 31).

20) Dokumente RGW, East Berlin, Staatsverlag der Deutschen Demokratischen Republik, 1971, p. 147.

21) CMEA expert O. T. Bogomolov explains the principle of socialist internationalism as follows: "In terms of practical politics, the needs of each socialist nation are bound up harmoniously with the needs of the socialist community as a whole, and national and international factors are balanced out properly against one another. It is just as impossible for the pursuit of the genuine national interests of a socialist nation to be in opposition to the needs of the socialist community as a whole as it is for the pursuit of international interests to work to the detriment of the particular interests of the individual socialist nations" (Theorie und Methodologie der internationalen sozialistischen Arbeitsteilung, East Berlin, 1969, pp. 37-38).

22) See A. Ushakov, Der Ostmarkt in Comecon (documentation), Baden-Baden, 1972, p. 469.

23) Aussenhandel (Moscow), 1972, No. 4, p. 7.

24) See Socialist World Market Prices, Leyden, A. W. Sijthoff, 1969, p. 51.

25) See Berend, op. cit., p. 24.

26) Conversion of capital investments in machinery and construction and of current production costs from Polish zlotys to clearing rubles (the clearing unit of "Haldex") requires no less than 60 coefficients. See Ausch, op. cit., p. 188.

27) Imports of the most crucial commodities in intra-CMEA trade are shown by the following figures: 72 percent of machine tools, about 100 percent of bituminous coal, 72 percent of crude oil, 82 percent of iron ore, 74 percent of construction metals, 82 percent of wood, etc. (Aussenhandel [Moscow], 1973, No. 9, p. 3).

28) See Eurostat, 1973, No. 4, pp. 10-13.

29) The production of the multinational corporations in the West grows twice as fast as the social product and 40 percent faster than Western exports. See L. Turner, "The Multinational Corporations," Futures, June 1971, Vol. 3.

30) Credits granted by the International Investment Bank (founded in 1971) cost two to three times as much.

31) During the five-year period from 1971 to 1975, Soviet deliveries will increase as follows, as compared with the preceding five-year period: crude oil, from 138 million to 243 million tons; natural gas, from 8 billion to 33 billion cubic meters; electricity, from 14 billion to 42 billion kilowatt-hours; iron ore, from 72 million to 94 million tons (Mezhdunarodnaia sotsialisticheskaia valuta stran-chlenov SEV [International Socialist Currency of the Member Nations of CMEA], Moscow, 1973, p. 68).

32) The share of the Soviet Union in world trade in 1955 was 4.4 percent, i.e., it was sixth behind the United States, Federal Republic of Germany, Great Britain, France, and Japan. In 1971, the Soviet Union, with a share of 4.0 percent, fell behind Italy and Holland to ninth place. See Aussenhandel (Moscow), 1973, No. 5, p. 56.

33) Estimate based on General Industrial Statistics, 1960-1968, United Nations, 1971.

34) See UN Statistical Yearbook, 1972. In 1970, foreign trade per capita in the CMEA was U.S.$170, including $101 for the Soviet Union and an average of $352 for the other member nations; in contrast, per capita foreign trade in the EEC countries was $930 (see Monthly Bulletin of Statistics, February 1972).

35) From the Resolution of the Twenty-Fifth Session of the Council on the Comprehensive Program (Neues Deutschland, August 7, 1971).

36) Ibid.

37) Ibid.

38) Ibid. For the period of the current 1971-1975 plan, the "adjusted" world market prices of 1965-1969 are in force.

39) Ibid.

40) See Rozliczenia miedzynarodowe [International Settlements],

collection of articles, Warsaw, 1970, p. 332.

41) Unlimited technical credits and the lack of any other countermeasure caused obligations to shoot sky high at certain times during the year. Deliveries slowed at the beginning of the year and picked up again at the end (Rozliczenia międzynarodowe, p. 351).

42) On June 9, 1949, multilateral settlement agreements were concluded between the USSR, Poland, Czechoslovakia, and Finland. Poland was to deliver hard coal (worth 80 million rubles) and Czechoslovakia, farm machinery (worth 20 million rubles) to Finland in return for foodstuffs from the Soviet Union. The Soviet Union was to obtain Finnish frame houses, cut lumber, and ships for $100 million. Trilateral clearing agreements were concluded among the USSR, Burma, and Czechoslovakia, and Bulgaria, the German Democratic Republic, and Romania.

43) See the Hungarian economist S. Ausch: "Switching over from bilateralism to a system of multilateral trade and payment requires fundamental qualitative changes in the domestic economies of the CMEA nations as well as in their external relations" ("Problems of Bilateralism and Multilateralism in the External Trade and Payments System of the CMEA Countries," in Vajda and Simai, op. cit., p. 61).

44) See A. Zwass, Finanse, 1963, No. 10, p. 5; and M. Kaser, Comecon, Oxford University Press, 1957, p. 169. The volume Rozliczenia międzynarodowe estimates the total settled balances at 2 percent of the total turnover (p. 354).

45) Documents of the CMEA, English version, East Berlin, Staatsverlag der Deutschen Democratishen Republik, 1971, pp. 174-175. The quotation is from the amendment of December 18, 1970.

46) The name "International Bank of the Socialist Countries" was rejected in an earlier stage of the discussions.

47) Cuba joined the CMEA banks on January 22, 1973.

48) "...a few months before the establishment of the EPU only 30 percent of intra-European trade was free from quantitative restrictions.... By early 1957, about nine-tenths of intra-European trade was quota-free" (R. Hinshaw, "Toward European Convertibility," in Essays in International Finance, Princeton, N.J., November 1958, p. 16).

49) "The rules on the basis of which the monthly nets were balanced out were defined in percentage in a gold-credit ratio, as it was called.... In the last three years of the EPU, the gold-credit ratio was 75:25. This was referred to as a hardening of the settlement procedures in the EPU..." (G. Schleiminger, "Europäische Zahlungsunion," in Enzyklopädisches Lexikon für das Geld-, Bank-, und Börsenwesen, Frankfurt am Main, 1967, p. 514).

50) This situation is described as follows by the former director of the Research Institute of the Polish Ministry of Foreign Trade: "Technically considered, the settlement system of the CMEA nations is multilateral. However, this did not carry with it a multilateralization of turnover, since trade relations remain bilateral. Under these conditions, multilateral settlement is reduced to a mere formality" (J. Soldaczuk, Handel międzynarodowy a rozwój gospodarczy w socjalizmie [International Trade and Economic Development in Socialism], Warsaw, 1970, p. 217).

51) In 1963, before the IBEC began its activities, the author of this book wrote: "Measures must now be taken to insure that the transferable ruble has the economic prerequisites for its transferability on the socialist market. Giving a new name to the clearing ruble will not change the present situation. The success of the settlement system on which we have set our sights requires that the considerable differences in currency value in intra-CMEA trade be eliminated. Otherwise, international trade will still be based on bilateral agreements. Under these circumstances, bilateral balancing will be the rule, and a transfer of balances to a third country the exception. A system of multilateral settlements based on no real economic foundations can only be maintained by constraint, without any notable success" (A. Zwass, "Monetary Functions in the Foreign Trade of the Socialist Countries," Finanse, 1963, No. 10)

52) See Svatopluk Potač, "Present Stage in the Development of the International Bank for Economic Cooperation," Zahraniční obchod, 1972, No. 11, p. 19. However, a positive balance of 7.7

billion koruny was again reached at the end of 1973 (Hospodárské noviny, October 12, 1973, p. 1).

53) Seventy percent of the bilateral surpluses and deficits, amounting to no less than $46.4 billion, accumulated in the EPU since its founding, were cleared by multilateral and temporary compensations, while 30 percent of these balances were covered by payments in gold or dollars, or by credits advanced for that purpose (Schleiminger, op. cit., p. 514).

54) In 1965, settlement credits amounted to 85.3 percent of the total credits (Adam Zwass, Pieniądz dwóch rynków [Money of Two Markets], Warsaw, 1968, p. 350). In 1970 and 1971, these figures tended to diminish, but in 1972 rose again to 86 percent, which was higher than the 1965 level.

55) K. Nasarkin, Aussenhandel (Moscow), 1970, No. 1, p. 50.

56) Documents of the CMEA, p. 178.

57) The Soviet economist O. Shelkov observes: "As regards the function of the transferable ruble as a reserve medium, it may be said that the planned nature of foreign trade relations in the socialist countries makes unnecessary such a hypertrophied development of this function as is seen in the case of some of the currencies of the capitalist countries" ("The Transferable Ruble as an Instrument of Socialist Economic Integration," Aussenhandel [Moscow], 1972, No. 8, p. 25).

58) The director of the Czech State Bank, S. Potač, says: "The IBEC does not undertake the financing of imports and exports as occurs on the capitalist market, neither in the case of deliveries of machinery nor in the case of capital investment projects. Commodity circulation is tied directly to money circulation" (op. cit., p. 20).

59) The East German economist Professor Karl-Heinz Domdey describes this limited importance of holdings in transferable rubles as follows: 'Its [the transferable ruble's] present shortcomings are seen in the fact that, even in the IBEC, its mechanisms for the exchange of goods and for employment as funds are both limited" (op. cit., p. 485).

60) See K. Nasarkin, "Ten Years of the International Bank for Economic Cooperation," Aussenhandel (Moscow), 1973, No. 10, p. 15.

61) See A. Zwass, Pieniądz dwóch rynków, p. 353.

62) See L. Pechacek, "Current Questions of the Convertibility of the Transferable Ruble into Gold and Convertible Currencies," Finance a úvěr, 1969, No. 9, p. 532.

63) Ibid.

64) See Potač, op. cit., p. 20.

65) Ibid.

66) Ibid.

67) The Western model for the IBEC — the EPU — formed its capital stock (U.S.$350 million) in convertible currency, not in settlement units. This capital was used for special credits to cover payments gaps, not for settlement purposes.

68) Ekonomicheskaia gazeta, 1972, No. 6, p. 21.

69) J. M. van Brabant, "Long-Term Development Credits and Socialist Trade," Weltwirtschaftliches Archiv, Vol. CVII, p. 107.

70) P. Glikman, Rachunek ekonomiczy we wspólpracy krajów RWPG w dziedzinie inwestycji [Economic Accounting in CMEA Cooperation in Investments], Warsaw, 1970, p. 49.

71) See van Brabant, op. cit., p. 119.

72) Documents of the CMEA, p. 223.

73) Ibid.

74) J. Konstantinov, "The Comprehensive Program in Action," Aussenhandel (Moscow), 1972, No. 10, p. 7.

75) Ibid., p. 7.

76) See Documents of the CMEA, op. cit., p. 229. The official gold content of the transferable ruble, 0.987412 gram pure gold, is the standard used here.

77) Article III of the Agreement.

78) See F. Kozma, Die weltwirtschaftlichen Beziehungen der beiden Europas und die sozialistische internationale Zusammenarbeit, Budapest, Kossuth Publishers, 1970, p. 11.

79) From an interview for the journal Życie gospodarcze, July 26, 1970, p. 1.

80) Z. Fedorowicz, "International Investment Bank," Bank i kredyt, 1971, No. 1, p. 2.

81) Article II of the Agreement.

82) This was the opinion given by the Polish Bank president

CMEA Monetary Institutions and Steering Instruments 157

in the quoted interview. Events have since borne him out. Of the total credits granted in 1972, the share of credits granted in convertible currencies was 39.5 percent (Życie gospodarcze, February 4, 1973) at a set share of 30 percent foreign exchange in the capital stock.

83) Ibid.

84) In the European Investment Bank, whose founding principles were taken into account in the preparing of the IIB documents, the amount of capital paid into the founding stock, which was raised to $1.5 billion on April 26, 1971, was 250 million accounting units at the end of 1970; this represented a negligible fraction of the 1,813 million accounting units sum of loan and guarantee contracts concluded as of December 31, 1970. See European Investment Bank, Annual Report, 1970.

85) Documents of the CMEA, p. 225.

86) See European Investment Bank, op. cit., p. 116.

87) In this connection, it would be useful to consider the opinion of Professor Otto Pfeiderer: "the Agreement of Bretton Woods... significantly provided only for liberalization of commercial payments on current account but not for that of capital transfers.... Virtually unlimited freedom of international capital movements, it must be admitted, exist — up to the most recently imposed restrictions almost only for two countries in the whole world, the Federal Republic of Germany and Switzerland" ("Control of International Capital Movements," Intereconomics [Hamburg], December 1972, pp. 375-376).

88) L. Rusmich, "Currency Relations in the CMEA," Aussenhandel der Tshechoslowakei, 1970, No. 10, p. 3.

89) See J. Konstantinov, op. cit., p. 7, and Życie gospodarcze, February 4, 1973, p. 10.

90) See Die Wirtschaft (East Berlin), October 11, 1972, p. 35.

91) G. Kadow, "The Activity of the International Investment Bank," Panorama (Linz), special edition, Gesellschaft für Ost und Südostkunde, 1972, p. 58.

92) Trybuna ludu, November 19, 1973, p. 2.

93) See L. Skibinski, "The International Banks of the CMEA," Gospodarka planowa, October 1972, p. 632.

94) See the Economic Bulletin of the TASS News Agency, November 17, 1971, pp. 10-11: "Almost 90 percent of the known reserves of basic materials in the USSR are in the sparsely populated Eastern territories; the other 10 percent are in the European USSR, which consumes 80 percent of the fuel. Calculations show that the fuel shortage in the European part of the USSR in 1980 will be almost four times that in 1970." Hence: "In the present period, the fuel problem of the CMEA countries can be solved only if every country raises financial means for equipment and machinery."

95) See D. Zademidko, CMEA Representative of the Soviet Union, in Trybuna ludu, August 29, 1972.

96) Documents of the CMEA, p. 226.

97) J. Kleer, "The Agenda of the CMEA," Polityka, July 4, 1972.

98) See G. Kadow, op. cit., p. 55.

99) The International Investment Bank, Moscow, 1972, p. 10.

100) O. I. Tarnovskii and N. M. Mitrofanova, Stoimost' i tsena na mirovom sotsialisticheskom rynke [Cost and Price on the World Socialist Market], Moscow, 1968, p. 84.

101) Ibid.

102) Bogomolov, op. cit., p. 156.

103) See Socialist World Market Prices, p. 109.

104) The European people's democracies have only 1 percent of the crude oil deposits of the CMEA, only 8.2 percent of its coal reserves, and 1.9 percent of its iron ore deposits (Rolf C. Ribi, Comecon, Zurich, 1970, p. 320).

105) From the commentary of the Soviet representative to the Budapest conference, B. Ladygin; see Socialist World Market Prices, p. 181.

106) Ibid., p. 53.

107) From statements by the Romanian representative, G. Siclovan, p. 41.

108) Ibid., p. 29.

109) Ibid., p. 62.

110) Documents of the CMEA, p. 57.

4. Monetary steering instruments of East-West trade

1. The Nonconvertible Currencies and International Economic Relations of the Planned Economies

1.1. Improvement of East-West Relations and the Backwardness of Payments Instruments

Most countries take a positive view of East-West trade and would like to see it grow. The Western nations are primarily interested in opening up new sources of raw materials and new markets, while those in the East are mainly concerned with importing modern capital goods and up-to-date techniques. The problems specific to East-West trade derive from the fact that the trading partners belong to fundamentally different economic systems. With this in mind, an unbiased analysis of the viability of the steering instruments used in relations between the two systems is certainly justified.

The most salient feature of the socialist system is the strict separation it maintains between the domestic economy and foreign trade. The practical effect of this separation is the almost total isolation of the monetary system and price structures in the CMEA area from the international market. Neither the national currencies nor the transferable ruble — the collective currency of the CMEA — have direct access to the world market. The official exchange rates of the planned economies have no function in international trade.

The Eastern European nations settle intra-CMEA trade on the basis of adjusted world market prices, while trade with the West — which accounts for about one-third of their total foreign trade — is settled in Western currencies on the basis of current prices of the partner country. Trade with the Eastern bloc comprises barely 5 percent of the total foreign trade of the Western nations.

1.2. Advantages and Disadvantages of a Currency with No Foreign Trade Function

One advantage of this type of currency is that the CMEA countries are not exposed to the unpredictable ups and downs of the international monetary system. Their domestic economies are relatively free to grow unimpeded, and economic policy can be carried out smoothly without recurrent balance of payments difficulties. The volume of money in circulation is not determined by the balance of payments and hence is not affected by external events over which national policies have no influence. In relations with the West, the planned economies are borrowers and thus usually reap a profit from the frequent monetary devaluations. (1) The Soviet Union, whose currency reserves consist mostly of gold, realized especially high profits from the two dollar devaluations and the rises in the price of gold that followed, thereby accomplishing what it had been striving in vain for years to obtain through official means.

On the negative side, however, a currency excluded from foreign trade activity has none of the considerable advantages of a convertible currency. Because of their shortage of foreign exchange and the nonconvertibility of their currencies, the Eastern nations must resort to barter, or at least to an effective balancing of reciprocal deliveries. Payment terms, rather than comparative cost advantages, become the overriding consideration in choosing a trading partner. Since no credit and capital market exists in the CMEA countries, there is no chance to evolve a deliberate export policy based on generous credit advances. (2) The currencies of the planned economies are used neither as reserve currencies by other countries nor as international clearing instruments, and this disadvantage is not offset by an increased utilization of foreign credits. All in all, the price paid by the Eastern nations for a stable domestic currency is an inability to develop an effective foreign trade policy and to cope effectively with the fluctuations of the world market.

1.3. Convertible and Nonconvertible Currencies and the Volume of Foreign Trade

While the share of CMEA countries in world trade has remained at a stable 10 percent over the past twenty years, the industrially developed market economies have increased their share from 60 percent in 1950 to 67 percent in 1960 and 72 percent in 1970, despite frequent currency crises. (3) The volume of Eastern bloc trade with the developing countries is much lower than that of the West. In 1970, the planned economies delivered goods worth U.S.$5 billion to the developing countries and received the equivalent of $3.2 billion in return; the corresponding figures for the West were $43 billion and $41 billion, respectively. (4)

The underdeveloped monetary system of the planned economies is not the only reason for their small slice in international trade. The main cause is the subsidiary role given to foreign trade within the overall economic framework of the centrally planned economies. In recent years, however, there have been distinct signs that this is changing. The monetary aspect of foreign trade suffers from general neglect at the broader level, so that any number of free-wheeling pragmatic solutions are always at hand.

1.4. The Reorganization of the International Monetary System with Eastern Bloc Membership

1.4.1. Problems in the East

The isolation of the Eastern currencies from the international monetary system is a logical consequence of the limited function assigned to foreign trade in the Eastern countries, although the political leanings toward isolation and autarky have also contributed their share to this state of affairs. Whereas in the West restrictions on convertibility are normally the result of a shortage of foreign exchange, in the Eastern countries the reverse is true. Tsarist Russia, Eastern Europe, and the Balkans were all totally integrated into the international monetary system before their economic systems were transformed.

The Eastern nations are also gradually coming to the realization that foreign trade is no place for ideological battles (5) and that a viable currency is needed if trade is to be effectively pursued. As long as foreign trade was regarded merely as a stopgap measure, and it was believed that autarky, though impossible on a national level, was an attainable reality within the broader area of the CMEA and that multilateral clearing through the IBEC was sufficient for flourishing trade activity, the Eastern countries were able to get along without such a currency. These notions, however, did not stand the test of reality. The drive toward autarky meant forgoing the introduction of up-to-date techniques and thus a slower effective economic growth. The creation of a so-called transferable CMEA currency changed nothing in the fundamental premise of foreign trade — namely, bilateralism.

Voices in favor of integrated world trade and a single worldwide monetary system are now heard in the East as well as the West. A high official of the Hungarian National Bank observed: "In the period of the second scientific-technical revolution — however different the socio-economic systems of the various countries in the world may be — different countries must be even more aware of the unity of the world market." (6) At the same time, a unified monetary system encompassing both economic blocs is stressed: "Transferability and convertibility are essential preconditions for real business calculations and for serious contacts between partners," and "in the framework of East-West contacts it is a Western as well as an Eastern task." (7)

Although such sentiments are by no means rare in the people's democracies, their practical realization is largely blocked by political dogmatism and a real lack of currency reserves.

The Soviet Union, the only CMEA country that has foreign exchange and gold, would never allow the requirements of a convertible currency to undermine the basic structures of its social order. (8) Even today, the Soviet Union still covers deficits in its underdeveloped foreign trade with domestically mined gold. The question of whether the guiding principles of a planned economy are compatible with a free world market in goods, services, and capital has never really been resolved. Yet one non-CMEA planned economy, Yugoslavia, where decentralization has proceeded far beyond the CMEA norms, and Romania, where the exact opposite is the case, have both set their sights on convertibility. On December 17, 1972, Romania became a member of the International Monetary Fund and the World Bank. Even China — a centrally planned economy par excellence — surprised everyone by attempting to pass off its own currency in foreign trade transactions. In 1968, the following agreement was made with the strongest trading partners in Western Europe: "The German, Swiss, Belgium, and English banks, etc., shall maintain accounts in Chinese currency in the Bank of China in London; these accounts will always be freely transferable into the currency from which they originated, i.e., into deutsche marks for Germany, etc. These clearing currencies may then be used to pay for goods moving in either direction." (9)

A broader agreement was reached in August 1972 between the Central Bank of China and the Bank of Tokyo; it stipulated that settlements between the two countries should henceforth be made in yen and yuan. The importing country will decide which currency is to be used. The yen-yuan exchange rate was set at 135.84 : 1 (10), with the proviso that any change in the official exchange rate of either of the two currencies would necessitate a revision of this rate. Each bank has the right to convert its net annual balance in the other bank into pounds sterling. Many Japanese commercial banks have since followed the Bank of Tokyo's example. (11)

China applied for membership in the IMF at the IMF meeting in Nairobi in September 1973. Although the currencies of Yugoslavia, Romania, and China are still a long way from convertibility, one thing is quite clear: In contrast to the traditional view that only essentially decentralized economies would be able to cope successfully with the mechanism of a convertible currency, it now seems that the specific structural features of the system are less of an obstacle to convertibility than political considerations.

1.4.2. Problems in the West

Domestic factors aside, the Eastern nations justify their aversion for the existing international monetary system on the grounds that it is unstable. Although the recurrent crises support this opinion, the view that the "currency crisis is a result of the deepening general crisis of the capitalist system as a whole" (12), a view especially prevalent in the Soviet Union, does not stand up to scrutiny. Western problems are not the result of an economic crisis but the effect of rapid economic growth — perhaps too rapid — and the lack of an internationally coordinated economic policy.

The Bretton Woods Agreement foundered on the unwillingness of the participating nations to observe the rules they themselves had laid down and on the problem of capital flows — a problem to which insufficient attention was given at Bretton Woods, since at that time it was not a timely issue. It is uncertain whether the crisis will soon be overcome, although there has certainly been no lack of suggestions, from the good to the mediocre. (13)

The two-tier system for the price of gold was adopted in March 1968, and later in 1970, special drawing rights (SDRs) were instituted. Neither measures, however, afforded a lasting solution; indeed, they were bound to fail, as long as the leading nations were unwilling to take the political steps necessary to restore international stability. At this writing, the market price of gold has reached a level that not even the most radical advocates of a price increase, such as R. Harrod, M. A. Halperin, J. Rueff, or E. Salin, would have dared propose. (14) Yet the rise in the price of gold has not led to an accumulation of currency reserves with stable value, as its advocates had expected; instead, monetary uncertainty has deepened, and the central banks have stopped converting currency into gold. On August 15,

1971, when the United States suspended the convertibility of dollars into gold, the official gold price lost its basic raison d'être, and the status of the dollar as a key currency has been seriously compromised. (15)

Traditional reserve media increasingly have had to be replaced by fiduciary money, which may be created, distributed, and even destroyed, according to hard and fast rules. Yet despite the techniques proposed to restore international liquidity, structural disequilibria in the balances of payments still remain, and these must be eliminated. For this, numerous political negotiations are necessary — for example, between the United States, on the one hand, and Japan and the EEC, on the other — but because of the political problems, a quick solution is very unlikely. In any event, there is no need to fear that any radical restrictions will be placed on the free movement of goods and capital (one of the West's outstanding achievements) even if more international coordination is found to be necessary to avoid imbalances in some countries. (16) Indeed, all parties are well aware of how much this international freedom of movement has contributed to the economic prosperity of the postwar era. It therefore would seem desirable that a revamped currency system should embrace the entire world market, i.e., that it should also take into consideration the needs and capacities of the planned economies. The conditions for the creation of such a worldwide system will be discussed in the next sections.

2. The CMEA Nations and the International Monetary and Credit Institutions

2.1. The Planned Economies and the International Monetary System Between the World Wars

The almost total isolation of Eastern currencies from international trade and capital flows has a troubled history behind it, in which attempts to integrate the Eastern economies into the world market alternated with tendencies toward isolation and autarky. During the years between the world wars, flaws (which persist today) in the Western currency system made the participation of the planned economies difficult. However, there is little reason to believe that a nation would experience difficulties in participating in the Western currency system merely because it had a centralized economy.

After its brief and ill-starred attempt to create a money-free economy under war communism, the Soviet Union adopted the New Economic Policy and, at the same time, announced its readiness to help in restoring the international monetary system after its utter and total collapse during the war. In 1922, the Soviet Union attended the conference at Genoa, where it fought for the retention of the ruble exchange rate set by the monetary reform and joined ranks with Western nations in an unsuccessful attempt to restore the gold standard. The Soviet reentry into the international division of labor soon bore fruit. In 1930, trade reached 73 percent of its prewar volume, a high point for the period between the wars. (17)

The Soviet flirtation with the market mechanism, first on the national and then on the international level, did not last long, however. The drive for autarky and the suppression of the regulatory mechanisms of the market in favor of centralized steering forced foreign trade back down to 30 percent of its prewar volume by 1933. (18) The national currency was reduced to a purely technical instrument for facilitating fulfillment of the plan, and all ties with the international currency system were severed.

Although the reorganization of the Soviet Union into a centrally planned economy was to a large extent ideologically motivated, it must be said that, at the time, the economically shattered Western nations were hardly able to offer an attractive alternative. The attempt to restore the gold standard (albeit with modifications) failed. An almost permanent currency chaos took hold and shook the very foundations of the international division of labor, driving the world even more deeply into the Great Depression. There should be little wonder, then, that the decision was made to seal off the Soviet economy, coming as it did at a time when the world market was foundering in the disintegrating swamp of bilateral clearing and when the notorious beggar-thy-neighbor policy had replaced healthy, efficiency-promoting competition as the international modus operandi.

2.2. The Planned Economies and the Reorganization of the International Monetary System after World War II

Although the decision of the Soviet Union to enter the international monetary system during the interim between the wars was a direct corollary of the New Economic Policy, there was nevertheless no necessary connection between the USSR's post-World War II attempt to enter the international monetary system and the way its economic system had evolved. At the time the Soviet Union was participating in the preliminary discussions for a new currency system, domestic preconditions for internationalizing the ruble and decentralizing economic decisions were nonexistent. Nevertheless, its participation was meant to be taken seriously, and, indeed, the fact that many of its proposals were accepted by other nations bears this out. The discussion centered on two basic reorganization proposals: the "Preliminary Draft Outline of a Proposal for an International Stabilization Fund of the United and Associated Nations," by the American Assistant Secretary of the Treasury Harry White, and the "Proposal for an International Clearing Union," by J. M. Keynes.

The Soviet Union favored the American proposal, although much of Keynes's project resurfaced in the CMEA's International Bank for Economic Cooperation (IBEC) twenty years later. In Keynes's proposal, as in the IBEC today, mutual claims and obligations were to be balanced out in a clearing union. In both cases, the export surpluses of some countries and the import surpluses of others were to be bridged by means of credits. For this purpose, Keynes proposed the issuance of bankors. The IBEC relies on the transferable ruble. Keynes was more farsighted, however, for in his proposal the capital stock was not to be constituted by these bankors, which were meant as a mere settling unit. Indeed, the IBEC foundered on the attempt to use a settlement currency as capital. While the IBEC pays interest to creditors and charges borrowers, Keynes wanted to charge interest to both, a policy which would have hit the United States particularly hard, since after the war it was cast consistently in the role of a lending nation. One may suspect that the Soviet Union probably rejected the Keynesian project because it wanted no part of any system based on fiat money, although it made no explicit statements to that effect. The Soviet Union still lays great store on gold as a means of payment.

Soviet suggestions concerning the International Monetary Fund were geared to the needs of the planned economies. It wanted to keep to a minimum the regulatory function of the IMF and the encroachments on the autonomy of the member nations that that function would entail. Thus, a member was to be allowed to take its own interests into account in setting exchange rates, and members were to be granted the right to alter par values without IMF approval, provided such a change "would not affect the international transactions of members of the Fund." In this way, it was intended to make the par value an internal affair of the planned economies and to isolate the domestic currency from the influence of the international market. (19) Another Soviet proposal had to do with a reduced gold subscription quota — normally 25 percent of the total — for those countries that had suffered substantial losses from military occupation. Of course, the Soviet Union was given one of the five executive positions on the Board of Directors, which was to be filled by the most influential member nations.

Nevertheless, the Soviet Union did not ratify the Bretton Woods Agreement because of the dominance of the United States, nor has it revised its position since that time. Poland resigned from the IMF and the World Bank on March 17, 1950, for the alleged reason that the Monetary Fund had not lived up to the expectations of its founders and that the World Bank had rejected its application for a loan of $600 million. (20) Even before that, in February 1950, the executive director for Poland and Czechoslovakia terminated his functions in the Board of Directors after the latter rejected his demand that the membership of Nationalist China be rescinded. A further conflict arose in 1952 when the IMF initiated discussions with all members that had not yet assumed all the convertibility obligations pursuant to Article VIII, including Czechoslovakia. Czechoslovakia refused to submit economic statistics to the IMF, claiming reasons of security. When Czechoslovakia changed the par value of the Czech koruna in 1953 without first consulting with the IMF, this was used as a pretext for barring that country from any further utilization of IMF funds. In a letter dated May 4, 1955, Czechoslovakia announced its resignation from IMF membership. (21)

Cuba, whose expulsion was continually up for discussion because of repeated infractions of the statutes, announced its resignation in April 1964. (22) About eight years later, just when Cuba had become a full member of the CMEA, Romania, one of the latter's founding members, joined both of the Bretton Woods institutions — the only CMEA nation to do so. It became the 122nd member of the IMF, with a capital subscription quota of $190 million, and the 122nd member of the World Bank, with a capital subscription of $162.1 million, in December 1972.

Other CMEA nations are currently considering membership. In the following section, we shall examine the difficulties they could encounter in taking such a step.

2.3. The Planned Economies and the Political Balance of Power in the IMF

The Soviet Union's official reason for not ratifying the Bretton Woods Agreement was the dominance of the United States in both the IMF and the World Bank. With its quota of $1,200 million, the Soviet Union would have had a proportional vote of only 12.37 percent in addition to 3.04 percent it could count on from Poland and Czechoslovakia (1.52 percent each). (23) The United States, on the other hand, with its initial quota of $2,750 million, would have had 27 percent of the votes; moreover, it would have enjoyed an effective blocking power in the most important decisions, which according to the statutes required 80 percent of the votes for passage. The dominance of the United States, however, derived principally from its economic power and hence the strength of the dollar, which the IMF statutes had institutionalized as a key currency.

Since that time, the power relationships in the IMF have shifted considerably. The 21.95 percent of the votes controlled by the United States is now counterbalanced by the 27.44 percent of the six original EEC countries and Great Britain. In addition, the 1969 amendment of the IMF statutes makes a majority of 85 percent necessary for major decisions. Ordinarily, a broad consensus is sought among the members, and formal vote counts have been quite rare except in elections. (24) An indication of the fading status of the dollar as a key currency is the decreasing number of dollar drawings from the IMF. From 1947 through 1961, these amounted to 65 percent of total drawings, but in 1971, only $10 million were drawn — about the equivalent of the drawings made in Austrian schillings. (25) In March 1973, an IMF member, the Federal Republic of Germany, for the first time set the par value of its currency in terms of special drawing rights. Other nations followed suit.

The Eastern countries' rejection of the IMF unquestionably made it easier for the Western countries, particularly the United States, to establish their dominant positions on the international money and capital markets (26), just as the entry of the Eastern nations into the Fund, even at this late date, would doubtless still be capable of undermining the hegemony enjoyed by the Western superpowers in the IMF.

2.4. The Planned Economies and the Goals of the Bretton Woods Agreement

Even if there should be no major obstacles, at least in organizational terms, to the entry of the Eastern bloc nations into the IMF, it still remains to be determined whether the goals of the international monetary organizations and those of the planned economies are ultimately compatible.

In contrast to the institutionalized nonconvertibility of the Eastern currencies, Article I of the statutes (Articles of Agreement) states that the chief goal of the Bretton Woods Agreement is "to assist in the establishment of a multilateral system of payments with respect to current transactions between members, and in the elimination of foreign exchange restrictions which hamper the growth of world trade." The member nations are accordingly asked to assume all the obligations set forth in

Article VIII. This means that "each member shall buy balances of its currency held by another member if the latter, in requesting the purchase, declares: (i) that the balances to be bought have been recently acquired as a result of current transactions; or (ii) that their conversion is needed for making payments for current transactions." Limitations on the freedom of exchange operations in the scarce currency can follow only after consultation with the Fund. (27)

Stable and uniform exchange rates should unify the convertible currencies. Article IV, Section 4, requires the member nations "to collaborate with the Fund to promote exchange stability, to maintain orderly exchange arrangements with other members, and to avoid competitive exchange alterations." (28)

Thus, the establishment of currency convertibility and the maintenance of a stable exchange rate are conditio sine qua non for participation in the IMF, regardless of the economic system of the member nation.

2.5. The Planned Economies and the Functioning of the IMF

A nonconvertible currency is quite obviously an appreciable obstacle to the active participation of a member in IMF operations. After all, the national currencies, not gold, constitute the major share (75 percent) of the reserves from which the IMF draws to advance credits to a member with balance of payments difficulties. The debtor nation purchases the amounts of its partners' currencies it needs from the Fund and credits the Fund with an equivalent sum in its national currency at its central bank; repayment is effected through the repurchase of the country's own currency with gold or with convertible currencies.

Even if its currency is nonconvertible, a member may raise its quota and gain access to the Fund's facilities by selling its own currency to the Fund for foreign exchange or gold and then later repurchasing it. No other country will draw inconvertible currencies, however, and this could cause the IMF problems, especially in view of the economic weight carried by the Soviet

Union. But the same difficulties that stem from nonconvertibility are encountered even by members with market economies that are unable to bring their currency and payments policies in line with the goals of the IMF because of a chronic shortage of foreign exchange.

2.6. Article XIV of the IMF Statutes — A Gateway to Membership for All

In 1943-1944, when the Bretton Woods Agreement was drawn up and later passed, currency convertibility and fixed exchange rates were a distant goal. The United States was the only nation able to fulfill the conditions for these two objectives, and hence, at that time, the dollar was the only currency for which there was a demand. Transitional provisions had to be created if the IMF was to begin functioning at all. These provisions are set forth in Article XIV of the agreement, which stipulates that, for a transitional period, members "may maintain and adapt to changing circumstances restrictions on payments and transfers for current transactions." So far, only 27 of the 124 member nations have fully met the requirements and become full-fledged Article VIII countries. For example, the Federal Republic of Germany, one of the world's leading industrial powers, did not assume the obligations spelled out in Article VIII until February 1962. Since Article XIV leaves it largely up to the member nation itself to determine how fast it will dismantle its restrictive policies, "the terms of the article, which was originally intended only for a transitional period after the war, have come to serve as a general license authorizing weaker countries to maintain their restrictions on payments and transfers." (29)

Since Article XIV makes no distinction among the different reasons for imposing payments restrictions, the planned economies could also invoke this article to their advantage. Over the long term, however, they would have to expect the other members to use the Fund to pressure them into relaxing their restrictions. Regardless of their status, the member nations are also obligated to keep the Fund regularly informed on certain national data, such as official holdings of gold and foreign exchange at home and abroad, total exports and imports of merchandise, international balance of payments, etc., as it deems necessary for its operations.

2.7. Advantages of Membership for CMEA Countries

The amount of credits the CMEA nations can obtain from the CMEA banks is very limited; in addition, credits are usually tied to goods deliveries. The IBEC grants short-term credits in transferable rubles to bridge temporary imbalances in intra-CMEA trade and in the nonconvertible currencies to the extent allowed by the modest amount of foreign exchange in its capital stock ($72 million). It also advances credits in convertible currencies to cover shortages in foreign exchange in trade with the West. The International Investment Bank grants middle-term and long-term investment credits in proportion to the composition of its basic capital stock (70 percent in transferable rubles and 30 percent in convertible currencies). This means that a borrower will be restricted in advance in the choice of markets for procuring needed capital goods. There are three basic causes for the modest credit facilities of the CMEA: the restrictive concept of foreign trade; the general limitation of CMEA currencies to domestic functions; and the lack of national and international markets for money and capital. There is not even a viable credit mechanism for current trade transactions. Investment credits are granted by the IIB from a pool (called capital). In this way, borrowers obtain equipment and machinery for capital development projects approved by the bank. The value of the deliveries, expressed in transferable rubles, represents the credit debt.

The IMF, on the other hand, can count on quota inpayments of $28.6 billion, in addition to another $6 billion in credit from the Club of the Ten, as specified in the General Agreement to Borrow. The World Bank raises its funds principally on the international capital markets and can rely on capital subscriptions of up to $26.6 billion from its member nations. Gold subscription is the only effective capital contribution of the IMF members. According to O. Emminger, "the countries involved could obtain the gold sums necessary for a subscription indirectly from the Fund itself." (30) At the end of November 1972, the gold quota was 6,884.4 million SDRs (31) but the drawings made by November 1972 alone amounted to 25,410 million SDRs. (32) As long as drawings do not exceed 25 percent of the quota within a twelve-month period, they can be made without any conditions; beyond that, economic conditions are imposed. On the whole, the debts of a member should not exceed 200 percent of its quota, although the executive directors of the Fund are empowered to make exceptions to this rule, and indeed have done so. An additional source for bridging payments gaps are the SDRs. The total sum of SDRs issued between 1970 and the end of November 1972 was 9,315 million. (33)

The case of Yugoslavia is a good example of how the IMF's facilities can be used to meet balance of payments difficulties. That country's gold subscription is $44.7 million; by November 1972, it had drawn $397.5 million. (34)

Credit conditions are also more favorable in the IMF than in the IBEC. About 80 percent of the settlement credits granted by the IBEC have repayment periods of only three months, while in the IMF the repayment terms are usually between three and five years. The IMF offers more favorable interest rates than the IBEC — if a comparison of interests borne by different forms of credit can be said to have any meaning at all. Depending on their period of repayment, credits in transferable rubles bear interest of 3.25 percent to 5 percent per year, while credits in convertible currencies are charged at the prevailing rates on the international capital market. The IMF, on the other hand, charges a transaction fee of 0.5 percent for every drawing. Interest must be paid only on drawings exceeding the cash subscription sum, and the rate is set in accordance with the duration and size of the loan. For example, the interest rate is 2 percent for a drawing of 50 percent of quota for a half-year; for each additional half-year, the rate is raised by 0.5 percent.

The World Bank is cast in an even more favorable light when compared with the International Investment Bank. The IIB can grant credits only within the limits of its founding capital (because of the long-term nature of credits, the weight of repayments is negligible). This sum is nominally $1,380 million, but in 1971-1972, only $470 million were granted. The founding capital of the World Bank is only a small sum by contrast. Credits are financed principally by the issuance of bonds on the international capital markets and by the rediscounting of bonds. In 1959, the conditions governing the payment of subscription quotas by the member nations were relaxed even further: only 1 percent of the total quota must be paid in gold or U.S. dollars, while 9 percent must be paid in the national currency. The remaining 90 percent is a guarantee and represents the collective responsibility of the members for the World Bank's bonds. In the fiscal year 1971-1972 alone, the World Bank circulated thirty issues of bank bonds worth $1.744 billion, as compared to $1.368 billion in 1970-1971 and $735 billion in 1969-1970. (35) All told, by the end of 1972, the World Bank had granted 855 loans worth $18.4 billion, including $5.5 billion in the period from 1970 to 1972 alone. (36) Yugoslavia, for example, has so far received 13 loans amounting to $377 million. (37)

The developing countries (group II) receive especially favorable credit opportunities and subscription terms in the International Development Association, which was established as a subsidiary of the World Bank. At the initial subscription of June 6, 1967, the seventy-nine developing countries (group II) paid in $248.6 million, of which 90 percent was in their nonconvertible currencies. In return, for a handling fee of 0.75 percent per annum, they receive interest-free credits with a maturity of up to fifty years and no repayment required for the first ten years.

Yugoslavia also belongs to group II, and Romania will surely claim this status too, as it has already done in the General Agreement on Tariffs and Trade (GATT), which it joined in October 1971. Australia, Japan, New Zealand, and Austria have already conceded Romania this prerogative. (38)

3. The Relation of Eastern Europe to the International Foreign Trade Organizations

Like world monetary and credit institutions, international trade organizations are also open to all United Nations members, regardless of their social or economic system. No one called into question the participation of the Eastern allies of World War II. Actually, after an initial period of collaboration, the planned economies withdrew, as they had done with the IMF and World Bank, but they are once again participating on a broad scale.

In 1946, the Soviet Union and Czechoslovakia were invited to participate in the founding committee of the International Trade Organization, whose specific function was to be that of implementing the liberalization program for international trade proposed by the United States in December 1945. Although Trygve Lie, first Secretary General of the United Nations, ascribed a special importance to East-West relations, and Italy was prepared immediately to ratify the ITO charter, it was ratified by neither the Soviet Union nor the Western countries. (39)

Bulgaria, Poland, Romania, and Czechoslovakia were all invited to the World Trade Conference in Havana in 1947 (40), but only Poland and Czechoslovakia, which even at that early date had an extensive tariff system, accepted. In the end, Poland did not sign the Havana charter, so Czechoslovakia turned out to be the only Eastern nation represented among the twenty-three founding nations of the General Agreement on Tariffs and Trade concluded on October 30, 1947. Since the GATT is more loosely organized than the IMF, Czechoslovakia — and Cuba — were able to retain their memberships, and when the question of membership came up later for the other CMEA nations, they found the decision to join much easier to make than it had been with the IMF.

Romania attended all the meetings of the GATT council and the Committee on Trade and Development as an observer from 1957 on, and in October 1971 it became a full member. Poland had a loose status with the GATT as an associated member from 1960 to 1966 and became a full member in June 1967. From 1966, Hungary had the status of an observer in the GATT; in 1969, it applied for full membership, which it received in August 1973. Finally, Bulgaria has had an observer status since 1967.

Aside from the German Democratic Republic, whose absence from the international organizations has been motivated by purely political considerations; the Soviet Union has been the only CMEA country that has kept aloof from the GATT. The turn of the CMEA countries to the GATT is therefore all the more noteworthy, since its objectives are actually just as much at variance with the principles of a planned economy as those of the IMF.

Whereas the IMF seeks the multilateralization of foreign trade through across-the-board convertibility of all currencies and regulated exchange rates, the path chosen by the GATT is the lifting of trade restrictions and preferential treatment of its member countries. Thus, Article I states that "any advantage, favor, or immunity granted by any contracting party to any product originating in, or destined for, any other country, shall be accorded immediately and unconditionally to the like product originating in, or destined for, the territories of all other contracting parties." (41)

The key point in the agreement is the most-favored-nation status, which entails multilateral reductions in customs tariffs; bilaterally negotiated tariff reductions must be extended to all GATT members. This proviso serves as a special incentive for the Eastern countries, which would like to take advantage of these provisions without sacrificing anything in return.

Although the Havana charter devotes a special section to the question of government-administered foreign trade and associated trade policy, only a few quite general provisions were ultimately adopted. (42)

In a country where all foreign trade has been nationalized and hence automatically placed on a quota basis, albeit informally, where prices are centrally determined, and where surpluses or deficits in foreign trade activity are accounted for in the national budget, customs tariffs do not mean very much. At most, they are a formal device for price formation, although this can also be achieved by more direct means.

The system of reciprocal privileges in the GATT overlooks the specific features of East-West trade, since the concessions a planned economy is able to offer to a GATT partner have nothing to do with preferential tariff treatment in the usual sense, although the Soviet Union, Hungary, and Bulgaria formally instituted their own customs system on the basis of the 3,500 tariff items of the Brussels tariff schedule.

The planned economies are just as interested in the most-favored-nation status which they can obtain from the market economies as they are in the facilities for obtaining credits in the form of foreign exchange from the IMF. The GATT developed a formula, similar to Article XIV of the IMF statutes, which will enable the planned economies to take out GATT membership. Thus, Poland and Romania agreed to increase imports from their partner countries in return for tariff privileges. Hungary, on the other hand, was able to offer a genuine customs tariff as a basis for its membership in the GATT.

4. A "Marshall Plan" for the Soviet Union

At the end of World War II, Eastern Europe and the Soviet Union were on the brink of economic ruin. The advocates of a broadly liberalized trade and currency convertibility were quite aware that the Eastern nations would have the greatest difficulties to overcome if such a policy were implemented. It is therefore no coincidence that Harry White, the author of the IMF proposal, advocated generous economic aid to the tune of $5 billion for the Soviet Union; this was intended to help make it easier for the USSR to meet the requirements of the IMF. From an unpublished memorandum of March 7, 1944, Richard Gardner learned that the proposed aid was to be granted without any political conditions attached. In a letter of November 30, 1945, White explained the reasoning behind his proposal: "The major task that confronts American diplomacy and the only one of any real value in the major problems that confront us is to devise means whereby continued peace and friendly relations can be assured between the United States and Russia." (43) His letter concludes with the statement: "Everything else in the field of international diplomacy pales into insignificance beside this major task." (44) White's proposal found a powerful supporter in Henry Morgenthau, Secretary of the Treasury, who wanted to double the proposed amount of Soviet aid. In his letter to the president of the United States accompanying White's memorandum, he expressed his hope that the presentation and implementation of a reconstruction program drawn up by the United States for the Soviet Union would go a long way toward alleviating many problems in U.S.-Soviet relations. (45)

The plan fell through, however; instead, an even wider-ranging plan for aid — but one restricted to Europe — was put into effect.

Although the European Reconstruction Program submitted by George Marshall, then Secretary of State, on June 5, 1947, and adopted on April 4, 1948, was limited to Europe, it gave a mighty boost to world trade and thus to the international division of labor, and countries that it did not directly concern could hardly avoid feeling its repercussions.

Originally, Poland, Czechoslovakia, and Hungary thought it would be possible to accept the Marshall Plan and intended to be present at the Paris conference where the practical guidelines were to be drawn up for its implementation. The USSR was invited to Paris personally by British Foreign Minister Bevin, at least for an exchange of opinions. (46) But the discussions that took place between England, France, and the USSR in late July 1947 foundered. The Soviet Union, having already rejected membership in the International Monetary Fund because of the dominance of the United States, was even less willing to accept American leadership in European reconstruction, which would of course have encompassed Eastern Europe. In the end, Poland, Hungary, and Czechoslovakia also withdrew their assent.

Thus, the World War II alliance between the Western European democracies and the Soviet Union came to an end, although it might well have served as the basis for any number of projects requiring political and economic cooperation after the war. Political motives, quite well known, caused and ultimately widened the rift. Western economic policy had embarked upon a new course.

5. The Economic War

In 1947, when the Marshall Plan was being discussed, there was still a reasonable hope that the Eastern and Southeastern

European nations would maintain their traditional economic relations with Western Europe despite the momentous upheavals in their social and economic systems. After an initial lull just after the war, trade between the Eastern European nations and the West increased rapidly in 1947 and continued to expand well into 1948.

Share of Western Trade in Total Foreign Trade
(in percent) (47)

	Bulgaria	Czechoslovakia	Hungary	Poland	Romania
1946	17	78	30	30	—
1947	18	86	53	61	12

By 1949, however, the trade war, which had set in during the interim, brought about an abrupt decline. The embargo on strategic goods, especially raw materials and capital goods, along with the general proscription on credits, dealt a severe blow to East-West relations. Thus it cannot be stressed strongly enough that Western experts in Eastern affairs are absolutely wrong when they claim that the cold war, and not internal political factors, were responsible for the creation of the bloc of centrally planned economies.

When the United States introduced restrictions on all deliveries to Europe as of March 1, 1948, the Eastern countries were already a solid bloc. The events in Czechoslovakia in February 1948 merely added the finishing touches. Formally, the Eastern bloc was created by treaties between the Soviet Union and Romania (February 4, 1948), Hungary (April 16, 1948), and Bulgaria (March 18, 1948). The policy of containment could no longer effectively impede this development, and could even less undo it once it was completed.

Thereafter, the United States also used the Marshall Plan for its embargo policy. Article 117(d) of the plan gave the United States the power to block the delivery of embargoed goods even to nations of Western Europe if any likelihood existed that they would find their way to a third country. (48)

	1948	1949	1950	1951	1952	1953	1954	1955 (49)
			1948 = 100					
U.S. exports to Eastern Europe (including China)	100	36	16	0.1	—	—	—	—
Western European exports to Eastern Europe	100	143	112	128	127	136	167	189
Marshall Plan aid	—	100	60	36	21	20	10	7

The embargo list, jointly compiled and in force since January 1, 1950, made the policy of containment the common concern of all the Western nations. The United States ceased all exports to the East. Western Europe, on the other hand, reduced its Eastern trade only for the duration of the Marshall Plan. When the latter had run its course, attitudes toward trade with the East abruptly changed, and the positive arguments for its development were again stressed.

Whereas in 1949 the ratio of U.S. economic aid to Europe to European exports to the East was still about 6:1, by 1953 it had fallen to 1.5:1. The situation reversed itself the very next year, and henceforth American aid was to far exceed the volume of exports to the Eastern countries. (50)

Western exports to the Soviet Union underwent a net decrease (by 30 percent) only in 1950. By 1952, they had again risen sharply. The effect of the embargo policy was more directly discernible in the other Eastern European nations.

The severance of cooperative ties between East and West in international economic organizations and the transformation of the Marshall Plan into an instrument of the roll-back policy toward the emergent Eastern bloc had a tremendous influence on

East-West relations and the international balance of power. The Western European countries, helped back on their feet by American aid, now sought political emancipation as well.

Their new-found economic independence found expression in the creation of the European Economic Community and European Free Trade Association, organizations for economic integration and cooperation, in which the United States did not participate. The seeds for later conflicts and currency crises were already sown.

The embargo neither prevented the political integration of the Eastern nations nor seriously impeded their economic development; nevertheless, it did leave a permanent mark on the scope and structure of East-West trade and helped to deepen the rift in the world economy, now irrevocably split into two systems.

The people's democracies were forced to find markets in the East and to strengthen their autarkic tendencies. (51) In 1953, the share of Eastern trade in the total foreign trade of some of the CMEA countries already showed a considerable increase over 1948, as may be seen from the following table. (52)

	Bulgaria	Czechoslovakia	Hungary	Poland	Romania
		(in %)			
1948	83	33	34	46	71
1953	86	78	76	70	84

The CMEA was created in 1949 as the Eastern answer to the Marshall Plan. Although it was unable to unify the national planned economies into a single economic supersystem, it did lay the groundwork for the common market that later emerged. Most of the foreign trade of the CMEA nations was intrabloc trade; trade with the West was restricted to only the most urgently needed goods and up-to-date equipment and techniques. Thus, trade with Western nations maintained a more or less constant share of the total foreign trade of the Eastern countries; there were, after all, still some rough edges on the state's foreign trade monopoly.

The International Bank for Economic Cooperation was unable to develop into a banking institution in the Western sense. To facilitate its activities, it evolved special trading practices and settlement procedures, designed only for the CMEA, which are now serving as obstacles to closer East-West relations. A unified worldwide infrastructure for international trade and credit transactions would be much more difficult to institute today than it would have been after World War II, but, by the same token, today both sides are much more aware of the importance of East-West trade for growth and prosperity than they were twenty or thirty years ago. All things considered, then, the climate is incomparably more favorable today for solving these problems than it was in the past.

6. The Expansion of Economic Relations Between East and West

Embargo and the credit proscription were the weapons of the United States in the cold war, although their use ran counter to Europe's economic interests. When the Marshall Plan could no longer be used as an instrument of economic coercion, the Western European nations soon began to explore ways to open up the vast Eastern market. Ideological factors yielded to commercial interests (53), and the different economic system prevailing in the East merited consideration only to the extent that it affected problems of pricing, settlement, credit conditions, etc.

Once bellum mercantorium had given way to pax mercantoria, bilateral and multilateral agreements began gradually to emerge in East-West relations; the Western nations began to vie for markets by offering attractive credit terms, while on the other side of the fence developments in the East fed directly into these efforts. Economic reforms undermined autarkic tendencies; industrial enterprises were given broader powers of decision; and a general awareness set in that foreign trade had an important role to play in improving overall economic efficiency. In particular, it became clear that the Western market alone held the key to closing the ever-widening gap in technology, and of course the credit facilities offered by the West fit in perfectly.

The Economic Commission for Europe (ECE) of the United Nations undertook some fruitful measures to improve East-West trade. It was the only international agency to be concerned with these problems throughout all the years of economic warfare, and later, when a thaw finally set in, it moved into the center of activity. In its first discussions in 1951, the ECE evolved a line of negotiations — namely, bilateral discussions within a multilateral framework — that was destined to prove useful in later years. (54) In 1953, the ECE hosted numerous discussions among experts from twenty-four countries. Lists of goods were exchanged as a basis on which imports and exports might later be expanded. (55)

A special meeting of the commission was arranged in the summer of 1959 to discuss technical and organizational problems and payments mechanisms in East-West trade; later, this agenda was referred to an ad hoc committee for further study. More parleys in September 1963 and December 1964 dealt with tariffs, most-favored-nation status, and the prerequisites for multilateralization of payments.

Reciprocity was a special problem. In the East, where prices and import quotas are normally set by central authorities, the tariff is not really an instrument for implementing foreign trade policy; hence the question arose of what the East could offer in return for the special tariff privileges accorded by Western nations. A solution was found: it was declared that the Eastern nations would be considered to have met their obligations in this respect if they helped to put East-West trade on a long-term basis, with balanced but steadily increasing flows in each direction. (56) Later the GATT employed this principle as a frame of reference in its negotiations with the planned economies.

The ECE initiated the first discussion of measures that would permit the transfer of balances and the convertibility of currencies in East-West trade, but unfortunately came to no agreement on these questions. Opinions were especially far apart on the question of reciprocity of preferential treatment. There were fourteen ECE members and fourteen different positions on the matter, and all diverged from the opinion of the ad hoc committee. Austria, Greece, Italy, and Spain were completely negative, while Scandinavia and the three CMEA countries (Czechoslovakia, Hungary, and Romania) took quite favorable views. (57) Austria felt that "it would not be advisable to lay down hard and fast rules for East-West trade" and that "every country should pursue the path it deems necessary in the light of its internal situation to achieve an optimal development of East-West trade on the basis of mutual advantage." (58) On the other hand, Holland, which had promised its support to the recommendation of the ad hoc committee, demanded multilateralization of payments in the planned economies as a conditio sine qua non for the liberalization of East-West trade. (59) To date, the problems of reciprocity and liberalization remain unresolved.

Other efforts in the sphere of East-West trade originated with the UN Conference on Trade and Development (UNCTAD) and the GATT, but these lie outside the scope of the present study. One effort of the European Parliamentary Assembly deserves mention, however. The Hahn committee was set up to investigate the possibilities for promoting East-West trade. In its report, the committee names two basic conditions which must be met to attain this goal: (1) A nation must be willing politically to embark upon a trade policy with long-term goals; and (2) it must have flexible instruments suited for implementing this policy. (60)

The political willingness found expression in the decisions of Western European governments to lift the embargo as rapidly as possible, to expand credit facilities, and to place economic relations with the CMEA countries on a long-term basis. In 1954, Great Britain became the first country to provide a legal framework for the projected trade boom with the East, which in fact was already on its way. France, Italy, and the Federal Republic of Germany later followed suit. After some countries took the initiative to remove more items from the embargo lists, multilateral agreements followed. The second major revision of the COCOM lists (61) in 1958 marked the effective end of the era of economic warfare. Ultimately, only products considered strategic in a narrow sense by all parties remained on the lists. (62)

Quota restrictions on Eastern imports were also gradually

relaxed, and import regulations were for the most part aligned with those already in force for other imports. Great Britain once again set the pace. In 1964, imports from Bulgaria, Poland, Czechoslovakia, and Hungary were liberalized; Romania and the Soviet Union in May 1969, and the German Democratic Republic in January 1970 were included in this list. (63) Today, about 96-97 percent of Soviet exports to Great Britain are free of restrictions. (64) In January 1961, France lifted all import restrictions from 600 to 919 tariff items (65), and today over 90 percent of all tariff items are free-traded. The Federal Republic of Germany completely liberalized all imports from the East in 1970 (66), and Austria has long since liberalized most of its trade with the Soviet Union, Romania, and Poland, with total liberalization scheduled for January 1, 1975.

The United States was the last to discover the Eastern market. In the 1960s, less than 1 percent of its total exports went to the East (67), and in 1970 its share in total exports of the Western industrial nations to the East was still not quite 4 percent. (68) The conspicuous absence of the United States on the Eastern markets was less the result of the Export Control Act of 1949 than of a lack of interest on the part of American business. About 1,200 products can be exported without license, and less than 0.5 percent of license applications in the first months of 1970, amounting to $170 million, were refused. (69) Yet trade remained low. Recently concluded trade and credit agreements between the Soviet Union and the United States, however, indicate that the United States intends to waste no time in making up this lost ground. Under a deal concluded in April 1973 between the American Occidental Petroleum Corporation and the Soviet Union, the USSR will import $8 billion worth of goods (70); this is almost 90 percent of the total imports of Eastern Europe from the Western industrial nations in 1970.

7. Settlement and Payments Procedures in East-West Trade

7.1. Clearing

Clearing is actually an invention of the market economies. It was used when free exchange of currency broke down or when foreign exchange was placed under full government control.

Clearing is a higher form of exchange compared with primitive barter in which one item is exchanged for another without the use of money. Through clearing, a series of bilateral claims and liabilities can be offset, provided that they are all with the same partner and that their net sums balance out. Clearing is effected through some central office, usually the central banks of the two countries involved, which also keep an eye on trade flows and endeavor to avoid surpluses or deficits. Where temporary imbalances do occur, they also take the necessary stopgap measures.

After the world economic crisis had put an end to the free flow of goods and money and some nations had partially reverted to barter in natura, clearing offered an attractive way out of an apparently hopeless situation. The first clearing agreements concluded by Switzerland with Austria and Hungary in 1931 found many imitators. In 1935, thirty-five clearing agreements were already on the books. (71)

During World War II and the immediate postwar period, clearing was the primary mode of settlement among the Western nations as well as between West and East. In the West, however, clearing is obviously at crosscurrents with the system as a whole, and is resorted to only in extreme situations. In the planned economies, the situation is otherwise; superficially, at any rate, clearing seems to fit in easily with the general structure of things.

Both the justification of clearing and its procedures differ in the two economic systems. In a market economy, a government temporarily assumes functions that ordinarily reside with the private sector until conditions for normal multilateral trade and payments flows are restored. (72) Indeed, when international trade and the world monetary system were restructured after World War II, the highest priority was given to the restoration of convertibility as a precondition for multilateral trade, and to this end the International Monetary Fund and European Payments Union were created.

The planned economies, in contrast, use the clearing system

even under normal conditions and regard it as compatible with their overall economic structures. (73) The system of settlements had undergone a few reforms over the course of time — for example, multilateral clearing was introduced into intra-CMEA trade; yet the basic principle has been retained. The Comprehensive Program regards clearing as the optimal settlement procedure for the next fifteen to twenty years. (74)

This view actually derives from a conservative concept of a planned economy in which the state has an absolute monopoly over foreign trade and currency, and the anonymity of freely moving money and foreign exchange is seen as imperiling plan fulfillment. However, as the planned economies develop into modern industrial societies in which technical progress and a rational division of labor are prerequisites for satisfactory growth and a decent level of employment, the ideological dismissal of foreign trade is giving way to a more realistic conception, and ways and means are being sought to step up foreign trade relations without neglecting the requirements of a planned economy.

Nevertheless, it would be unrealistic to think that the Eastern powers will unconditionally submit to the requirements of the international payments and monetary system in its present form. Most likely, East and West will have to sit down together and hammer out a new system acceptable to both.

7.2. Clearing Procedures in East and West

Since the reasons for the existence of clearing in the two systems are fundamentally different, one might expect that the practical procedures for effecting it would also differ. In contrast to the situation in the planned economies, the assumption of control of foreign exchange by the market economies was not accompanied by a strict quota system. The lists of goods accompanying trade and payments agreements were never binding; even when restrictions were most stringent, they represented only what was possible — that is, the items on the list were those that a given country had a special interest in exporting or importing in the event a business transaction was concluded.

No obligation to deliver was stipulated, although licenses to trade were required. The import and export flows with a partner country quite often failed to balance out, and temporary stopgap measures had to be applied. Even the nonconvertible currencies that existed among the market economies were able to move more freely in an international context than were the Eastern currencies. There was always one exchange rate for the settlement currency (even if it was not always stable), and often convertible money or gold was used to offset balances, especially in multilateral clearing. As restrictions on goods were gradually relaxed, the use of convertible currencies for payments became a growing practice, and trade became progressively more liberalized until it ultimately developed into the totally free trade system we have today.

In the planned economies, the quotas are obligatory, and are set in accordance with the input-output balances of the economic plan; thus, a tendency toward autarky is in a certain sense inherent to the CMEA. The goods that may be exchanged with the West are limited in variety and quantity. Imports can be increased only if there is a corresponding increase in exports or if foreign credits have been offered. The domestic market is cut off from the world market, as is the domestic currency, which functions entirely independently of the unit of settlement. Hence, national price structures have no influence on international market prices, and vice versa. In contrast to the European Payments Union, there are no bridges in the CMEA between the settlement currency of the multilateral CMEA clearing office and the convertible currencies. Liberalization of trade is not a goal. Negative and positive balances arising in intra-CMEA trade cannot be offset by those arising from East-West trade.

7.3. East-West Trade at the Crossroads Between Clearing and Settlement in Foreign Exchange

The specificity of the different settlement procedures in East-West trade to their respective systems was not noticed until the end of the fifties. It became evident only after currency convertibility was restored in the West and after the CMEA settlement system was isolated once and for all from the international market. Distinct conflicts began to arise between the restrictive Eastern settlement system and the needs generated by growing trade with the West. At the time, it was primarily the West that was critical of the limits placed on payments and settlements in East-West trade. The Western nations were the stronger trading partners because of the high quality and variety of goods they had to offer and because their currencies were stronger. The Eastern nations were often driven into debt; they could avert deficits neither by appropriate monetary devices nor by attractive export offers. Hence, imbalances were more serious in East-West trade than in intrabloc trade on either side.

Nowhere is this brought out more graphically than in swing procedures. The swing is a practical arrangement whereby interest-free credits are used to offset temporary imbalances between trading countries. The limit is usually set at 10 percent of the trade volume. In actual fact, however, the negative balances of the socialist countries in trade with the West have been considerably higher. In 1957, they were 14 percent, and after convertibility was restored they rose to over 20 percent during the early sixties. (75) In intra-CMEA trade, on the other hand, the import-export imbalances have been much smaller: for the corresponding period from 1960 to 1965, they reached 10 percent only once (1962), and were much lower in the other years. (76) Multilaterally settled foreign trade in the CMEA still accounts for only about 3 percent of the total trade.

7.4. The Evolution of the Settlement System

7.4.1. The ECE Clearing Office

In 1956, an international clearing office for offsetting mutual claims and liabilities was created following a proposal by an international committee of central banks. This office began operation in July 1957 under the auspices of the ECE. Claims and liabilities that arose were to be reported to the clearing office every three months. However, the office had no broader powers to cover the balances; that responsibility fell to the central banks of the respective countries.

Since the balances did not offset each other multilaterally — hardly surprising, under the circumstances — the ECE clearing office turned out to be just as ineffective as other precursors of the European Payments Union and the CMEA clearing office that existed before the IBEC. Between 1957 and 1968, a total of $136 million from thirty-one countries was cleared, including $33.6 million from the countries of the European monetary agreement, $34.1 million from the CMEA countries and the remainder from other nations. (77) The clearing office was most active during the first three years of its existence. By 1965-1966, however, over 40 percent of the balances filed with it could no longer be offset, since the countries involved were unable to come to an agreement. Thereafter, the clearing office was used less and less, until in mid-1968, its settlement activities ceased entirely. The office was formally dissolved in October 1970.

The failure of the ECE clearing office had its counterpart in the IBEC, which had been empowered by Article IX of the Agreement of October 22, 1963, to make settlements in transferable rubles for nonmembers, an operation in which it proved ineffective. In both cases, the basic problem of multilateral clearing between West and East cropped up again. Clearing is basically a barter in quantities; multilateral settlements function only when the supply of exports and the demand for imports, on the whole, balance out one another in terms of quantity. However, since the goods offered by the Eastern nations quite often do not meet Western needs, a settlement in terms of pure values frequently founders due to the lack of a standard price system. This problem remains even when settlements follow in convertible currencies.

7.4.2. Swap and Switch Operations

The gaps between Eastern demand for imports from Western nations and the limited ability of the Eastern nations to offer the West suitable goods in return grew wider and wider as time passed. The interest charged on swing, originally intended as a way to prevent the Eastern nations from incurring major debts, only deepened the difficulties of the debtor nations without contributing anything toward overcoming the payments deficits.

To enable exports to grow at all, the swap arrangement had to be devised. (78) These operations, originally intended for bridging temporary payment gaps, were also unable to eliminate the root problem. For example, in dealings with Austria, the Eastern nations swapped more than $73 million up to 1969, and were unable to pay back about $71 million of this sum because of their chronic shortage of foreign exchange. The Austrian National Bank, on the other hand, was able to buy back the full amount swapped, $18 million. (79)

Transit transactions were introduced to multilateralize clearing and to activate frozen clearing overhangs of third countries. For example, a Western firm which found itself in the position of creditor vis-à-vis an Eastern nation would import goods from an Eastern partner that it itself did not need but that were needed by a third country, to which they would then be reexported. The additional costs incurred would run from 2 percent to 6 percent, and were to be borne by the Eastern partner. (80) It was not long, therefore, before this roundabout path was abandoned and the clearing claims were handled by means of switch transactions in convertible currency. (81) In this way, switch transactions came to bear many resemblances to transactions in foreign exchange, such as in financial switchings. In such cases, the clearing claims would not be sold to an importer of Eastern goods but to banks or trading companies for convertible currencies at a discount. Nevertheless, switch was still a relatively cumbersome and involved operation. (82)

Because of the lack of anything better, switch transactions became extremely common in the 1960s, and their volume even increased by 15 percent per year. Special trading companies were established. Alongside the notorious switch traders, such as the Bank Contrade of the Swiss Bank Union, the Bank Hoffman for Trade and Effects in Zurich, and the Dutch Bank Unie in Amsterdam, Austrian traders such as the Banking House Winter, the Allgemeine Warentreuhand AG (affiliated with the Credit Anstalt Banking Society), and the Transmerx Export-Import

Company (affiliated with the Länderbank), etc., set up offices. Although no official statistics are available on the volume of switch trading, private estimates for 1967 run to $150 million in Zurich, $120 million in Vienna, $100 million in London, and so on. (83) According to the estimates of the Allgemeine Warentreuhand AG, switching transactions amounting to $200 million were concluded in Vienna. (84)

Switch trading doubtless helped to alleviate the growing imbalances in East-West trade. In 1964, the Austrian positive trade balance with Eastern Europe was 430 million schillings, 32 percent of which was cleared in switching and transit transactions. In 1966, these transactions amounted to 72 percent, with a surplus of almost a billion schillings. (85) For the years 1966 through 1971, Austria's average receipts in settlement currencies from switching operations were 53 percent of total exports to Eastern Europe; its expenditures amounted to 62 percent of the imports from these countries. (86)

Generally speaking, compared with the former strictly bilateral clearing system, switch operations represented a distinct step in the direction of multilateral East-West trade. Nevertheless, bilateral clearing definitely predominated until well into the 1960s, and Western interests surely had a hand in retaining it. (87)

The Eastern countries saw their export opportunities improved by bilateral trade agreements, since the export needs of the Western partners caused them seriously to examine the possibility of imports from the East. In the five-year period from 1959 through 1964, two-thirds to four-fifths of the foreign trade of Bulgaria, Romania, Czechoslovakia, and Hungary with Western Europe took place on the basis of bilateral agreements. (88) Eighty-four percent of the trade of the Federal Republic of Germany with the East in 1964 was on this basis. (89)

In the past few years, both sides have modified their attitudes toward bilateralism and the emergency solution of switch operations. The latter had caused the Eastern countries considerable expense, since they had to pay the difference (sometimes as high as 30 percent) in the value of a claim in clearing currency and the value in foreign exchange. The Western nations, especially Austria, also began having more serious conflicts with the statutes of the International Monetary Fund, which required special approval if the switching system was to be maintained.

Contrary to the course of development in intra-CMEA trade, in which bilateral clearing was restructured into multilateral clearing and the currency was modified accordingly, East-West clearing found itself thrown back more and more on the international settlement system of the market economies. Clearing balances were made transferable through switch trading, clearing accounts were transformed into deposits, and obligations became normal credits that could be immediately offset by another trading transaction, even if often with a considerable discount. It is little wonder, then, that foreign exchange came increasingly to be used as a means of settlement in East-West trade, and clearing accounts with the West were transformed into deposits in a settlement currency that, in practice, functioned just as a convertible currency.

Thus, the director of the Hungarian National Bank, Dr. Bela Markowits, observed: "Since in Hungary the settlement dollar is regarded in every respect as the U.S. dollar, it is a matter of indifference to the Hungarian exporter whether he receives a clearing dollar or free foreign exchange for imported goods, as far as the currency aspect is concerned." (90)

7.4.3. Foreign Exchange Settlements in East-West Trade

The changeover to settlements in foreign exchange unquestionably marked a step forward in East-West trade. It paved the way for liberalizing trade and foreign exchange flows and for extending the trade and credit facilities long in use in the market economies to the Eastern nations as well. Finally, it gave the Western powers more direct access to the East, and the Eastern nations a freer choice of foreign markets from which to draw their imports.

It is no coincidence that Great Britain broke first ground in the push eastward when it eased trade and credit restrictions, and was also the first Western European country to lift restrictions on East-West settlement procedures. In the early postwar years, Britain had already made the facilities of the transferable pound available to almost all the socialist countries of Eastern Europe. The Federal Republic of Germany, France, and Italy, which had made their currencies partially convertible long before general convertibility was restored, also extended these facilities to the socialist countries. (91) Thus, during 1963-1968, the Soviet Union was able to use its surpluses from trade with the Federal Republic of Germany (1.9 billion deutsche marks) to cover imports from other Western countries, while Poland was able to do the same with its surplus of 285 billion deutsche marks during 1967-1970. (92)

Studies by the ECE for 1964 have shown that the Soviet Union made free use of its holdings in the currencies of the Federal Republic of Germany, Denmark, France, Great Britain, Italy, Japan, Canada, New Zealand, and the United States for settling its accounts with other countries; it also settled its balances from bilateral clearing with Belgium, Holland, Norway, and Sweden at year's end in freely convertible currencies. The other socialist countries were allowed to transfer freely their holdings in the currencies of the Federal Republic of Germany, Belgium, Great Britain, Holland, Italy, and the United States. (93)

A report of the ECE secretary shows that in 1970 approximately two-thirds of East-West trade was settled in freely convertible currencies. (94) Bilateral clearing was used to settle only 9 percent of Poland's foreign trade with the Western industrial nations, but 70 percent of its trade with the developing countries. (95) Clearing has endured the longest as a settlement procedure in the trade of Austria and Finland with the East (with the balances left over from swings offset in freely convertible currencies). Swiss trade with the Eastern nations (except that with the Soviet Union), Scandinavian trade with the German Democratic Republic, and Benelux trade with the Soviet Union all are settled by clearing. (96)

Since 1971, relations between Austria and the Eastern nations have undergone some notable changes. Austria has agreed to settlements in freely convertible currencies with the following countries: the Soviet Union (January 1, 1971), Hungary (November 23, 1971), Bulgaria, Poland, and Czechoslovakia (January 1, 1972), and Romania (July 1, 1973). Clearing has been retained as a settlement procedure only in trade with the German Democratic Republic, although even in this case the dollar has been replaced by the schilling as the settlement currency. Short-term trade credits are also granted in schillings.

In making the transition to settlements in foreign exchange, every effort was made to retain some of the obvious advantages of clearing. The agreement between Austria and the USSR concluded on August 5, 1970, stipulated that the Soviet Union was not to use its proceeds from exports to Austria for purchases in third countries. (97) A mutually satisfactory agreement with insurance against price fluctuations was concluded with Poland (98) and Romania. A protective clause permits corrective measures to be taken when difficulties arise in trade flows. (99)

To recapitulate, it may be said that, although settlements in foreign exchange have certainly simplified payments flows between the two economic blocs, the practice has not brought about any fundamental changes in the Eastern foreign trade system or in relations between the two blocs. The Eastern currencies are still nonconvertible, and the CMEA countries still suffer from a chronic shortage of foreign exchange. The government still maintains total control of the flow of commodities and foreign exchange. Settlements by means of convertible currencies have not essentially brought the Eastern market any nearer to integration into the world market. An Eastern nation's surpluses or deficits in trade with the West still have only a negligible direct influence on the domestic economy. As a long-term forecast, however, we may reasonably expect that the planned economies will give priority to those industries producing exportable goods so that they can thereby be assured of the foreign exchange they need for vital imports.

Another reason for the shift to foreign exchange as the medium of settlement in the CMEA was that the transit and switching operations that developed out of the clearing system proved to be more cumbersome than covering deficits straight off with foreign exchange. (100) The decision was further facilitated by the fact that the shift to foreign exchange would make more Western credits available for bridging payments gaps.

The relaxation of quota restrictions on exports to the West was another advantage for the East that could be expected from the shift to foreign exchange. Recent agreements between the Soviet Union and the three Scandinavian countries (Norway, Sweden, and Denmark) no longer contain quota schedules; instead, they emphasize a common desire to improve trade. The Western partners promised to forge ahead with their liberalized policy on Soviet imports, and the Soviet Union pledged to increase exports from the Scandinavian countries. Thus, the following observation is quite apposite: "Those forms of multilateralism in which Socialist countries participate are not consciously designed as a move away from bilateralism. Rather they are resorted to in order to make their bilateralism workable with a minimum of inconvenience and inefficiency." (101)

It may therefore be doubted whether settlements in foreign exchange will be able to establish any better conditions for the multilateralization of East-West trade than the multilateral settlements of the IBEC were able to do for the multilateralization of intra-CMEA trade. But one thing is clear: settlements in foreign exchange in East-West trade do not mean the multilateralization of trade. We can, however, expect that the conditions of East-West trade will be brought more and more closely into line with those governing trade among the Western nations, and that the same will happen in the sphere of credits as well.

8. Credit in East-West Relations

8.1. Introductory Comments

As the changeover was made from bilateral clearing to settlements in foreign exchange, modern credit relations were also gradually emerging from the practical stopgap arrangement of the swing transaction. However, this development was largely confined to the industrialized countries of Western Europe, which then began to extend the credit system that had emerged in Western trade to trade with the East.

In no other areas did the economic differences between the two systems become more apparent than in credit relations. The domestic circumscription of the currencies of the planned economies, their shortage of foreign exchange, and their grossly underdeveloped capital and money markets made it impossible for the Eastern countries to grant anything but short-term credits tied to specific goods. As soon as the ideologically determined restrictions on East-West trade had been lifted, however, a tremendous upswing took place in credit advances from Western nations to their Eastern partners. The Western nations vied for the attractive Eastern markets and outdid one another with the generosity of their credit offers. The CMEA nations could allow themselves to be selective, or at least partially so, and took advantage of their position to bargain over the credit terms and to enter actively into the international money market.

8.2. Historical Background of Credits to the East

Credit bans were an effective and frequently used weapon of economic warfare. Thus, during the period between the wars, the refusal of the Soviet Union to acknowledge tsarist debts or to offer compensation for nationalized foreign property, assessed at almost 12 billion gold rubles, was countered with a credit blockade which remained in force until 1926.

From that point on, however, credit transactions with the Soviet Union expanded rapidly. Belgium, Denmark, France, Great Britain, Italy, Japan, and Austria granted generous credit terms to the Soviet Union, and by 1931 the volume of credits advanced by these countries had reached 1.4 billion rubles. (102) These did a great deal to stimulate foreign trade, which reached its highest level of the period between the wars in that same year. Thereafter, credit transactions — and with them, foreign trade — declined abruptly. (103)

The same pattern was repeated after World War II with the entire Eastern bloc, with the difference that, for a short period at the war's end, it seemed likely that the Eastern bloc would participate in the international monetary and trade system. The United States considered a generous credit assistance to the

Soviet Union and granted large amounts of credits to Poland and Czechoslovakia. In 1946, the Soviet Union obtained from Sweden the first postwar finance credit not tied to specific products, worth one billion kronor and with a fifteen-year period of repayment and the unusually low interest rate of 2.375 percent annually. (104)

This brief period of eased relations, however, was followed by a period of total credit proscription to which the United States had given legal force by a 1945 law that tightened the Johnson Act of 1934. Accordingly, any credit from private American sources to countries that were delinquent in their financial obligations to the United States under the lend-lease treaties was punishable as a crime. (105) Bulgaria was the only Eastern European country that had not incurred any of these debts, and thus was the only country not affected by this law.

The Bern Union (106), a pool of government export insurance institutions, also intervened in credit relations with the East in the late fifties by setting an upper limit of five years for the repayment of suppliers' credits and of eight years for investment credits (107); but the unabating bitter competition for Eastern markets made these conditions unenforceable. The Bern Union could do no more than keep a record of every credit contract of the OECD countries with a repayment term exceeding five years. This was done for all borrowers, not merely the Eastern nations.

Unlike other Western nations, the United States maintained its hostile economic policy until the early 1970s. As late as 1964, when most of the Western European nations had already abandoned their common policy of restrictive credits to the East, the United States passed the Foreign Aid and Related Appropriations Act which prohibited the Export-Import Bank from financing exports to Communist countries and from guaranteeing such credits. (108)

Great Britain's dissenting attitude is best seen in a statement of then Prime Minister Sir Alec Douglas-Home to President Johnson in the same year: "Great Britain does not wish to wage economic warfare with the Communist nations, neither on account of buses for Cuba nor long-term credits for Russia." (109) At that time, the British government had not only lifted all restrictions, but in 1964 had decided to provide government guarantees for the foreign trade of the Soviet Union. Soon thereafter, these guarantees were extended to the other Eastern countries.

On June 19, 1964, the British government Export Credit Guarantee Department (ECGD) guaranteed its first export credit to a CMEA country (Czechoslovakia) with a repayment term of twelve years (110), and in September 1964 a guarantee was given to credit granted to the USSR with a maturity of fifteen years. (111) From 1963 through 1965, Great Britain granted a total of $185 million in credits to the Eastern bloc. (112) Since then, assumption of guarantees for credits with maturities up to seventeen years and interest at the rate prevailing on the capital market have become an established practice in Great Britain's dealings with the Eastern nations. (113)

In 1963, France still took the position that credits with over five years' maturity amounted to economic aid. Soon thereafter, however, France repatterned its credit policy after the English example. In 1964, negotiations were initiated with the Soviet Union on a guarantee for long-term trade credits, and in October 1964 France granted the Soviet Union a major credit (3.5 billion francs) with a 7-year maturity. (114) In 1966, the maturity on credits to the Soviet Union was raised to 8.5 years (115), and the same credit terms were extended to the other CMEA countries. From 1963 to 1970, France granted $1 billion in credits for the financing of its exports to the socialist countries. (116)

Until 1961, Italy had had an aggressive credit policy toward the Eastern nations; in that year, a credit line of $100 million was granted to the Soviet Union (117), and Bulgaria, Poland, Romania, Czechoslovakia, and Hungary received credits with maturities of up to twelve years. Thereafter, Italy tended to adopt a more restrictive attitude. Recently, however, it has opted for an extremely liberal policy toward the East by arranging a large-scale credit for the construction of the Soviet automobile factory in Togliattigrad.

One by one, other Western European nations that had formerly maintained a conservative policy toward the East now entered into competition for Eastern business. The Federal Republic of Germany was one such country. Because of the conditions laid down by the Allied military authorities, the Federal Republic of Germany was prohibited from granting any credits to the East until 1963 (Poland was the sole exception). Since 1964, the Federal Republic of Germany has also granted credits to other Eastern nations for imports from Germany, when it could be demonstrated that other foreign offers were already in competition. (118) The repayment terms, which generally were not permitted to exceed five years, could in these matching cases, as they were called, be extended to eight years.

The Federal Republic of Germany's credit business with the East has been in full swing since the mid-sixties. Bulgaria and Romania were the first to benefit from Bonn's generous credit policy, but later the ambitious credit advances to the Soviet Union, most of which were tied to specific goods, went far beyond anything that any other Western European country had ever offered.

The United States was the last to enter the credit business with the Eastern nations. In August 1971, a law was finally passed that lifted the ban on credits and guarantees. The earlier laws remained in force only for those countries that were engaged in armed conflict with the United States. Since then, the United States has granted and promised credits on an unprecedented scale.

8.3. The Scope of Credits to Eastern Nations

No complete official statistics are available on either side as to the volume of credits granted by OECD countries to Eastern nations, although a rough idea is provided by the credit contracts reported to the Bern Union for the years 1959 through 1970. (119) According to these statistics, the volume of credits to the East and their share in total credits granted by OECD nations have risen sharply, in step with the growing share of capital goods in the total volume of world trade (120) and total exports to the East. (121)

Of the total of 19,188 million accounting units (122) of credits guaranteed from 1959 through 1970, 2,674 million accounting units — 13.9 percent — was advanced to the CMEA nations; 1,672 million — 8.7 percent — went to the industrialized nations of Western Europe; and the rest went to the developing countries. CMEA countries received 40 percent of the total credits granted and guaranteed by the OECD countries to European nations, at an average credit maturity of 7.26 years, which was not much different from the European average of 7.95 years. The Soviet Union was the leading borrower from both OECD countries (1,443 million accounting units, or 7.5 percent) and EEC countries (815 million accounting units, or 9.6 percent), followed by Romania, with 510 million accounting units' worth of credits from OECD countries, and Poland, with 259 million units.

The rapid expansion of credits guaranteed by Western nations to Eastern countries is significant. From a volume of 45 million accounting units in the first year (1963), guaranteed credits rose to 218 million and 357 million accounting units in the next two years, and by 1969 had reached 545 million accounting units. Since 1970, the six EEC countries have been involved in Eastern credit dealings on a massive scale. The credits guaranteed by the EEC reached 1.6 billion accounting units in 1970 and rose further to 2 billion accounting units in 1971. At the end of 1971, total EEC credits granted to Eastern nations exceeded $3 billion, and for that year were just barely less than the volume of EEC exports to the East. (123)

The most active Western lender during the period from 1959 through 1970 (according to the statistics of the Bern Union) was Great Britain, with 5.4 billion accounting units (including 0.6 billion accounting units to CMEA countries), followed by Japan (124), 3.8 billion accounting units (0.3 billion accounting units to Eastern nations); France, 3.5 billion accounting units (1 billion to Eastern nations); and the Federal Republic of Germany, 2.7 billion accounting units (0.2 billion to Eastern nations). Austria was in tenth place with 0.2 billion accounting units (57 million to Eastern Europe). Great Britain's credits also had the longest maturity, with an average of 8.6 years (8 years with the

East), followed by France, with 7.8 (7.5 with the East); Japan, 8.7 (6.3 with the East); Federal Republic of Germany, 8.5 (7.6 with the East); and Austria, 8 years (7.3 with the East).

8.4. Historical Review of the Major Credit Transactions

8.4.1. The Soviet Union and Poland Invigorate Their Credit Policy

Fearing political dependence and an excessive interest burden, the Eastern countries accepted almost no credits from the West after World War II, and often did not take full advantage of those credit agreements they did conclude. For example, in 1946 the Soviet Union let a favorable Swedish credit go unutilized. The aversion of the former Polish Party leader to Western credits is well known, and on his account Poland was obliged to curtail grain imports from 1966 through 1970, a measure that proved to be disastrous for stockraising and domestic meat supply. During the 1960s, both countries fundamentally revised their attitude and have now declared a special interest in credits for the import of industrial equipment. The Soviet Union would like to obtain credits for capital goods for tapping energy sources and would repay the credits with the products of the financed plant.

In 1961, when the other Western industrial countries were still pursuing a conservative credit policy vis-à-vis the Eastern bloc, Italy granted the USSR a credit of $100 million, which by Italian standards was very high. Five years later, Italy financed an automobile factory in the Soviet Union with a planned output of 600,000 Fiat cars annually, at that time the largest project ever undertaken with Western aid ($363 million). Even the repayment term, fourteen years, was far longer than the terms customary at that time.

Italy is now one of the Soviet Union's biggest creditors. The exchange of goods between the two countries amounted to about 180 billion lire in 1971, and in October 1972 the Soviet debt to Italy was about 1,000 billion lire. (125)

During the same period, when the Western credit markets

were being opened to the CMEA nations, France also got into the credit business with the Soviet Union, and in October 1964 granted a credit line of 3.5 billion francs to be used for the purchase of French equipment for the petrochemical and petroleum industries, etc. Through further credits in the following years, France was able to dispose of one-third of its capital goods exports in the Soviet Union. (126) A credit agreement concluded in October 1971 for 1.5 billion francs opened the way for the Renault Works to participate in the construction of a truck factory on the Kama River. Soon thereafter, France approved an 800 million franc credit granted by the Banque de Paris in cooperation with Dutch banks and intended for the financing of a cellulose factory with an annual output of 500,000 tons as a joint venture of the five CMEA countries. Today, about two-thirds of the French deliveries of equipment to the Soviet Union are financed with guaranteed credits. (127)

The Federal Republic of Germany is on the point of becoming the biggest creditor of the Soviet Union. The German-Soviet credit agreements go far beyond the limits of bilateral relations, particularly those specified for the financing of the exploitation of Soviet natural gas deposits, which amounted to over 1.2 billion deutsche marks each. The project provides 20 billion deutsche marks over twenty years to finance the tapping of the deposits. The recipients will be the Federal Republic of Germany, Italy, and Austria. Negotiations are currently in progress on a large-scale credit of 3 billion deutsche marks for the construction of a metal works near Kursk by the enterprises Salzgitter AG and Korfstahl AG. (128)

After prolonged negotiations carried out simultaneously with the United States and the Federal Republic of Germany in which great stress was laid on a reduction in interest rates, the Soviet Union concluded an agreement to deliver in April 1974 on the basis of cash payment.

Great Britain began credit dealings with the Soviet Union quite early, but they remained rather modest in volume. In July 1972, a major credit deal of over £200 million was concluded for the Soviet purchase of equipment from Great Britain. Most of the machinery will be replacements for obsolete equipment in the Soviet textile industry; a smaller portion is for chemical plants. (129)

Pursuant to the agreement, 80 percent of all capital goods deliveries to the Soviet Union by Great Britain shall be financed with credits. It is forecast that these deliveries will double in volume within two years. The repayment periods are between five and eight years. The interest rate of 6 percent is especially generous compared with the usual 7 percent. British money and capital markets have a special importance for the Soviet Union since they provide the setting for Eurodollar transactions. (These will be discussed in the next chapter.)

But by far the greatest credit facilities for the Soviet Union are now being offered by the United States. Whereas from 1963 through 1965 the Soviet Union had to finance its huge grain purchases by the sale of a total of $1.5 billion in gold (130), in 1972 it obtained a credit of $500 million from the Commodity Credit Corporation at interest rates between 6-1/6 percent and 7-1/8 percent (131) for grain purchases, in addition to a subsidy of $300 million from the American government. A credit agreement concluded in March 1973 for $225 million with a maturity of sixteen years provides for deliveries for the construction of a truck factory on the Kama River and for the tapping of new oil reserves.

American-Soviet credit relations are still in their infancy, but improvement in political relations between the two countries and the growing interest of American business in large-scale Soviet projects foretoken their rapid expansion. Studies are currently in progress on a mammoth project for opening raw materials reserves in Siberia, the total cost of which is estimated at $45 billion; a large portion of the necessary machinery imports is to be financed with American credits.

Japan currently is advancing to a lead position as lender. The Soviet list of demands runs to a total of $4.8 billion, of which $1.050 billion had already been accorded by May 1974.

Between 1964 and 1969, the Soviet Union received long-term credits from the West amounting to 1.16 billion rubles ($1.29 billion at the prevailing exchange rate) (132); of this sum, 463 million rubles were from Great Britain.

The major credit agreements have been concluded since 1970. The Soviet Union's balance of payments deficit rose sharply from $0.1 billion in 1971 to $1.2 billion the following year. Most of this deficit was covered by Western credits, while a smaller portion was met by the sale of $325 million in gold. (133)

At the end of 1970, the estimated total indebtedness of the Soviet Union to the Western nations was $4 billion. The amount rose to $5 billion and $7.1 billion, respectively, in the next two years, and the debt service rose correspondingly from 11 percent of exports at the end of 1970 to 22 percent two years later. (134) During the same period, however, the currency reserves of the Soviet Union rose from $2.2 billion in 1971 to $4.4 billion in 1973 thanks to stepped up gold production. Reserve holdings of approximately $5 billion are projected for 1975. (135) The Soviet Union has not yet assumed the role of lender to the Western industrial nations, although it has functioned in this capacity vis-à-vis the socialist countries. Yugoslavia received a credit of $1,300 million, although only $500 million has been claimed, while the developing countries received a total of $5.6 billion for the period 1954 through 1968. (136)

During the years of economic warfare, Poland was the least affected by the American credit ban. The first American credit to Poland, amounting to $77 million, was granted in 1946. Other credits followed between 1957 and 1959. After 1959, Poland received a number of bound credits on very favorable terms, principally for grain purchases; by 1964, these had totaled $500 million. (137)

From that time until 1972, Poland sought almost no further credits from Western nations. Then the new Polish leadership accepted a credit from the First National Bank of Chicago and the Export-Import Bank, amounting to $19.8 million, for the construction of two meat-processing plants by the Alan Scot Corporation of Chicago. (138) Soon thereafter, the Export-Import Bank and the Chase Manhattan Bank granted Poland two credits of $8.9 million and $4 million for the purchase of various machinery. (139) Negotiations are currently in progress for a large-scale credit for mining Polish copper deposits, to be provided by the Manufacturers Hanover Trust Company of New York in a joint venture with banks of other countries. (140) Manufacturers Hanover Trust also recently financed a $30 million project for the expansion of two cement factories, and the Export-Import Bank has just announced that Poland will be treated on an equal basis with Western countries as far as its credit ceiling is concerned. (141)

Since the mid-1960s, Poland has obtained credits on favorable terms from Great Britain, France, and Italy. In February 1965, the British Lloyd Bank, Limited granted a credit of $45 million for the financing of machinery imports for a nitrogen plant in Puławy (142); in 1969, Poland received a credit guaranteed by the British government of $48 million for the purchase of various capital goods. And in July 1971, the banking houses of Lazard Brothers and Company and Morgan Grenfell and Company, in conjunction with British Petroleum, offered a bound credit of $20 million with a ten-year maturity period for the construction of an oil refinery in Gdańsk; British Petroleum was to provide the crude oil for this plant (3 million tons annually for ten years). (143)

In 1972, the National Westminster Bank granted the Polish government two credit lines of £5 million and £10 million (144), and in the same year Barclay's Bank International, Limited, provided a credit line of £15 million to finance 85 percent of import orders of up to £50,000 until 1973. (145)

France participated in Polish capital development with a bound credit in 1968 for $45 million for the financing of a fertilizer factory in Włocławek (146) and another investment credit in 1972 for 1.5 billion francs. During his visit to Poland in late October 1973, then French Finance Minister Giscard d'Estaing promised to increase this loan to 2.25 billion francs.

In 1966, Italy granted a bound credit for the purchase of licenses, machinery, and know-how for production of the Fiat 125p. (147)

After unanswered political questions had been cleared up, the Federal Republic of Germany quickly became Poland's leading creditor; as a consequence, Poland's trade deficit with the Federal Republic of Germany increased abruptly from 6 million deutsche marks in 1971 to 464 million deutsche marks one year later. (148) A deficit of 1 billion deutsche marks is expected for 1973. A nonbound credit of 1-2 billion deutsche marks is currently being discussed.

Credit relations with Austria are expected to develop smoothly, since the Austrian Kontrollbank concluded an agreement to finance joint capital development ventures with the Bank Handlowy in June 1973.

Poland's total indebtedness in 1970 is estimated at $1.75 billion with a debt service (for an average interest on credits of 6.5-7.5 percent for the years 1968-1971) of 12 percent of the annual export. The share of long-term credits in this total also increased from 11 percent in 1966 to about 40 percent in 1971. (149) By the end of 1973, Poland's indebtedness will probably have reached $3 billion.

Poland's trade balance reflects the expanded volume of imports made possible by these credit grants. It has moved from a slight surplus in 1971 to a deficit currently estimated at $800 million. Various measures have been tried to reduce the burden of the debt service; for example, foreign investment credits may now be utilized only if the investment project will yield a net surplus in foreign exchange from later exports made in repayment.

So far, Poland has never granted credits to the Western industrial nations; but its credits to the developing countries amounted to $500 million at the end of 1970. (150)

8.4.2. Attempts of Bulgaria and Romania to Reduce Their Indebtedness

Bulgaria and Romania established credit relations with the Federal Republic of Germany quite early. Thus, Bulgarian exports to the Federal Republic of Germany showed a net increase over the previous years of 65.8 percent in 1964, 41.9 percent in 1965, and 96 percent in 1966. (151) At the end of 1970, the Bulgarian trade balance with the Western industrial countries showed a deficit of about $580 million. (152) For 1973, a deficit of $900 million is envisioned.

Bulgaria has received other long-term credits from France, Great Britain, and Japan. In addition to the government-financed participation of the Renault Works in Bulgarian automobile production, Bulgaria received two credit lines of 40 million francs in July 1972. In 1972 it also received a bound credit from the Westminster Bank for £25 million to finance a joint venture (153), and a Eurodollar credit from ten major Japanese banks for $25 million. (154) The Commerz Bank AG, together with its international partners, the Banco di Roma and Crédit Lyonnais, granted a middle-term credit for $15 million (155) to the Bulgarian Foreign Trade Bank.

With total credits of $510 million, Romania ranks after the Soviet Union as the leading recipient of credits (Bern Union statistics as of June 1970). The Federal Republic of Germany, contributing a total of 1.3 billion deutsche marks, heads the list of creditors. (156)

In addition, Romania has received long-term credits from France (63 million in 1965 for financing the purchase of industrial equipment) (157), Great Britain (bound credits for £5 million for the financing of an irrigation project), and especially the United States. In 1972 alone, Romania borrowed $40 million from the Commodity Credit Corporation (with a maturity period of three years) for the purchase of grain, cotton, tobacco products, etc.; other credits amounted to $20 million for the purchase of aircraft, $13 million for the import of machinery from the United States (158), and $28.8 million for equipping a new tire factory in Floresti. (159)

Romania's balance of trade deficit with the West has been a cause of concern. Although the record level of $1.4 billion (160) at the end of 1970 was reduced through drastic measures, the deficit for 1972 was still around $130 million, most of which was from trade with the Federal Republic of Germany. Accordingly, in June 1973, the Federal Republic of Germany promised two additional credits (in particular, a credit of 200 million deutsche marks from the Reconstruction Loan Corporation) to fund this debt. (161)

8.4.3. Czechoslovakia's Conservative Credit Policy

In contrast to the other CMEA nations, Czechoslovakia has

consistently maintained a conservative position with regard to credits from the West, with the exception of a brief period in the late 1960s. In the decade from 1950 to 1960, the total sum of Western credits amounted to only $14 million (162); from 1964 to 1967, this figure increased to about $100 million. (163) With a total of $155 million, Czechoslovakia is well to the bottom of the Bern Union list for the years 1969-1970.

In 1964, Czechoslovakia concluded two long-term credit agreements, one with a British bank consortium for $11 million for outfitting a machine-tool factory and one with Italy for $6.7 million (twelve-year maturity period) for constructing a precision-tool factory. (164) The Banque de l'Union Européene and the Banque Française du Commerce Extérieur made an additional contribution to the outfitting of Czech industry by advancing a bound credit of 30 million francs to the chemical industry at a repayment term of seven years.

The 1971-1975 five-year plan is further testimony to Czechoslovakia's cautious foreign trade policy. Sights are set on a small balance of payments deficit with the CMEA countries and the West in order to build up foreign exchange reserves. (165) The present trend in CMEA trade is actually in this direction, while Czechoslovakia's trade debt to the West is increasing. The Soviet Union demanded in strong terms that Czechoslovakia clear its trade deficit and gear its production toward export to cover Soviet needs. (166)

In terms of net balance, Czechoslovakia is actually a creditor nation; it has helped finance the tapping of new fuel deposits in the Soviet Union with $500 million, and granted generous credit aid amounting to $1.1 million to developing countries during the years from 1954 to 1968. Czechoslovakia ranks second next to the Soviet Union in this respect. (167)

8.4.4. Hungary's Credit Policy

Like Romania and Bulgaria, Hungary also found itself obliged to dig into funds reserved for financing capital development investments to check the steadily growing cumulative balance of trade deficit with the West, which amounted to $1 billion at the end of 1972 ($225 million in 1971 (168) and $181 million in 1972). Other measures were also taken to reduce the deficit.

In connection with its economic reforms, Hungary's policy on foreign credits took a new turn, with focus on the following major guidelines: (169)

1) Achievement of equilibrium, preservation of status as a good credit risk, and protection of the Hungarian economy from the disruptive influences of the instability of Western currencies. The guidelines of the Fourth Five-Year Plan (Articles 49 and 59) therefore stress selectivity in granting and accepting international credits. Both the purpose and the source of credits are now regularly subjected to careful scrutiny.

2) Centralization of credit acceptance. Hungarian enterprises are permitted to accept credits only after approval from the National Bank. Short-term credits are generally not approved. Approval is given only for large-scale purchases of capital goods. However, the National Bank, not the particular enterprise, functions as the borrower. It alone negotiates with the foreign partner banks. Credit offers from foreign trading companies or financing companies are ordinarily not accepted.

3) Separation of credit transactions from trade transactions. Hungary's policy is aimed at paying off imports from abroad immediately so as to obtain more favorable price and delivery terms. At the same time, the Hungarian National Bank often negotiates a credit with a foreign bank quite independently of the foreign firm, and the foreign bank usually limits itself to the function of mediator between domestic and foreign enterprises.

4) The acceptance of foreign credits is viewed as a means for improving the structure of the national economy and for modernizing those branches of the economy producing for export. Therefore, long-term bound credits are given preference.

Hungarian economic policy adopted two new objectives: increased economic cooperation with the West and the restoration of stability to a precarious foreign exchange and balance of trade situation. Although other CMEA countries have also embarked upon this relatively new path in East-West relations, Hungary, with more than 300 cooperative agreements (including

100 with the Federal Republic of Germany and 50 with Austria) leads the way. Like Romania, Hungary made it possible for foreign firms to accumulate up to 49 percent of the basic capital stock in Hungarian enterprises. Pursuant to the terms of these agreements, Hungarian and foreign enterprises commit themselves to seeking third markets to dispose of their products and in this way help Hungary to improve its balance of trade. As a result of this realignment in its foreign trade policy, Hungary became the first CMEA nation to begin issuing long-term bonds. The proceeds from this operation plus credits from the International Investment Bank have been used to modernize and expand Hungary's most important industry — the manufacture of buses. (170)

8.4.5. Close Credit Relations Between the Federal Republic of Germany and the German Democratic Republic

Credit relations of the German Democratic Republic (East Germany) with the West have been mainly with the Federal Republic of Germany (West Germany) because of the special favors extended by the latter. The exchange of goods between the two German states was defined as intra-German trade in the "Berlin Agreement" (the Berlin Abkommen), and that definition is retained in the Basic Agreement of May 11, 1973.

Although formally the German Democratic Republic has received no long-term credits from West Germany, the temporary overdraft allowances provided for in bilateral trade have been widely utilized by East Germany, with the result that the outstanding balance from swing transactions is increasing steadily. An agreement reached in December 1968 stipulated that at the beginning of each year swing transactions were to amount to no more than 25 percent of the business of the German Democratic Republic with the Federal Republic of Germany in the preceding year. This agreement is to run until 1975. As a result, credits granted through swing rose from 200 million deutsche marks in 1968 to 620 million in 1973. (171) Actually, East Germany overdrew its swing limit regularly, so that at the beginning of 1973, its intra-German trade deficit was 1.8 million deutsche marks. (172)

Thus, swings perform the same function as a long-term credit but have no maturity period and carry no interest. (173)

The German Democratic Republic also raised long-term credits on the international capital market. In 1965, Humphreys and Glasgow, Limited, and the French firm ENSA financed a fertilizer plant, and in 1970 France advanced a bound credit of 550 million francs with a maturity period of seven years for the purchase of 10,000 railroad cars.

Japanese banks have also been interested in the East German market. The Japanese International Investment Bank, together with the International Mutual Bank and Bank of Tokyo, granted East Germany a credit line of $45 million in 1972.

The importance of East Germany in EEC trade, especially that with West Germany, induced the EEC to approve long-term, five- to eight-year credits for trade with the German Democratic Republic.

9. Eastern Activity on the International Money Market

9.1. The Attempt to Influence the Interest Rate

As a consequence of the increased flow of credits from the West, the interest rate often creates balance of payments difficulties for the Eastern countries. Accordingly, CMEA nations have endeavored to get the interest rate reduced, especially since the rates charged in intra-CMEA trade lie far below a realistic market level. Only the IBEC, followed recently by the IIB, has brought its interest rates more closely into line with the market, although only against the determined resistance of Romania, Bulgaria, and Mongolia. The bulk of investment credits, however, continue to bear 2 percent in the CMEA. In contrast, Western interest rates, which of course move in response to the interest yielded by deposits and to the rate of inflation, as well as to supply and demand, have risen to exorbitantly high levels.

The Soviet Union is especially anxious to obtain interest rate reductions in its bilateral negotiations with Western nations (174), and quite recently Hungary and the German Democratic Republic put forth similar demands in Helsinki at the Conference for Security and Cooperation in Europe. (175) Any reduction in the interest rate must be financed by government subsidies, however, and only Great Britain (176), Italy, and France — considered as more favorable credit markets in the East — have been willing to meet these demands in order to promote Eastern trade. The Federal Republic of Germany (177) and the United States (178) have so far emphatically rejected such a request. Japan has also granted the Soviet Union credits at reduced interest rates (6.375 percent); as of May 1974, the total was $1,050 million. The Federal Republic of Germany has offered the strongest opposition to budget-financed reductions in interest rates. In gas pipeline deals, manufacturers, in agreement with the banks, could calculate interest reductions into their final prices (the credits were granted at 6.25 percent interest). But Germany did not wish to set a precedent. Opinions varied. The West German foreign minister stated in Budapest in April 1974 that his nation was prepared to grant middle- and long-term credits but at terms prevailing on the capital market.

For a time it was thought that the Federal Republic of Germany might build up the instruments of a government interest policy such as exists in the United States and Japan. The American Export-Import Bank advances credits to cover 45 percent of the amount of a credit request at a rate of 7 percent (as of February 4, 1974; before that date, the rate had been 6 percent); the interest is financed on the money market. Another 45 percent is covered by commercial banks at the market interest rate. The more costly interest is paid off first, the cheaper later.

The Japanese Export-Import Bank operates in a similar fashion and can count on interest-free allocations from the national budget. The credits from the Export-Import Bank and the commercial banks are paid back at the same time. The West German Reconstruction Loan Corporation is being considered as the possible executor of the government interest policy. However, its honorary President J. Abs noted that this institution does not even begin to have funds of the magnitude required by the Soviet Union (over 16 billion deutsche marks) and furthermore would be unable to lower the current interest rates of 14 percent to the 6 percent expected by the Soviets.

The controversy around interest reductions continues, and even though the EEC proposed a gentlemen's agreement to maintain a 7 percent lower limit on middle- and long-term credits, the tough competition being mounted for Eastern markets makes chances very slim that such an agreement will be upheld.

Another way to improve credit facilities is to found branch bank offices in the West or expand those already existing.

9.2. Eastern Europe's Bank Network in the West

Through their branches in the West, the CMEA countries seek to improve their contacts with the world market, to procure credits on the international money and capital markets at more favorable terms, and to accumulate profits and hence foreign exchange income by taking on routine banking functions. The branch offices in the West are also used for settling foreign trade with Western nations. While the Soviet Union elected to pursue these goals through its own bank network, the other CMEA nations have preferred cooperation with the Western banks.

The largest and oldest Eastern bank in the West is the Moscow Narodny Bank. It was founded in 1916 as a branch of the Cooperative Russian Bank in London, and transformed by the Soviet government in 1919 into an independent bank with a capital stock of £250,000. (179) After a decline in its operations during the 1930s, it has now once again stepped up its activities. Its staff has increased from 30 in 1959 to 300 at present. At the end of 1971, its assets amounted to almost £400 million, with a profit of £1.2 million, a capital stock of £7 million, and reserves of £3 million. (180)

The principal activity of the Moscow Narodny Bank is the financing of East-West trade. However, the bank also participates in consortia for the supplying of credits to the German Democratic Republic, Hungary, the International Bank for Economic

Cooperation, etc. It has expanded its activities to North Africa and South America, reactivated a branch founded in Beirut in 1963 (181), and established a new branch in Singapore in 1971. Another branch is planned in Canada.

The Banque Commerciale pour l'Europe du Nord in Paris is another old Soviet bank in the West; it was founded in 1921 by Russian emigrants and bought four years later by the Soviet government. It deals principally in foreign trade transactions between the Soviet Union and France (182), but also handles all other traditional banking operations, as does the AG Vozkhod Trade Bank, founded in Zurich in 1966 for the sale of Soviet gold.

The objectives of the East-West Trade Bank AG, established in Frankfurt on November 11, 1971, are much more wide-ranging. In addition to creating the financial groundwork for expanding Soviet-German relations, it will also offer comprehensive banking services. Its capital stock amounts to 20 million deutsche marks, 55 percent subscribed by Gosbank, 30 percent by the Foreign Trade Bank, and 5 percent by each of three foreign trade enterprises — Promsyr'eimport, Tekhmashimport, and Eksportles. (183) It handles all banking transactions of East-West trade, but also deals in trade among the Western nations. "Its special concern is the support of small and medium-sized enterprises in their efforts to establish contacts between East and West." (184)

The special function of this bank is to serve as a funnel for Russian diamonds into Germany. Its main office is therefore in Frankfurt, in the new building of the Frankfurt Diamond Exchange; it advances credits to private dealers, especially jewelers, for financing their inventories. (185)

The East-West Trade Bank is also involved in the sale of Soviet gold. On April 1, 1974, the Donaubank AG began operations in Vienna with a founding capital of 100 million schillings, 60 percent of which has been subscribed by the Soviet Foreign Trade Bank. Except for the top officials, it is staffed by Austrians.

The steady improvement in economic relations between East and West should induce a further expansion of the Soviet banking network in the West. A Soviet bank is scheduled soon to be opened in Luxembourg, while the establishment of independent banking institutions in New York (186) is being considered.

With the exception of the German Democratic Republic and Bulgaria, all the other CMEA nations also have banks in the West, some of them established long ago. All have recently stepped up their operations considerably, and new steps are being undertaken to expand the existing banking network in cooperation with Western credit institutions, so that in the future it will not be necessary to rely on the services of the notorious Moscow Narodny Bank. Poland, Romania, and Hungary have been the most active in this respect.

Poland has branches of its Bank Handlowy in Belgrade, London, and New York, and a smoothly functioning network of PKO banks in France and Israel, which are engaged primarily in money transfers for Polish citizens and a few other foreign exchange operations. Through these banks, the first attempts were made to set up joint credit institutions with Western banks.

In January 1971, Poland joined forces with six Western banks — Kleinwort Benson, Limited, London; Banque Occidentale pour l'Industrie et le Commerce, Paris; Banco Popular Español, Madrid; Banco Sicilia, Palermo; Bank of Tokyo, Limited; and Bank für Arbeit und Wirtschaft, Vienna — to found a limited liability company, CENTROFIN (now CENTRO), whose home office is in Vienna. Each of the founding companies has an equal share in the capital stock of 65 million schillings. The principal concern of the bank is the financing of East-West trade, especially trade with Poland. (187)

In March 1973, the German-Polish Central European Bank AG was founded in Frankfurt am Main, the first joint venture between a West German bank and an Eastern bank. The Polish Bank Handlowy has subscribed to 70 percent of the founding capital and the Hessische Länderbank Girozentrale, to 30 percent. (188) The new bank will focus on promoting Polish-German economic relations and helping the Bank Handlowy to gain a foothold on the international money market.

Romania forged its own integration into the international monetary system both by entering the International Monetary

Fund and the World Bank, and by cooperating with Western banks. In February 1972, an agreement to found the Romanian-French Bank was signed with Crédit Lyonnais, and a year later a British-Romanian bank was opened. The founding capital of the French-Romanian bank was 20 million francs, half of which was subscribed by the eight largest French banks. (189) The British-Romanian bank has a capital of $7 million, half of which is subscribed by the Romanian Bank for Foreign Trade, 30 percent by Barclay's Bank, and 20 percent by Manufacturers Hanover Trust. (190) Both banks were founded to promote business with all Western nations and to stimulate the exchange of goods and monetary transactions with France and Great Britain.

Not only had Hungary gone further with its domestic reforms than any other CMEA country, it was also extremely active on the international finance markets. It was the first Eastern nation to issue Eurodollar bonds and has recently opened branch offices in Paris and Zurich. In September 1968, a bank consortium was formed with Yugoslavia. The traditional collaboration with Austrian banks was given a special boost. In early 1972, the Centralwechselstuben AG, which had been in operation in Vienna since 1918 and had its home office in Budapest, was reorganized into the Central-Wechsel-und-Creditbank AG and expanded considerably. As part of this reorganization, the bank's own capital was raised from 105,000 to 40 million forints, while that of the Vienna branch was raised from 4 to 12 million schillings. In addition to its customary functions as an exchange bank and savings institution, it is now handling more and more large-scale credit transactions. During the three years prior to 1971, it raised its balance from 212 million to 690 million schillings. (191)

At the beginning of 1973, the Austrian Kontrollbank and the Hungarian Foreign Trade Bank concluded a skeleton agreement for cooperation in financing joint ventures by Austrian and Hungarian firms in third countries. The Hungarian National Bank, Limited, was opened in London on October 17, 1973, with a capital stock of £1 million. Its shareholders are all Hungarian banks: the Hungarian National Bank with 60 percent of the shares heads the list, followed by the Hungarian Foreign Trade Bank and the Ländersparkasse with 15 percent each, and the Central-Wechsel-und-Creditbank AG with 10 percent.

The Hungarian National Bank, Limited, is a fully accredited British bank. With its establishment, the London office of the Hungarian National Bank was closed. The bank presently has a staff of fourteen. It will maintain close contact with the international money market and keep an eye on developments in the Western monetary and currency system. Above all, the new bank will promote Hungarian exports to England and third countries by offering credit assistance, including joint credit operations with Western banks. It will also be active on the Western European foreign exchange markets. (192)

9.3. Eurodollar Bonds of the Eastern Nations

The CMEA nations are no newcomers on the Eurodollar market. The Moscow Narodny Bank led the way when it first offered Eurodollars to its European correspondents in 1955. Today it is one of the four leading banks on the London Eurodollar market. But the first bond on the Eurodollar market was not issued until 1971, when Hungary floated a bond for $25 million in May 1971. More than eighty Western European banks, including three Austrian banks, underwrote the issue. (193) Its maturity was ten years at 8.75 percent. (194) Encouraged by its initial success, Hungary issued another bond for $50 million with a maturity of fifteen years and an interest yield of 8.5 percent through an international consortium composed of the Moscow Narodny Bank, the British National Westminster Bank, the London Morgan Grenfell Banking Company, the Bank of America, and the Frankfurter Bank. The bond was oversubscribed. (195)

The IBEC has been especially active on the international capital market. During a three-month period in 1972, it received three middle-term Eurodollar credits from various banking consortia: $20 million from the Société Générale, Paris, and the Société Générale de Banque, Brussels, in February; $60 million from the Crédit Lyonnais and the Banco di Roma in March; and $40 million from the Moscow Narodny Bank, the National Westminster Bank, and the Morgan Grenfell in April 1973. (196)

The chief activity of the IBEC on the international money market, however, is the procurement of short-term money. It currently maintains correspondent relations with 200 banks in all countries. In 1972, its sight and time deposits transactions ran to $22 billion. (197)

9.4. The Western Banks in the Eastern Nations

Generally speaking, a Western banking institution, because of the Eastern economic system, will not be as free to grow in the East as its counterpart in the West. The first branch office of a Western bank in a socialist country was established by Crédit Lyonnais. (198) German banks soon followed suit. In January 1973, the Dresdner Bank AG opened a branch in the Moscow Hotel Intourist, and soon thereafter the Deutsche Bank AG opened an office in Hotel Metropol (199), followed by the Frankfurter Kommerzbank AG. The Finnish Osake Paukki Bank and the Italian Banco Commerciale are also now active in Moscow.

With the expansion of economic relations between the United States and the Soviet Union, the major American banks also began to show an interest in the Eastern market. The Chase Manhattan Bank was the first to begin operations in Moscow, and was later followed by Wells-Fargo. The Bank of America has also applied for permission to open an office.

By mid-1973, twenty Western banks had submitted applications to the Soviet Gosbank. The New York Stock Exchange has also shown an eagerness to establish a foothold in this virgin economic territory; in November 1972, it sent representatives to the Soviet Union to find out what role the stock exchange could play in the development of trade relations with the Soviet Union. (200)

Since by no means all the Western nations are represented by branch offices in the CMEA countries, the Financial Square in Vienna is fast becoming an important center for East-West contacts. In addition to the 200 branches and a like number of representatives of foreign firms, including 80 American companies, 16 international banks have established branch offices in Austria for better access to Eastern markets. These include branches of powerful worldwide institutions such as the Export-Import Bank of the United States, the Kommerzialbank AG, an affiliate of the Chase Manhattan Bank in Vienna, the Bank of America (201), the Bank of Tokyo (202), etc.

Of course, in the East, where no capital market exists, the Western banks cannot perform the same functions as the Eastern banks do on the international money market. (203) They are engaged principally in the settlement of payments and the handling of credit transactions generated by trade, cooperation, and credit agreements.

They are also the conveyors of industrial techniques and commercial know-how, and their role should not be underestimated. Thus, for example, the German banks are especially vital to business in pipelines and natural gas. The Deutsche Bank leads a consortium of 100 West German firms with financial interests in such projects.

By their readiness to advance credits to the CMEA nations, the French banks have given a potent shot in the arm to the Eastern operations of private industrial firms. Recently, they have even extended their activities beyond purely financial transactions and are now attempting to sound out export possibilities, especially in the Soviet Union, through their branches in the Eastern nations, with an eye toward putting Eastern trade on a long-term basis and hence providing greater security for their credit dealings. This is precisely the purpose of the bank consortium GISOFRA, founded in 1971 by the leading French banks (Société Générale, Crédit Lyonnais, Banque Nationale pour le Commerce et l'Industrie).

The banks of the other Western powers join the French banks in this interest in financial projects and in the search for new markets for Eastern exports to the West, and the number of their branch offices in the East is growing daily. Thus, the increasing cooperation among banks of both economic systems is gradually constituting a new industrial basis that is destined to play a key role in the development of East-West trade and in the world monetary system.

Notes

1) There are exceptions to this rule. When the pound sterling was devalued in November 1967, the IBEC lost $1.5 million.

2) This one-sidedness in credit relations cannot be maintained over the long term, however. On his return from a hard round of negotiations with the Soviet Union, former Secretary of State Petersen declared: "We also said to them that we thought it was appropriate as well that U.S. firms get credit from the Soviet Union" (U.S. News and World Report, August 28, 1972, p. 40).

3) International Financial Statistics, January 1973, p. 19.

4) Ibid., p. 97.

5) "All economic relationships are unhappy, but the less personal and political they are the more tolerable they are," observed Peter Wiles (Communist International Economics, Oxford, 1968, p. 531).

6) J. Fekete, Vice-President of the Hungarian National Bank, "Some Connections Between the International Monetary System and East-West Economic Relations," Acta Oeconomica, 1972, Vol. 2, No. 9, p. 160.

7) Professor Imre Vajda, International Economic Relations, Proceedings of the Third Congress of the International Economic Association, London, 1969, p. 131.

8) But Handelsblatt of March 2, 1973, reported that Alchimov, the Soviet Deputy Minister of Foreign Trade, declared at a Soviet-American trade conference in Washington that the Soviet Union's membership in the IMF "is being considered."

9) See E. Boettcher (ed.), Wirtschaftsbeziehungen mit dem Osten, Stuttgart, Reihe Kohlhammer, 1971, p. 141.

10) The yen-yuan ratio was changed to 130.25 : 1 in connection with the devaluation of the dollar in February 1972 (Biulleten' inostrannoi kommercheskoi informatsii, February 24, 1973).

11) Biulleten' inostrannoi kommercheskoi informatsii, August 29, 1972.

12) See A. Anikin, "Capitalist Economics in the Monetary and Financial Crisis," Voprosy ekonomiki, 1972, No. 2, p. 63.

13) In his message of greeting to the IMF meeting in September

1972, Nixon stated that "at least two academic proposals are available for every penny."

14) See the Frankfurt discussions of the List Society, March 5-6, 1965 (Fundamentale Fragen künftiger Währungspolitik, Tübingen, 1965).

15) Exactly forty years earlier, in 1931, the old gold standard broke down when Great Britain withdrew from gold parity, and with it went the pound sterling's status as a key currency.

16) The former president of the Austrian National Bank pointed out correctly that the currency problem in the West "was a matter of too much freedom and too little coordination" (W. Schmitz in a report presented to a joint meeting of the Donaueuropäischen Institutes and the Peutinger Collegium in Munich, March 21, 1972, p. 28).

17) Vneshniaia torgovlia SSSR za 1918-1940 [Soviet Foreign Trade, 1918-1940], Moscow, 1960, p. 14.

18) Ibid.

19) See M. Orlowski, Kursy walutowe — pieniądz — kapital [Exchange Rate, Money, and Capital], Warsaw, 1972, p. 215.

20) See Rozliczenia międzynarodowe [International Settlements], Warsaw, 1970, p. 287.

21) See J. Keith Horsefield, The International Monetary Fund, 1945-65, Vol. I: Chronicle, Washington, D.C., pp. 359-364.

22) See Otmar Emminger, "Internationaler Währungsfonds," in Enzyklopädisches Lexikon für das Geld-, Bank- und Börsenwesen [hereinafter referred to as Enzyklopädisches Lexikon], Frankfurt am Main, 1967-1968, p. 828.

23) See Rozliczenia międzynarodowe, p. 286.

24) See Emminger, op. cit., p. 831.

25) International Financial Statistics, January 1973, p. 12.

26) See Richard Gardner, Sterling-Dollar Diplomacy, New York, 1956, p. 295.

27) Emminger, op. cit., pp. 827, 838.

28) Ibid., p. 836.

29) Ibid., p. 838.

30) Ibid., p. 829.

31) A special drawing right is equivalent to the U.S. dollar of December 1946.

32) International Financial Statistics, January 1973, p. 12.
33) Emminger, op. cit., p. 7.
34) Ibid., pp. 8, 10.
35) The World Bank, International Development Association, Annual Report, 1972, p. 79.
36) Ibid., p. 3; Enzyklopädisches Lexikon, p. 794.
37) See S. Rączkowski, Międzynarodowe stosunki finansowe [International Financial Relations], Warsaw, 1972, p. 370.
38) See Lumea, January 1, 1973. As reported in the Neue Zürcher Zeitung, November 29, 1973, Romania made its first drawing from the IMF in November 1973 in an amount of $47.5 million.
39) See R. Nötel, "The Role of the United Nations in the Sphere of East-West Trade," Economia internazionale, November 1965, p. 645.
40) See Claus-Dieter Rohleder, Die Osthandelpolitik der EWG-Mitgliedstaaten, Grossbritanniens, und der USA gegenüber den Staatshandelsländern Südosteuropas, Munich, 1969, p. 35.
41) See Herbert Schicht, "GATT," in Enzyklopädisches Lexikon, p. 582.
42) See Nötel, op. cit., p. 644.
43) Gardner, op. cit., p. 7.
44) Ibid.
45) Of historical interest in this connection is a statement by Lloyd George dating from 1920, after he signed the first trade agreement with the Soviet Union: "We were unable to rebuild Russia with force; I hope we shall be able to do it with trade" (cited in Kultura [Paris], 1973, No. 10, p. 41).
46) See B. Kiesewetter, Der Ostblock, Berlin, 1960, p. 33.
47) Ibid., p. 32.
48) See Gunnar Adler-Karlsson, Western Economic Warfare, 1947-1967, Stockholm, 1968, p. 23.
49) Ibid., pp. 26, 36, 46.
50) Ibid., p. 46.
51) The Hungarian economist Imre Vajda has correctly observed: "Embargo and, in its turn, autarky are but twins, offspring of the same spirit, tendencies which reinforce and apparently justify each other" ("The Problems of East-West

Trade," in International Economic Relations, p. 121).

52) See Kiesewetter, op. cit., p. 36.

53) The deputy president of the Hungarian National Bank has put the issue quite clearly: "Differences in policy and ideology cannot hinder acknowledgement and recognition of economic realities" (Acta Oeconomica, 1972, No. 9, p. 160).

54) See The Work of the Economic Commission for Europe, 1947-1972, United Nations, New York, 1972, p. 19.

55) Ibid.

56) See Analytical Report, Geneva, 1971, p. 56.

57) See Nötel, op. cit., p. 655.

58) Ibid., p. 656.

59) Ibid., p. 657.

60) Proceedings of the European Parliamentary Assembly, March 6, 1968. See J. Stolte, "East-West Trade in the Seventies," Studies on the Soviet Union, 1970, No. 29, p. 25.

61) COCOM is an acronym for Coordinating Committee for East-West Trade Policy, an institution founded in August 1951 for the supervision of the embargo conditions in East-West trade.

62) G. Adler-Karlsson, Der Fehlschlag, Vienna, 1971, p. 158.

63) See Analytical Report, p. 123.

64) See W. Tscheklin, Aussenhandel (Moscow), 1970, No. 6, p. 12.

65) See K. H. Standke, Der Handel mit dem Osten, Baden-Baden, 1968, p. 211.

66) See West-Ost-Journal, 1970, No. 5, p. 2.

67) Die Wirtschaft, 1973, No. 10, p. 22.

68) Ibid.

69) Speech given by Deputy Secretary of State P. H. Trezise, December 29, 1970, published in Handel zagraniczny, 1971, No. 4, p. 138.

70) See Die Presse, April 14, 1973.

71) See Rozliczenia międzynarodowe, p. 198.

72) In 1937, when clearing procedures still dominated foreign trade, K. Blessing, later President of the German Federal Bank, had the following to say about the negative effects of clearing: "We totally abhor this system, because it is economically

destructive. It hamstrings our exports because it forces us to offset our balance of payments with each particular country on its limited market instead of on the world market as a whole; and it interferes with trade through its inherent bureaucratism" (see Koexistenz zwischen Ost und West, Vienna, 1967, p. 287).

73) See Chapter 2 of this book.

74) See Neues Deutschland, August 7, 1971.

75) See J. Wilczynski, "Multilateralization of East-West Trade," Economia internazionale, 1968, Vol. 21, No. 2, p. 302.

76) Ibid.

77) See Standke, op. cit., p. 82.

78) In this arrangement, the debtor nation puts up a sum in freely convertible currency as security and the creditor nation grants a supplementary credit line on this basis, thereby making possible the further exchange of goods. The foreign exchange security must be covered by equivalent amounts of deliveries within a specified time or it is forfeited to the lending nation.

79) See West-Ost-Journal, 1969, No. 5, p. 7.

80) Ibid., 1968, No. 2, p. 2.

81) A term for foreign exchange arbitration. Two types are distinguished: (a) export switching operations, in which an exporter of a country with convertible currencies interested in a transaction with an importer in a clearing country attempts to exchange the received clearing currency for convertible currency at a discount in a third country; and (b) import switches, in which the importer of a country with a convertible currency attempts to obtain clearing currency at a discount, which is then offered to a third country for payments to the country of settlement (from which he wishes to import) (see Enzyklopädisches Lexikon, p. 1585).

82) "Switch trading is hideously cumbersome and inefficient as a system, no matter how skilled and sophisticated the dealers themselves may be," The Economist, January 14, 1967, p. 144.

83) Ibid.

84) Die Presse, October 25, 1972.

85) West-Ost-Journal, 1968, No. 2, p. 2.

86) See J. Stankovski, "Der österreichische Transithandel," Quartalhefte der Girozentrale, 1972, No. 3, p. 245.

87) "...it would be unfair not to mention that, in too many instances, the Western trading partner itself insists on bilateral balancing" (A. Nove, "East-West Trade," in International Economic Relations, London, 1969, p. 103).

88) See E. Weber, Stadien der Aussenhandelsverflechtung Ost-, Mittel-, und Südosteuropas, Stuttgart, 1971, p. 174.

89) See Standke, op. cit., p. 41.

90) West-Ost-Journal, 1970, No. 1, p. 63.

91) Within the system, the holdings were freely transferable but not exchangeable for other foreign currencies, such as the U.S. dollar and Swiss franc. See Rozliczenia międzynarodowe, p. 368.

92) See E. Lederer, "Le financement du commerce Est-Ouest dans la République Fédérale d'Allemagne," Revue de l'est, April 1971, Vol. 2, No. 4, p. 153.

93) See Wilczynski, op. cit., p. 305.

94) See Analytical Report, p. 113.

95) Rączkowski, op. cit., p. 87.

96) See Analytical Report, p. 54.

97) See Die Presse, August 8-9, 1970.

98) See J. Staribacher, "EWG, EFTA, Comecon," Europagespräch in Wien, 1972, p. 55.

99) See Wiener Zeitung, April 11, 1973, p. 7.

100) See Wilczynski, op. cit., p. 316.

101) Ibid.

102) See Aussenhandel (Moscow), 1970, No. 5, p. 6.

103) See Chapter 2 of this book.

104) See Rączkowski, op. cit., p. 392.

105) See Rohleder, op. cit., p. 76.

106) At the annual meeting which took place on June 4-8, 1973, thirty institutes from twenty-four countries of all continents were represented at the Bern Union; the chairman is Dr. H. Haschek, General Manager of the Austrian Kontrollbank.

107) See Enzyklopädisches Lexikon, p. 81.

108) See Rohleder, op. cit., p. 78. Six years later, H. Trezise,

Undersecretary of State, demonstrated in his talk of December 29, 1970, that the credit ban had undermined the competitiveness of American exports (see Handel zagraniczny, 1971, No. 4, p. 138).

109) See Adler-Karlsson, Der Fehlschlag, p. 197.
110) See Board of Trade Journal (London), June 26, 1964.
111) The Manchester Guardian, September 9, 1964.
112) See Standke, op. cit., p. 191.
113) See Rohleder, op. cit., p. 75.
114) See Standke, op. cit., p. 277.
115) See Biulleten' inostrannoi kommercheskoi informatsii, October 28, 1971, p. 8.
116) See Mirovaia ekonomika i mezhdunarodnye otnosheniia, 1973, No. 11, p. 33.
117) "Eastern European Foreign Trade," Reports of the Federal Office for Foreign Trade Information, Cologne, 1961, No. 148.
118) Reports of the Federal Office for Foreign Trade Information, Appendix to the NfA, 1971, Vol. IV, p. 7.
119) The data cover only guaranteed credits with a maturity of over five years, not total credits granted. A considerable share of guaranteed credits in 1970 was not reported until 1971.
120) The share of capital goods in world trade grew from 20 percent to 30 percent in the period from 1955 to 1968 (see D. Stentzel, "Export Credit Insurance — A Comparison," Intereconomics, 1972, No. 1, p. 18). The ratio of long-term credit to total exports rose from 3.8 percent in 1964 to 8 percent in 1969 in Japan, from 2.2 percent to 7.5 percent in France, from 2.6 percent to 6 percent in Great Britain, from 1.0 percent to 2.5 percent in the Federal Republic of Germany, and from 0.2 percent to 1.7 percent in Austria (from Bern Union statistics).
121) The share of goods of classes 5, 6, and 7 (principally machinery and equipment) in Soviet imports from the Federal Republic of Germany grew from 87.4 percent in 1965 to 93.3 percent in 1970; from France, from 77.8 percent to 85.7 percent; and from Italy, from 74.6 percent to 84.0 percent in the same period (see K. Bolz and B. Kunze, Wirtschaftsbeziehungen zwischen Ost und West, Hamburg, 1972, p. XIV).

122) One accounting unit = 1 U.S. dollar before the realignment.

123) See H. Geiger (President of the Deutschen Sparkassen und Giroverbandes, Bonn), "Währungsprobleme und Wirtschaftsbeziehungen in Europa," West-Ost-Journal, 1973, No. 2, p. 16.

124) Japan reported no new credits in 1969 and 1970.

125) See Die Presse, October 31, 1972, p. 9.

126) See Standke, op. cit., p. 277.

127) Mirovaia ekonomika i mezhdunarodnye otnosheniia, 1973, No. 11, p. 33.

128) Wirtschaftswoche, May 18, 1973, p. 20.

129) See Financial Times, July 21, 1972.

130) See Foreign Report, December 1965, p. 2.

131) Süddeutsche Zeitung, July 12, 1972.

132) See W. Alkhimov, "Foreign Trade Monopoly and Credit Relations of the USSR," Aussenhandel (Moscow), 1970, No. 5, p. 8.

133) See Michael Kaser, "Soviet Union," International Currency Review, July-August 1973, pp. 88-93.

134) Ibid.

135) Ibid.

136) See Rączkowski, op. cit., p. 389; Economic Survey of Europe, March 24, 1973.

137) See Rączkowski, op. cit., p. 397.

138) Washington Post, April 22, 1973.

139) Biulleten' inostrannoi kommercheskoi informatsii, April 26, 1973.

140) Radio Free Europe Research, May 25, 1973.

141) Report of the Austrian National Bank, May 21, 1973.

142) See U. Fox, Das Bankwesen der Europäischen Volksdemokratien, Wiesbaden, 1967, p. 163.

143) Trybuna ludu, July 6, 1971.

144) Financial Times, October 19, 1972.

145) Trade and Industry, March 22, 1973.

146) See Rączkowski, op. cit., p. 398.

147) Ibid.

148) Wirtschaftswoche, March 30, 1973, p. 16.

149) See A. Lipinski, "Ekonomiczne znaczenie kostów kredytów

średnio- i długoterminowych" [The Economic Significance of the Cost of Medium- and Long-Term Credits], Handel zagraniczny, 1973, No. 8, p. 261.

150) See Rączkowski, op. cit., p. 390.
151) Lederer, op. cit., p. 153.
152) Kurier (Vienna), March 10, 1972, p. 11.
153) Financial Times, October 19, 1972.
154) Ibid., June 2, 1972.
155) Die Presse, December 14, 1972, p. 10.
156) See K. Bolz, B. Kunze, and H. D. Wulf, "Ost-West Handel der EWG," Hamburger Weltwirtschaftsarchiv, 1972, p. 45.
157) See Standke, op. cit., p. 212.
158) Biulleten' inostrannoi kommercheskoi informatsii, May 22, 1973; Die Presse, April 12, 1973.
159) Handelsblatt, June 28, 1973, p. 4.
160) Kurier, March 10, 1972, p. 11.
161) Süddeutsche Zeitung, June 27, 1973, p. 1.
162) Pravda (Bratislava), May 20, 1963, p. 2.
163) Večerni Praha, August 9, 1968.
164) Handelsblatt, April 15, 1964.
165) Finance a úvěr, 1972, No. 2, p. 80.
166) Report of the Austrian National Bank, May 2, 1973.
167) See Rączkowski, op. cit., p. 389.
168) See prepublication text of the Economic Survey of Europe, April 24, 1973, p. 56.
169) Based on the talk given by T. Bačskai at the second meeting of Austrian and Hungarian economists in Vienna, November 14, 1973.
170) See West-Ost-Journal, 1972, No. 6, p. 18.
171) See Europa-Archiv, May 25, 1973, p. 354.
172) K. Bolz, "Handel oder Hilfe," Wirtschaftsdienst, 1973, No. 2, p. 57.
173) Otto Wolf von Amerongen, Wirtschaftswoche, March 23, 1973, in which he says: "I plead for the commercialization of swing transactions. And I mean more than charging them with interest."
174) The former U.S. Secretary of Commerce Peter G. Peterson

stated in an interview in U.S. News and World Report on September 4, 1972: "The Russians are great bargainers. When we were working on the grain deal, they wanted 10-year terms and 2 per cent interest."

175) See Pravda, July 7, 1973, p. 5.

176) In July 1972, Great Britain granted the Soviet Union a global credit at 6 percent interest. Great Britain also granted the Soviet Union a global credit insurance policy that, in effect, provided a 50 percent premium reduction over individual policies (see B. Kunze, "Die Kreditpolitik der EWG gegenüber den RGW-Staaten," Wirtschaftsdienst, 1973, No. 5, p. 258).

177) An exception was piping, on which an interest rate of 6.25 percent had been agreed. "This spectacularly low interest rate is unique and is attributable to the favorable prices for steel piping" (T. D. Zotčev, "Der Handel zwischen den System," Kieler Sonderdrucke, 1972, No. 38, p. 149). From the visit of German Secretary of State Wischnewsky and Foreign Minister Scheel to Poland in September and October 1973, it may be suspected that the West German interest policy was eased despite the resistance of the Chamber for Commerce and Industry (DIHT), especially in the case of credits intended for the opening of new sources of energy (see Rynki zagraniczne, September 18, 1973). The then Prime Minister Brandt observed: "If Bonn gives Warsaw a finance credit of a billion marks and assumes 4-4.5 percent of the current market interest rate, the highest burden of middle-term finance planning is not reached until 1979 and 1980" (Wirtschaftswoche, October 12, 1973, p. 16). The budget subsidy would then have to be about 500 million deutsche marks (Die Zeit, October 19, 1973).

178) Peterson: "We had to make it clear that any credit we offered would be on concessionary terms and through the regular approval procedures" (loc. cit.).

179) See Problèmes économiques, September 11, 1969, p. 10.

180) Press bulletin of the Moscow Narodny Bank, June 14, 1972. Polish economists describe the tasks of socialist banks in the West as follows:

a) They inform interested domestic circles on the economic situation of the host country, the usage of its market, and the regulations of foreign exchange and trade operations; they inform the economic circles of the host country on production and export possibilities, the functioning of a socialist economy, the organization of foreign trade, and the system of settlement.

b) They cultivate credit relations, encourage a reduction in the cost of credit, and make it possible to finance foreign trade with funds raised in the country in which they have their operations (see A. Dorosz and M. Pulawski, "The Turn of Credit to the East," Polityka, September 1, 1973, p. 18).

181) Ibid.

182) Three major French banks formed a community of interests with the Soviet Nordbanque early in 1971 to support Soviet-French plans for cooperation.

183) See Tagesspiegel, March 21, 1972.

184) See O. Louts, East-West Trade Bank, Frankfurt, "Einige Daten über den Aussenhandel der UdSSR mit den kapitalistischen Industriestaaten," Panorama (Linz), 1973, pp. 53-56.

185) See West-Ost-Journal, 1973, No. 2, p. 64.

186) Arbeiter-Zeitung, December 5, 1973.

187) West-Ost-Journal, 1971, No. 3, p. 20.

188) Wirtschaftsdienst, 1973, No. 4, p. 168.

189) Kredit und Kapital, 1972, No. 2, p. 233.

190) Handelsblatt, June 28, 1973, p. 4.

191) BfA/NfA, April 5, 1972.

192) See Vilaggazdasag, October 18-19, 1973.

193) See Arbeiter-Zeitung, June 17, 1971.

194) Handelsblatt, June 8, 1971.

195) Die Presse, August 21, 1973.

196) Tagesspiegel, May 16, 1972, and Financial Times, May 10, 1972.

197) Ekonomicheskaia gazeta, 1973, No. 22, p. 20.

198) On September 28, 1972, the President of Crédit Lyonnais, F. Bloch-Lainé, announced the decision to open a branch office in Moscow (Le monde, September 29, 1972).

199) See Wirtschaftswoche, May 18, 1973.

200) "The stock exchange is the most significant mediator between the financial markets and the largest American industrial concerns" (Die Presse, March 10-11, 1973).

201) The Bank of America has maintained relations with Bulgaria, the German Democratic Republic, Hungary, Poland, and Romania for years. Ties with these countries are cultivated by a special official attached to the Vienna branch office, and not by the Moscow office (Handelsblatt, July 24, 1973).

202) See Panorama (Linz), special edition, Gesellschaft für Ost und Südostkunde, 1973.

203) In an interview with the Viennese paper Die Presse after his return from the Soviet Union on January 25, 1973, David Rockefeller said: "A bonafide branch office cannot be established since the Eastern countries do not have convertible currencies."

5 | The outlook for East-West monetary relations

1. The Division of the World Currency System After World War II

There is no unified world monetary system and hence no uniform infrastructure for international trade. However, the division of the world into two blocs was based not on de facto currency convertibility, but on whether a given nation was willing to accept convertibility as a future goal. Thus, the economically strong countries, i.e., those whose currencies are convertible and thus may be used as payments and reserve media, and countries whose currencies are still a long way from achieving convertibility exist side by side in the institutions created by the Bretton Woods Agreement (the IMF and the World Bank). The long membership of nations with nonconvertible currencies in the IMF derives from Article XIV of the IMF statutes, which grants all member states a transitional period for achieving convertibility. The net effect of Article XIV has been to perpetuate the membership of numerous countries without convertible currencies. (1) In quite another light, the CMEA nations (with the exception of Romania, 1972) declined participation in the international monetary and credit institutions because they could not reconcile convertibility with their economic system.

The origin of the two monetary blocs is ultimately to be sought in the differences between the economic systems in East and West. The line is clearly drawn: on the one side, we have the industrial nations with convertible currencies and the developing countries for which convertibility is a desired goal, and, on the other, the Eastern bloc of nations, which emphatically rejected the manifest goal of the Bretton Woods Agreement.

The Bretton Woods Agreement was originally intended for all United Nations members. Other Eastern European countries besides the Soviet Union participated in the preliminary discussions, and some even joined the IMF as founding members. Participation in a world currency system intended to bring some order into international monetary relations and offering cheap credit assistance to members in temporary payments difficulties was at that time attractive to many, from Poland and Czechoslovakia, which had begun negotiations before their social transformation and continued them thereafter, to the Soviet Union, with its highly centralized economic system.

The theme of convertibility, which runs throughout the IMF statutes, was at that time a tune of the future, even for Western Europe; it was hardly considered immediately practicable. The failure of the Soviet Union to ratify the agreement, and later the departure of Poland and Czechoslovakia, were rooted more in the political power relations of the postwar years than in any fundamental differences in outlook. The rift in the world monetary system grew deeper as more and more industrial nations adopted convertible currencies as more suited to the needs of a market economy. The CMEA countries helped to widen the gap by limiting their currencies to domestic transactions and creating a separate settlement system for the CMEA area, as well as setting up autonomous price structures and exchange rates that had no validity on the international market.

The division was still not so perceptible in the fifties, since the unwritten rules of East-West trade were not at all that different from the bilateral and multilateral clearing methods practiced in the West. (2) The sixties saw more radical contrasts emerge after the IMF began to thrive due to the success of the European Payments Union in restoring convertibility in Western Europe. The contrasts grew even sharper in the seventies, a time of steady expansion of trade, both between East and West and among the CMEA countries, and a growth of tourism, industrial cooperation, and credit relations.

With two currency systems (in one of which money has a purely domestic function) existing side by side, all trade suffers, but in East-West trade, in particular, the Eastern nation is at a permanent disadvantage because its currency is not convertible.

2. The Common Interest in a Unified Currency System

Both systems would only gain from a unification of the international monetary system, although admittedly the present division creates more serious problems for the East than for the West. The diverse currency systems mean that, in the CMEA, several methods of settlement must be used: multiclearing within the CMEA; bilateral clearing in trade with the other socialist countries and with a few Western nations; and settlements in foreign exchange in trade with Western industrial nations — with all the advantages and disadvantages for foreign trade, and particularly for solvency, that such a division entails.

Within the CMEA, some progress had undeniably been made. One example is the creation of the IBEC, which advances cheap credits to promote intrabloc trade and raises foreign exchange to stimulate trade between the CMEA countries and the West. Yet the Eastern nations would have to make a number of changes in their economic systems to achieve genuine multilateralization, even within their own settlement area. The Hungarian economist S. Ausch has justly observed that, even after the creation of a multilateral clearing office, the Eastern system of trade would remain inherently bilateral, since "no country operating with a system of direct plan instructions can renounce specifying the bulk of its bilaterally balanced export and import trade in terms of physical use values." (3) West German economist H. Giersch, who sees no prospects for a genuine multilateralization without convertibility, is of a similar opinion. (4)

Criticism of the existing settlement system continues to mount in the Eastern European countries, if for no other reason than because it is costly and unwieldy. The same country is often a debtor in one settlement area and a creditor in another. Clearing balances, including the multilateral balance in the IBEC, are not transferable. The efforts of Poland, and later of Hungary, to establish some link to the Western currency system by making the transferable ruble at least partially convertible have so far met with the unbending resistance of the other CMEA nations. Under present conditions, however, in which CMEA prices not only vary internally, but also vary appreciably from those used in East-West trade, even a partial convertibility of the transferable ruble is out of the question. The official fictional exchange rate of the transferable ruble is useless in such a situation, and a conversion coefficient acceptable to all the member nations would be a practical impossibility.

In terms of costs, the clearing procedure, including multilateral clearing, penalizes the creditor and works to the advantage of the debtor; it also encourages a certain laxness in meeting delivery schedules, since the delivering party can receive credits automatically at relatively low interest rates even if he is not punctual. For countries with surpluses, positive balances, which generally reflect planned but not yet delivered imports, are unrecoverable losses. The creditor also has the disadvantage that, even though he receives interest on his holdings, they cannot be used to offset plan target shortfalls caused by a supplier's failure to come through with the goods.

The exclusively domestic function of the CMEA currencies unquestionably put these countries at a disadvantage in trade with the West. For years, even after convertibility was restored in Western Europe, the Eastern nations, with their monopoly over foreign trade, settled their accounts with the West by means of clearing procedures and thus had to pay higher prices as well as any additional costs incurred from financing a negative balance through switch, swap, and transit transactions. The adoption of foreign exchange as a means of settlement eliminated some of these disadvantages, but also created new ones, especially for the West.

In contrast to its Eastern partner, a Western country with convertible currency usually can take advantage of the diversity and elasticity of the goods it has to offer to offset a payments deficit, and in urgent cases it can even call on the facilities of the IMF. In the planned economies, on the other hand, market elasticity is very limited. Unlike a Western country possessing a convertible currency, an Eastern partner cannot use its own currency to pay for imports. The shortage of foreign exchange is chronic in the East, since the goods offered for export cannot measure up to import demands. Moreover, the Western partners fear that if convertible currencies are used for settlement, the Eastern trading partner will accumulate surpluses which it will then use in a third country. Therefore, many Western countries (Austria is a good example) approved a change-over to convertible currencies in transactions with the East only on the proviso that an explicit clause be included in payments agreements. If it is the CMEA nation that runs up a deficit, more costly ways to raise funds must be found.

All in all, trade relations, between East and West reproduce some of the features of trade relations between the industrially advanced nations and the underdeveloped countries, and nowhere is this more apparent than in the commodity structure of the Soviet Union, Bulgaria, and Poland. Despite multilateral clearing offices in the CMEA and the use of foreign exchange as a means of settlement in East-West trade, commodity exchange with and among countries with nonconvertible currencies remains largely bilateral. (5)

East-West trade relations are not limited exclusively to the exchange of goods; now that the political climate is returning to normal and the CMEA countries are being accorded some of the trade prerogatives operative in the West, the economic relations between the two systems are coming more and more to approximate those existing among the Western nations. Trade in services, especially tourism, is expanding, and industrial cooperation is on the rise. Indeed, the nonconvertibility of the CMEA currencies and the fictional exchange rates have been particularly obstructive in negotiating cooperation contracts. Capital movements, which are quite indispensable for joint ventures, are encumbered by any number of restrictions, and the lack of any realistic exchange rate makes efficiency calculations for such projects almost impossible.

As a result, East-West industrial cooperation has its own unique features. The Western enterprises in the East are interested primarily in combining cheap Eastern labor with Western know-how. So far, cooperation agreements have generally been limited to the commitment of the Eastern partner to produce certain components of a final product or to supply the raw materials or initial material for its manufacture. In their turn, the Eastern countries participate in construction projects in the West by furnishing a relatively cheap labor force.

Although these cooperative ventures help to expand the export structure of the CMEA countries by including products that normally could find no way onto Western markets and have helped to alleviate Eastern shortages in foreign exchange through the sale of the products manufactured in third countries, both sides have been somewhat dissatisfied with the results.

Western countries will very rarely risk tying down large sums of capital and technological equipment in really long-term ventures. (6) Even though in some countries (e.g., Romania and Hungary) up to 49 percent of the operating capital of an enterprise may be in foreign hands, a merger of the state property of the Eastern partner with private capital has so far proven to be a practical impossibility.

The main obstacles to such a merger are not only the meager decision-making powers of Eastern enterprises but also the limited facilities available for the transfer of capital. Compensatory transactions, aimed at exploiting rich Soviet raw materials and energy reserves, offer much greater prospects. The most dramatic agreement — the exchange of equipment for large pipelines in return for natural gas — is already in the implementation stage, and negotiations are in process on further ventures of this type.

Cooperative agreements on a larger scale thus have not come about, and factors inherent to the respective systems undoubtedly have been partially to blame.

The isolation of the CMEA currencies from the international monetary system hit credit transactions the hardest, in both intra-CMEA and East-West trade. The inadequate ties between foreign trade and domestic production and the lack of any organic relationship between transactions in transferable rubles and transactions in the foreign exchange holdings of the international CMEA banks have been especially detrimental to trade. In the IBEC, the flows in these two units of currency run side by side without being joined by any realistic exchange rate. Differences between the exchange rates used for settling in the CMEA banks and actual exchange ratios are as high as 100 percent.

The types of credits granted by the IBEC in transferable rubles have not progressed beyond the technical short-term settlement credit. Long-term investment credits in transferable rubles are in fact still granted by the IIB in natura, just as they have always been under bilateral agreements. For every venture that has been approved for financing, a list of goods accompanies the capital or credit advanced.

Since no functioning capital market exists, the credit operations of the two CMEA banks in foreign exchange have taken on a form completely different from that which such transactions have on the world market. The IBEC accepts deposits from the major Western banks and employs 85-90 percent of these deposits for short-term credits to the CMEA countries. The IBEC members place their foreign exchange holdings at the bank's disposal only in exceptional cases. The difference between credits in rubles and credits in foreign exchange stands out even more conspicuously in the IIB. Its capital, which consists of 70 percent transferable rubles and 30 percent foreign exchange, may be used for credits only in the same proportion, and then only as long as there are no other available sources of financing. That portion of credit advanced in foreign exchange is supposed to be used to purchase high-quality machinery and equipment from the West, while the ruble credits are reserved for purchases within the CMEA. The two parts of these funds are correlated by means of a formal exchange rate for purposes of accounting. The limited uses of the ruble credit are reflected in the interest rate, which is lower for credits in rubles than for those in foreign exchange.

The disparities in credit facilities offered by the East and West are particularly evident in their reciprocal credit relations.

The Outlook for East-West Monetary Relations   241

The planned economies are always borrowers, never lenders. In the increasingly bitter competition over the attractive new Eastern markets, Western lenders are outdoing one another in their offers. The result has been a steep rise over the past few years in the interest and debt service burdens on the national incomes and the balance of payments of CMEA nations, with the cost of interest augmented even further by inflation in the West.

Eastern borrowers are often able to effect reductions in interest rates through budget subsidies granted to the Western lender by its government; in addition the relatively inexpensive credit facilities of the IMF and the World Bank are there for anyone who wishes to make use of them. Expanding East-West credit relations, the stepped-up activity of the planned economies on the international monetary markets, the increasing activities of the Eastern banks in the major world financial centers (7), and the establishment of the first Eastern branches of the major Western banks have stimulated interest on both sides in economic developments in the other bloc.

A CMEA country can no longer ignore fluctuations in the exchange rate (8), the price of gold, or the interest rates on the world markets, while the West must reckon with the economic efficiency, export potential, and solvency of the Eastern borrower. The Western nations must also be especially attentive to Soviet policy on the sale of gold (9), since it is certain to play a big role in any discussions on the future function of gold in a reformed world monetary system.

The lively monetary and credit relations that have emerged between the CMEA countries and the Western nations are pressing toward the integration of the two monetary systems. But for this ultimately to become a reality, the present international currency system will have to be modified, and some reforms will have to be made in the structures of the Eastern economies.

3. Preconditions for a Single World Monetary System

3.1. The Need for Reform in East and West

The creation of a unified worldwide currency system is a joint task of both blocs. The Western currency system, which is based on convertibility, and the economic systems of the CMEA countries, where currencies have a domestic function only, are both in need of reform. The market economies have a money and banking system tailored to an advanced international division of labor. But failure has invariably met all attempts to equip the world monetary system with economic and political stabilizers that could balance out uneven development among individual nations. In its present form, that system is certainly not suited to the specific needs of the planned economies, nor could it adequately serve as an international currency system for both sides. On the other hand, the Eastern monetary system meets the requirements of a centrally planned economy, but not those of an international division of labor on a broad scale.

Despite its need for reform, the Western currency system is doubtless better equipped for achieving an integrated international monetary system than its Eastern counterpart. However, the Eastern nations have serious objections to both the existing system and current reform proposals; so far, they have had to raise their objections as mere outsiders, although it would surely be more constructive if they were permitted to participate in the discussion of the reforms. If they were given a voice, a system agreeable to both sides could be worked out; we would then truly have one world monetary system. In the next section, we shall discuss the preconditions for creating such a worldwide system.

3.2. Needed Reforms in the West

Just after World War II, there seemed to be no inherent obstacles to the participation of the Eastern nations in the IMF and the World Bank. The failure of the Soviet Union to ratify the Bretton Woods Agreement cannot be attributed to the incompatibility of the Soviet economic system with the Western currency system, which, indeed, the Soviet Union had helped to create. The overriding reason was, rather, the political dominance of the United States and the status of the U.S. dollar as a key currency. These objections, however, no longer carry the same weight as formerly. Other problems have emerged to take their place, and the arguments used by the Eastern countries in their criticism of the Western monetary system have undergone corresponding changes.

The Bretton Woods Agreement, which for years provided the basis for an unprecedented expansion of foreign trade and toursim, has been shaken to its very foundations. Its cornerstone has crumbled: the key currency, the U.S. dollar, and the national currencies are no longer mutually convertible nor exchangeable for gold, and the former relatively stable exchange rate has been abolished. Today the dollar and gold are no longer unconditionally accepted as the key reserve media. The August 15, 1971, decision of the United States was public acknowledgment of the currency crisis that had long been smoldering beneath the surface, and provided the incentive for seeking means to overcome it. The two subsequent devaluations of the dollar, and the suspension of the dollar's convertibility into gold, deprived the dollar of properties indispensable to its functioning as a key currency: it is no longer a standard of par values for the other currencies, which more and more are being defined in terms of special drawing rights; and it is rapidly losing its preferred status as a reserve currency in favor of more stable holdings. Yet there can be no doubt that the replacement of the dollar as a key currency facilitates the transition to a new currency system, acceptable to East and West alike, even if this development is more the offshoot of chronic U.S. balance of payments difficulties than of any inherent reformist tendencies within the IMF.

Although equivalency among all currencies will continue to be unlikely in the future, a necessary condition would be the creation of a convertible Soviet ruble with a status more in keeping with the USSR's role as a world economic power. While the demolition of the dollar's reserve status was welcomed in the Soviet Union, a skeptical attitude was adopted toward certain tendencies, prevalent in the West, to replace gold, too, by fiduciary assets, for example, special drawing rights. The Soviet Union and the other Eastern countries have never concealed the fact that, for them, an international currency system without gold is inconceivable. Therefore, as early as December 1965 —

at a time when the central banks were still defending the official gold price of $35 per ounce — the Soviet Union demanded a rise in the price of gold in the Finance Committee of the UNCTAD. (10)

There seem to exist no clear ideas in the Eastern bloc on the future function of gold in a reformed currency system. At the International Conference for Trade and Industrial Cooperation held in Warsaw in June 1972, it was concluded, rather vaguely, that gold should continue to serve as an important reserve medium, although not on the same scale as heretofore. (11)

The Hungarian economist J. Fekete, who rejects the traditional gold standard, was of a similar opinion; yet he observed that, "by creating stable values for foreign exchange holdings, countries must be made interested in the lasting accumulation of such holdings. This can be achieved only if, as a final guarantee of the system, the direct relation with gold is maintained." (12)

A statement of the Subcommittee for Currency Matters and Payments Flows of the American Congressional Committee on Economics is fully in line with Fekete's comment: "Thus gold could easily continue for the time being to constitute an important share of currency reserves, although relative to the growth of total reserves, this share will diminish rather rapidly." (13) But the following statement of Professor Fritz Machlup will remain unacceptable to the Soviet Union as long as it is a major gold producer: "It will eventually be recognized by the world that gold has become a metal like any other metal, and should be discharged from its functions in the international monetary system." (14)

The Eastern nations have also made known their reservations concerning the creation of more flexible exchange rates. (15) This is no more than understandable, considering that the Eastern currencies are not subject to the ground rules of the world market, and that fluctuations in the exchange rates of the convertible currencies, over which the Eastern nations have no influence, threaten at any time to upset the stability so necessary to a planned economy and give rise to losses.

The demand, voiced by many Western economists, for more

flexible exchange rates actually works against the development of a single currency system. (16)

Even though the opinions of the planned economies on proposals for international monetary reform are those of outsiders, they do not diverge radically from the attitudes expressed by some of the most influential members of the IMF. There can hardly be said to be any genuine unanimity of Western opinion on this matter, however.

The positions of the representatives of the CMEA nations on the currency question reflect the importance these countries ascribe to reform efforts, as well as their desire to participate in development of a new worldwide system. As early as 1968, N. Patolichev, the Soviet Minister of Foreign Trade, stressed the need for reforms benefiting all the parties involved. (17) The Soviet professor Lubimov had a similar comment on these matters in 1972. (18) However, the planned economies must also institute reforms if the CMEA nations are to become a part of a revamped Bretton Woods system.

3.3. Reforms in the East

The real problem of Eastern participation in a reformed world currency system is not the varying importance attached to gold as a reserve (in this matter, France takes a more extreme position than the Soviet Union), nor does it lie with the unstable exchange rate; rather, the central issue is currency convertibility. Convertibility is the key to effective multilateral economic relations. The question is the extent to which the socialist countries, given their economic systems, can accept this imperative. Convertibility in the usual sense implies that the currencies of the planned economies would be traded on the world market as commodities at prices determined by the market mechanism. In addition, the CMEA currencies would have to be exchangeable for any domestic commodity, in which case the world market prices would have a strong influence on the internal price structures. In the present CMEA system, in contrast, production and distribution of commodities is centrally steered and prices are formed independently of the world market prices. The exchange rate is thus divested of all economic functions — above all, its capacity to influence prices.

The planned economies, so steered, could enter the existing monetary system on the basis of Article XIV of the Bretton Woods Agreement. That article, however, was intended only for those countries whose underdeveloped economies and shortage of foreign exchange made it impossible for them to meet the terms of Article VIII, one of which is currency convertibility.
If the planned economies did enter the world monetary system, Article XIV of the IMF statutes makes it mandatory that the Bretton Woods institutions place their facilities at the unlimited disposal of the planned economies without receiving monetary reserves from them, aside from their gold deposits. Romania did join the World Bank and the IMF on the basis of Article XIV, but the conditions it imposes are hardly befitting the prestigious position of the industrially advanced Eastern nations.

The participation of the Soviet Union would pose special problems. To quote a Hungarian expert on the question: "For those who know the situation, it will be clear without detailed argumentation that, for ideological, traditional, and, last but not least, defence reasons, the Soviet Union will not abandon in the foreseeable future its system of economic control based on direct, obligatory plan instructions.... Relying on its vast economic power and on its gold reserves, the Soviet Union is likely to prefer, in its relation with the capitalist countries, even in the future, the system of centrally controlled bilateral trade." (19)

Interestingly enough, Romania, whose economy is strictly centrally steered, is the only CMEA nation to join the two Bretton Woods organizations, while Hungary, which, of all the Eastern nations, has given widest range to the market mechanism, has not. Perhaps Romania's decision is to be understood in the context of its foreign policy, whereas Hungary has made known that it will never act independently of the Eastern bloc. The other Eastern nations (Poland, for example) seem to have been guided by similar considerations. Finally, as an added complication, the question of an effective common CMEA currency is still very much the subject of debate within the CMEA.

3.4. Is the Transferable Ruble the Key to the Entry of the Eastern Bloc into the World Currency System?

For the European Payments Union, the way to convertibility lay through multilateral clearing. At the same time, however, its member nations steered a course along a parallel path, so that ultimately it was the national currencies, not the EPU accounting unit, that were made convertible. The creation and effective assimilation of a collective currency into the international monetary system requires that the economies of the territory covered by such a currency be incorporated into an international framework, and that the particular nations renounce their rights of sovereignty in currency matters, in which they are especially vulnerable to outside intervention. Although there have indeed been various types of monetary unions in the past, sovereign nations have never accepted a collective currency [20], and no collective currency has ever found its way to the IMF. To be integrated into the international monetary system, the present accounting unit of the CMEA must possess all the attributes of a functioning national currency. In particular, it must operate as a uniform standard of value, i.e., all prices should be directly expressible in terms of it. In the CMEA, prices are independent of the exchange rates, which are determined by direct economic considerations; hence, no uniform price structure exists. This being true, the transferable ruble is also unsuitable as a uniform standard of value for the CMEA. It functions merely as a conversion factor by means of which prices may be expressed in terms of rubles, but without necessarily bearing even a rough correspondence to prices in the Soviet Union. In any case, the relation of the national currencies to the transferable ruble must by no means be conceived as an exchange rate in the Western sense.

Hence, for the common currency to be integrated into a world system, it is first necessary for a uniform system of value and price relations to be established within the CMEA and adjusted to those existing on the world market. In addition, it would be necessary to safeguard the exchange rate of the collective currency from short-term fluctuations, and that can only be done by means of the centrally guided intervention of a collective exchange fund.

The Eastern bloc, however, suffers from a chronic scarcity of foreign exchange that is less the consequence of economic weakness than of factors peculiar to the Eastern foreign trade system: first, two-thirds of foreign trade is settled by bilateral or multilateral clearing without the use of foreign exchange; and second, the Eastern bloc is permanently in debt to countries with convertible currencies because of its limited offering of goods. The only feasible remedy for these problems would be to place greater emphasis on the needs of the world market in planning, which of course means rethinking the role of foreign trade in the economy as a whole.

The foreign exchange reserves of the Eastern bloc, already quite meager, are distributed very unevenly. Only the Soviet Union, the world's second greatest gold producer, has the means to procure the necessary foreign exchange through the sale of gold. For this reason, the CMEA nations would not be able to participate in the creation of a collective foreign exchange fund to a degree that adequately reflected their economic capacities; furthermore, they are still quite a long way from a genuine concept of community in which the economically stronger partner would absorb costs incurred by the less developed nations. On the other hand, if all the Eastern nations were to participate in the IMF en bloc, with a single collective membership, the membership conditions could not give special consideration to the specific situation of the individual countries, which would vary according to their level of development.

As we have already pointed out, the CMEA would have to become far more market-oriented than it is at present for it to be able to join the world currency system as a uniform bloc, and not all the member nations are willing to do this. Least of all is the Soviet Union inclined to pursue such a course, since the share of foreign trade in its total social product is extremely small, and it has sufficient gold reserves to cover its payments deficits. Furthermore, to allow more play to market factors would require a far more radical reorganization of the highly centralized Soviet economy than of the economies of most of the other CMEA nations.

In a centralized economy modeled along Soviet lines, quantity will always have priority over value, and the bridging of gaps in plan fulfillment, not comparative advantages, will be the determining factor in foreign trade. It is impossible, on such a basis, to create a common price structure to which the exchange rate for a collective currency can be tied, and clearing will continue to retain its importance in Soviet foreign trade. Lastly, it may be said that the Soviet economic system provides no basis for the transferable ruble to evolve into a common convertible CMEA currency.

3.5. Diverse Views Within the CMEA

The East's present currency system is defended by those nations who wish to retain the basic principles of a centrally planned economy and rejected by those who desire far-reaching economic reforms. The latter camp is dissatisfied with the existing settlement mechanisms, which they view as obstacles to the multilateralization of trade. For them, the present CMEA monetary system is merely a temporary stage on the way to more advanced monetary and credit relations, with integration of the Eastern currencies into the international monetary system as the ultimate goal.

The Soviet Union sees the situation differently. (21) For it, the monetary system of the planned economies and foreign trade tied to commodity quotas have definite advantages; they reflect the superiority of the socialist system over the crisis-prone capitalist monetary system, and guarantee its continuing independence from the capitalist market and the stability of the collective CMEA currency. (22) Since the Soviet Union rejects any broad use of market mechanisms for steering the economy, it is only logical that it should oppose convertibility. (23)

Many Soviet arguments ground their objection to monetary convertibility in the view that it would necessarily lead to the abolition of central planning and the introduction of the steering instruments of the market. This line of reasoning is not very convincing, however. A changeover to convertible currencies would mean that the CMEA price structures for internationally traded goods would have to be adjusted to world market prices, but the state monopoly over foreign trade and its obligatory quota system could still be maintained. Although Soviet economists reject the merest suggestion of convertibility for the transferable ruble, they would still like to see it evolve into a "world currency that could serve as a means of international payments as the socialist system grows in size and strength." (24)

Understandably enough, the positions of the smaller CMEA countries are somewhat more subtle than that of the Soviet Union, whose foreign trade constitutes a negligible share of its total production, and who also has ample gold reserves. (25)

While the Soviet Union views the multilateral clearing of the IBEC in a positive light, the Hungarian finance minister criticized it. (26) In particular, he lamented the lack of economically realistic exchange rates. But, for these to exist, the price structures of the individual CMEA nations would have to be more akin than they are now. The Hungarian finance minister is in favor of a collective currency that would be linked to both the currencies of the CMEA nations and the Western monetary system. To achieve this goal, reforms would have to go beyond mere currency matters to a fundamental restructuring of economic relations within the CMEA and between the East and West. (27) Recent political developments in Hungary, however, indicate that a more guarded assessment of the monetary problem can be expected.

Poland, which was the first country officially to broach the monetary problem (28), is also critical of the way the transferable ruble functions. (29)

A collective CMEA solution that could lead to an integrated world monetary system through the creation of a convertible collective currency is therefore not in the cards, at least for the foreseeable future. It would not only encounter obstacles peculiar to each nation involved; it would also run up against more general problems that any community of autonomous states could expect to meet were it to undertake such a project. At the present level of integration, these general problems would be just as difficult to overcome as they have been in the EEC.

As things stand now, however, a solution at the national level is just as unlikely. Even a widely decentralized planned economy could not reconcile its basic principles with the IMF statutes, especially Article VIII.

Political considerations would also prevent a nation from going it alone, as Romania did. (30) A common solution would therefore not mean the integration of the CMEA en bloc into the world monetary system, but rather a joint position of all CMEA countries which would still leave each nation to seek membership on its own terms. Such a joint position would only be viable, however, if at the same time collateral reforms were made in the world currency system. A special statute for countries with state foreign trade monopolies, as exists in the GATT, would unquestionably facilitate such an accommodation.

4. The Outlook for the Future

The chances for integration of the Eastern countries into a worldwide monetary system were frivolously let slip away by both sides after World War II. If the Eastern nations had joined the International Monetary Fund or had remained members if they already were so, the international monetary system would have developed along quite different lines. The community of nations would then have had to take into account the special circumstances of those members with planned economies. Yet that would hardly have been difficult at a time when the detailed implementation of the Bretton Woods Agreement had still not been worked out.

Today the atmosphere is once again favorable for the integration of the CMEA countries into a worldwide monetary system. The Western system as delineated in the IMF statutes no longer exists, and the general contours of a new system are just now being worked out. Now, when everything is still in flux, it will be easier to look into the special needs of the planned economies than would be true in the contrary case in which one has to work with a system already firmly entrenched.

The conditions are also more favorable now in the East for a unified monetary system. New functions far beyond the traditional stopgap role are being given to foreign trade; in the past, a nation could import only goods which it did not produce itself and which were indispensable for plan fulfillment. Under such a restrictive foreign trade policy, the function of exports was to procure means of payment necessary for imports. More recently, the planned economies have come to acknowledge the importance of foreign trade as a vehicle of technological progress, and to realize that their ambitious growth goals will remain mere ambitions without technology and know-how from abroad. The Soviet Union is also well aware that its plentiful resources in raw materials and energy are quite attractive to the West. In principle the USSR still rejects the theory of comparative cost advantages, but in practice has been taking it increasingly into account. Within the CMEA, tendencies toward a multilateral foreign trade based on the transferable ruble have been gaining momentum, and, in trade with the West, settlements in foreign exchange are gradually replacing bilateral clearing. Now that clearing and switch transactions have been largely abolished, the way is clear for a true multilateralization of payments. Besides a more subtle and refined assessment of the role of foreign trade, the East is also tending to permit some play to market mechanisms. Without wishing to overstress the point, it would be reasonable to say that these trends indicate that a more realistic assessment of the advantages and disadvantages of strictly centralized planning is emerging, just as voices have long been heard in the West against excessive reliance on market mechanisms.

These developments, which are at least helping to establish a common language, if not common goals, have been reinforced by the easing of political tensions, the end of the cold war, and the de facto proliferation of economic relations and contacts in other areas. East-West trade is growing in volume with each year; new Eastern banks are being opened in Western financial centers; Western banks are setting up offices in Eastern countries; the Western industrial nations are engaged in vigorous competition in their credit offers to Eastern partners; and the latter have long since abandoned their fears of any large-scale indebtedness to the West. Cooperative agreements and joint

The Outlook for East-West Monetary Relations 253

ventures between private Western firms and Eastern state enterprises, financed by international banking consortia, are no longer a rarity. The climate is favorable for reforms on both sides.

The main problem, however, is still convertibility. In the preceding chapter, Soviet arguments against the convertibility of the transferable ruble were cited. But convertibility is much less of a problem in the East than is commonly thought in Western circles. Monetary integration on the basis of convertibility is possible, and the Eastern nations could easily accept a somewhat modified concept of convertibility. As P. Wiles noted, there is no reason why an Eastern or Western bank should not be able to make exchange transactions from rubles into other currencies. (31) The Soviet Union could control the flows of goods and services to and from the USSR simply by maintaining the state monopoly over foreign trade and by regulating trade in services, and the same could no doubt be done with capital flows. If the Soviet Union remained in control of these factors, it should experience no difficulties in covering any negative balance of payments with rubles.

Nevertheless, the Eastern countries could make concessions in one area: they could adjust their price structure for internationally traded goods and services to the price structures existing on the world market. In fact, this has already been attempted in many CMEA countries. In the Western monetary system, such adjustments have traditionally been left to the market mechanism, while the Soviet Union's state monopoly over foreign trade and its centrally steered economy have in the past effectively blocked them. The alignment of price structures in the planned economies to those of the world market would lead to realistic exchange rates. It should be understood, however, that payments imbalances in the Soviet Union could not be eliminated in a system such as the one outlined merely by adjusting exchange rates. Payments would still have to be balanced out by means of adjustments in the government-set quotas for foreign trade.

The West would have to agree to accept the rules of a new monetary system that was largely independent of the economic systems of the countries involved. In particular, for the East's sake, the West would have to rid itself of the prejudice that payments flows should be unrestricted; that makes sense only in a market economy, anyway. Thus, the new currency system would have to be a system organized along lines within which a multiplicity of subsystems could be created on a regional basis (for example, for all the Western industrial states) to serve the interests of a specific group of nations.

If the ruble were convertible, even only partially, the International Monetary Fund could continue to serve a useful function in an expanded currency system. The ruble would then augment the credit facilities of the fund and not merely increase the demand for IMF credits, which is what happens now in the case of Romania. The participation of the CMEA nations in special drawing rights would then present no problem.

Article XIV of the IMF statutes cannot serve as a basis for CMEA integration with the IMF. In the first place, the USSR would pose insoluble problems for the IMF by the sheer magnitude of its credit demands; but second, Article XIV was meant only to provide a transitional period toward free payments flows for the economically weak countries. The Soviet Union is not economically weak, and the intent of Article XIV in no way, either explicitly or implicitly, can be considered to pertain to the USSR.

It was not our aim in this study to offer any specific proposals for solving the problems we have outlined. Our objective was a more modest one: to delineate prospects for the expansion of monetary relations between East and West on the basis of an analysis of the monetary and currency problems of the Eastern nations.

If we were to allow ourselves a sweeping generalization, yet one quite to the point in the present situation, it would be that the time is ripe for a dialogue between East and West, beginning with parleys among professional economists, to draw up a blueprint for an integrated world monetary system in which every country could participate, regardless of its economic order.

Notes

1) See Section 2.7 of Chapter 4.

2) The number of bilateral clearing agreements concluded in the West increased from 200 in 1947 to 400 in 1950.

3) See S. Ausch, Theory and Practice of CMEA Cooperation, Budapest, 1972, p. 190. Elsewhere, Ausch also says: "In the CMEA, bilateralism will continue to exist even when centrally steered and decentralized economies exist side by side."

4) "We know by experience how much trade and welfare are limited by bilateralism and bilateralism is almost inevitable if there is no free convertibility of one currency into another" ("East-West Economic Relations and the International Monetary Problem," Acta Oeconomica, 1972, Vol. 9, No. 2, p. 204).

5) On this point, H. Giersch says: "To have more multilateralism in East-West trade we need a currency that is generally accepted as a means of settling deficits and surpluses" (ibid.).

6) See L. Kamecki, "The Possibilities of Reciprocal Trade and Industrial Cooperation Between the Socialist and Capitalist Countries," Problemy handlu zagranicznego, 1973, No. 3, p. 31.

7) The CMEA banks maintain contacts with 300 Western banks; the current foreign trade transactions of the IBEC are about $30 billion annually. The IBEC has already issued three bonds worth $140 million on the Eurodollar market. The conditions of Article XII of the statutes of the International Investment Bank enable the IIB to issue bonds on the international capital markets. In Western financial circles, it is already viewed as certain that the IIB will issue bonds totaling $1.3 billion on the world market. Three hundred million dollars are destined for the mining of Eastern Siberian copper deposits, while $1 billion is pegged for the expansion of the Eastern European oil and gas pipeline system.

8) See the opinion of Soviet Premier Kosygin: "Since we trade with all nations, we cannot avoid feeling the effects of currency crises" (Die Presse, July 6, 1973). The Soviet Union can even less afford to be indifferent to events on the world currency market since it has profited from the rise in the price

of gold and raw materials, holds large sums in hard currency, and recently appeared as a quite active money lender on the European market. Disposable foreign exchange reserves are placed on the short-term money markets in Luxembourg and London against a high 9-10 percent interest (see Frankfurter Allgemeine Zeitung, April 1, 1974).

9) According to estimates of the London gold trader Montagu, about 20 percent of the gold that appeared on the market in 1973 came from the Soviet Union. Although, in terms of mere quantity, the record of 311 tons of gold in 1965 remained unsurpassed (in 1973, it was only 280 tons), at that time the Soviet Union cashed in only U.S.$350 million, while in 1973 the corresponding figure was $824 million (New York Times, March 14, 1973).

10) See Tagesspiegel, June 21, 1966.

11) See Problemy handlu zagranicznego, 1973, No. 3, p. 47.

12) Acta Oeconomica, 1972, Vol. 9, No. 2, p. 159.

13) W. Schmitz, in his subcommittee report, Management im Kreditwesen, Festschrift für Hans Krasensky, Vienna, 1973, p. 287.

14) Professor Fritz Machlup, in his interview for the Hungarian journal Figyelö. See Acta Oeconomica, 1972, Vol. 9, No. 2, p. 196.

15) See, for example, S. Raczkowski, in connection with the CMEA Conference for Trade and Industrial Cooperation, Problemy handlu zagranicznego, 1973, No. 3, p. 46.

16) "The spurious fixed exchange rates only create difficulties in offsetting the payment balance and provide speculators with a risk-free option... one would only have to set up simple rules for a controlled float" (Professor G. Haberler in his talk in Vienna, September 11, 1973; see Die Presse, September 12, 1973).

17) See Problemy handlu zagranicznego, 1973, No. 3, p. 47.

18) K. H. Domdey, Geld- und Kreditprobleme im Kampf zwischen den sozialistischen und kapitalistischen Industriestaaten, Dresden, 1968, p. 495.

19) See Ausch, op. cit.

20) The seven members of the West African Currency Union and the five members of the Central African Economic Community and Customs Union, which also issue a collective cur-

rency, as well as the five members of the Central American Free Trade Area and the ten members of the Latin American Free Trade Association, are independently represented in the Bretton Woods institutions.

21) See <u>Mezhdunarodnaia sotsialisticheskaia valuta stran-chlenov SEV</u> [International Socialist Currency of the Member Nations of the CMEA], Moscow, 1973.

22) See the statement of W. Garbusov, the Soviet Finance Minister and Chairman of the Permanent Currency and Finance Commission of the CMEA: "The transferable ruble is a currency of the planned market.... Multilateral settlements by means of a collective currency, the transferable ruble, effectively shield the monetary flows on the international socialist market from the effects of crises in the capitalist currency system" (ibid.).

23) "The spontaneous market relations arising from currency convertibility are irreconcilable with the socialist planned economy.... Neither anarchic manifestations nor exchange into freely convertible capitalist currencies can be allowed.... In a planned economy, neither free trade nor free exchange of the transferable ruble are admissible" (J. Konstantinov, Director of the Department of Currency and Finance of the CMEA, and K. Laryonov, his predecessor, in <u>Kommunist</u>, 1973, No. 7, pp. 99-192).

24) <u>Mezhdunarodnaia sotsialisticheskaia valuta stran-chlenov SEV</u>, p. 18, and the Comprehensive Program.

25) The present gold production of the USSR amounts to about 240 metric tons per year; its reserves total 1,800 tons.

26) "The multilateral settlement system was created because bilateral clearing had become an obstacle to CMEA cooperation. However, the new clearing system has not yet been very effective, since the scope of multilateral trade continues to be negligible!"

27) See Ausch: "All this can emerge only as a result of gradual changes within the individual countries and in their cooperation, changes which must lead to <u>qualitative</u> transformation, <u>to the abolition of a system of direct plan instructions</u>" (op. cit., p. 182).

28) See the statement of the former general director of the Polish Finance Ministry, H. Kotlicki, Trybuna ludu, April 27, 1965.

29) "Holdings in transferable rubles are brought into being not because of the desire to create money resources for use at a later date, but because banks are obliged to accept them since, at the time, no usable goods are available." And, "A country may have holdings with the IBEC without being able to purchase goods, even if it is willing to pay a higher price" (J. Wesolowski, Finanse, December 1972). The criticism of S. Raczkowski is even more to the point: "The transferable ruble is the international money of the CMEA nations, however imperfect it may be.... It does not have a universal buying power that can be used at any time in any country and for any purpose" (op. cit., pp. 344-346).

30) Thus, the President of the Hungarian National Bank, A. Laszlo: "The joining of the IMF is a complex question, and this country will take joint steps in this direction with other socialist countries" (in a conversation with Die Presse, December 14, 1972).

31) George Garvy, Banking, Money, and Credit in Eastern Europe, New York, 1966, p. 119.

Bibliography

Adler-Karlsson, G. Der Fehlschlag. Vienna, 1971.
———. Western Economic Warfare 1947-1967. Stockholm, 1968.
Albrecht, D., and Weiss, H. "Die Aussenwirtschaft im ökonomischen System des Sozialismus." Sozialistische Aussenwirtschaft, 1968, No. 1.
Alkhimov, W. "Foreign Trade Monopoly and Credit Relations in the USSR." Aussenhandel (Moscow), 1970, No. 5.
Anikin, A. "The Capitalist Economy and the Crisis of the Monetary and Finance System." Voprosy ekonomiki, 1973, No. 2.
Ausch, S. "Problems of Bilateralism and Multilateralism in the External Trade and Payments System of the CMEA Countries." In I. Vajda and M. Simai (eds.). Foreign Trade in a Planned Economy. Cambridge, 1971.
———. Theory and Practice of CMEA Cooperation. Budapest, 1960.
"Der Aussenhandel Ost-europas." Mitteilungen der Bundesstelle für Aussenhandelsinformationen (Cologne), 1961, No. 148.
Berend, L. "Eastern European Economic Integration." In I. Vajda and M. Simai (eds.). Foreign Trade in a Planned Economy. Cambridge, 1971.
Bogomolov, O. T. Theorie und Methodologie der internationalen sozialistischen Arbeitsteilung. Berlin, 1969. (Translated from the Russian.)

Bohdanowicz, J. Neue Organisationsformen im polnischen Aussenhandel. Warsaw, 1971.
Bolz, K. "Handel oder Hilfe." Wirtschaftsdienst, 1973, No. 2.
Bolz, K., and Kunze, B. Wirtschaftsbeziehungen zwischen Ost und West. Hamburg, 1972.
Bolz, K., Kunze, B., and Wulf, H. D. Ost-West-Handel der EWG. Hamburg, 1972.
Brus, W. "Money in a Socialist Economy." Ekonomista, 1963, No. 5.
Brzák, V., and Maršikova, D. "New Methods of Management and Organization of Foreign Trade in Socialist Countries." Soviet and Eastern European Foreign Trade, 1970, Vol. VI, No. 3-4, pp. 214-267. (Translated from the Czech.)
Csikos-Nagy, B. "Incidence de la réforme économique sur le commerce extérieur Hongrois." Revue de l'est, 1970, No. 2.
Denezhnoe obrashchenie i kredit SSSR [Money Circulation and Credit in the USSR]. Moscow, 1970.
Dokumente RGW. East Berlin, 1971.
Domdey, K. H. Geld- und Kreditprobleme im Kampf zwischen den sozialistischen und kapitalistischen Industriestaaten. Dresden, 1968.
Dorosz, A., and Pulawski, M. "The Turn of Credit to the East." Polityka, September 9, 1973.
Emminger, O. "Internationaler Währungsfonds." Enzyklopädisches Lexikon für das Geld-, Bank- und Börsenwesen. Frankfurt am Main, 1967-1968.
"Europäische Investitionsbank." Jahresbericht, 1970.
Fedorowicz, Z. "International Investment Bank." Bank i kredyt, 1971, No. 1.
Fekete, J. Monetary and Credit Policy in Hungary. University of California Press, 1968.
———. "Some Connections Between the International Monetary System and East-West Economic Relations." Acta Oeconomica, 1972, No. 2.
Fox, U. Das Bankwesen der europäischen Volksdemokratien. Wiesbaden, 1967.
Frey, L. Mezhdunarodnye rashchety i finansirovanie vneshnei torgovli sotsialisticheskikh stran [International Settlements

and Financing of Foreign Trade of the Socialist Nations]. Moscow, 1960.
Fundamentale Fragen künftiger Währungspolitik. Tübingen, 1965.
Gardner, R. Sterling-Dollar Diplomacy. London, 1956.
Garvy, G. Money, Banking and Credit in Eastern Europe. New York, 1966.
Geiger, H. "Währungsprobleme und Wirtschaftsbeziehungen in Europa." West-Ost-Journal, 1973, No. 2.
Glikman, P. Rachunek ekonomiczny we wspolpracy krajow RWPG w dziedzinie inwestycji [Economic Accounts in CMEA Cooperation in the Area of Investment]. Warsaw, 1970.
Grossman, G. Money and Plan. University of California Press, 1968.
Guzek, M. Zasada kosztów komparatywnych a problemy RWPG [The Principle of Comparative Costs and the Problems of the CMEA]. Warsaw, 1967.
Haberler, G. A Survey of International Trade Theory. Princeton University Press, 1961.
Hoffman, O. V. "Verfassung und Aussenhandelsmonopol." Sozialistische Aussenhandelswirtschaft, 1968, No. 4.
Jaworski, W. Banki i kredyt w krajach socjalistycznych [Bank and Credit in the Socialist States]. Warsaw, 1971.
Kadow, G. "Die Tätigkeit der Internationalen Investitionsbank." Panorama (Linz), 1972.
Kamecki, L. "The Development Possibilities of Trade and Industrial Cooperation Between the Socialist and Capitalist Nations." Problemy handlu zagranicznego, 1973, No. 3.
Kaser, M. Comecon. Oxford University Press, 1957.
———. "Sovietunion." International Currency Review, July-August 1973.
Kiesewetter, B. Der Ostblock. Berlin, 1960.
Kleer, J. "On the CMEA Agenda." Polityka, July 4, 1972.
Koexistenz zwischen Ost und West. Vienna/Frankfurt/Zurich, 1967.
Konstantinov, J. "The Comprehensive Program in Action." Aussenhandel (Moscow), 1972, No. 10.

──────. "Currency and Financial Relations of the CMEA Countries." Aussenhandel (Moscow), 1972, No. 10.
Kosk, H. "The Search for an Aggregate Accounting Method for the Efficiency of Foreign Trade." Gospodarka planowa, 1972, No. 9.
Kozma, F. Die wirtschaftlichen Beziehungen der beiden Europas und die sozialistische internationale Zusammenarbeit. Budapest, 1970.
Kubiczek, F. "Modernisierung des Systems der Planung des Aussenhandels." Aussenhandel (Warsaw), 1972.
Kucharski, M., and Pruss, W. Pieniądz i kredyt w socjalizmie [Money and Credit Under Socialism]. Warsaw, 1971.
Kunze, B. "Die Kreditpolitik der EWG gegenüber den RGW-Staaten." Wirtschaftsdienst, 1973, No. 5.
Lederer, E. "Le financement du commerce Est-Ouest dans la République Fédérale d'Allemagne." Revue de l'est, 1971, Vol. X.
Lipinska, A. "The Economic Significance of Costs of Middle- and Long-Term Credit." Handel zagraniczny, 1973, No. 8.
Louts, O. "Ost-West-Handelsbank, Frankfurt." Panorama (Linz), 1973.
Machlup, F. Interview for the Hungarian journal Figyelö. Acta Oeconomica, 1972, No. 9.
Marketing in Hungary (Budapest), 1971, No. 3.
Mezhdunarodnaia sotsialisticheskaia valuta stran-chlenov SEV [International Socialist Currency of the CMEA Nations]. Moscow, 1973.
Michal, J. M. "Price Structures and Implicit Dollar-Ruble Ratios in East-European Trade." Weltwirtschaftliches Archiv, 1972, Vol. CVII.
Międzynarodowe stosunki ekonomiczne [International Economic Relations]. Warsaw, 1964.
Mises, L. von. Le gouvernement omnipotent. Paris, 1944.
Nasarkin, K. "Zehn Jahre der Internationalen Bank für Wirtschaftliche Zusammenarbeit." Aussenhandel (Moscow), 1973, No. 10.
Nattland, K. H. Der Aussenhandel in der Wirtschaftsreform der DDR. Berlin, 1971.

Nötel, R. "The Role of the United Nations in the Sphere of East-West Trade." Economia internazionale, 1965, Vol. XI.

Nove, A. "East-West Trade." In International Economic Relations. London/Melbourne/Toronto, 1969.

Ohlin, B. Die Beziehungen zwischen internationalen Handel und Bewegungen von Kapital und Arbeit in der Theorie der internationalen Wirtschaftsbeziehungen. Cologne/Berlin, 1966.

Orlowski, M. Kursy walutowe − pieniądz − kapital [Exchange Rates − Money − Capital]. Warsaw, 1972.

Pechaček, L. "Current Questions of the Convertibility of the Transferable Ruble into Gold and Convertible Currencies." Finance a úvěr, 1969, No. 9.

Pfeiderer, O. "Control of International Capital Movements." Intereconomics (Hamburg), 1972, No. 12.

Plowiec, U. "System of Controls in Foreign Trade." Ekonomista, 1971, No. 5.

Potač, S. "Present Stage of Development of the International Bank for Economic Cooperation." Zahraniční obchod, 1972, No. 11.

Raczkowski, S. Międzynarodowe stosunki finansowe [International Finance Relations]. Warsaw, 1972.

Ribi, R. Comecon. Zurich/St. Gallen, 1970.

Rohleder, C. D. Die Osthandelspolitik der EWG-Mitgliedsstaaten, Grossbritannien und Der USA gegenüber Staatshandelsländern Südosteuropas. Munich, 1969.

Rozliczenia międzynarodowe [International Clearing]. Warsaw. 1972.

Rusmich, L. "Die Währungsbeziehungen im RGW." Aussenhandel der Tschechoslowakei, 1970, No. 10.

Schelkov, O. "Der Transfer-Rubel als Instrument der sozialistischen Integration." Aussenhandel (Moscow), 1972, No. 8.

Schicht, H. "GATT." In Enzyklopädisches Lexikon für das Geld-, Bank- und Börsenwesen. Frankfurt am Main, 1967-1968.

Schmitz, W. "Management im Kreditwesen." Festschrift für Hans Krasensky. Vienna, 1973.

Scitovsky, T. Money and the Balance of Payments. London, 1969.
Senin, M. Sozialistische Integration. Berlin, 1972. (Translated from the Russian.)
Siemiatkowski, L. "Banking Reforms." Gospodarka planowa, 1969, No. 1.
Skibinski, L. "The International Banks of the CMEA." Gospodarka planowa, 1972, No. 10.
Sláma, J., and Vogel, H. "Niveau und Entwicklung der Kilogrammpreise im Aussenhandel der Sowjetunion mit Maschinen und Ausrüstungen." Jahrbuch der Wirtschaft Osteuropas, 1971, No. 2.
Slobin, I. Mirovoi sotsialisticheskoi rynok [The Socialist World Market]. Moscow, 1963.
Socialist World Market Prices. Leyden, A. W. Sijthoff, 1969.
Stankowsky, J. "Der österreichische Transithandel." Quartalhefte der Girozentrale, 1972, No. 3.
Staribacher, J. "EWG, EFTA, Comecon." Europagespräch in Wien, 1972.
Szász, I. Ungarns Rechtsnormen für den Aussenhandel. Budapest, 1970.
Stolte, J. "Ost-West-Handel in den siebziger Jahren." Studies on the Soviet Union, 1970, No. 29.
Sztyber, W. "Theoretical Basis for the Reform of Sale Prices in Socialist Countries." Eastern European Economics, Winter 1970-1971, Vol. IX, No. 2, pp. 91-131. (Translated from the Polish.)
Turner, L. "The Multinational Corporations." Futures, 1971, No. 3.
Uschakow, A. Der Ostmarkt im Comecon (documentation). Baden-Baden, 1972.
Vajda, I. "Integration, Economic Union and the National State." In I. Vajda and M. Simai (eds.). Foreign Trade in a Planned Economy. Cambridge, 1971.
———. "International Economic Relations." In Proceedings of the Third Congress of the International Economic Association, 1969.
Van Brabant, J. M. "Long-Term Development Credits and Socialist Trade." Weltwirtschaftliches Archiv, 1973, Vol. CVII.

Weber, E. Stadien der Aussenhandelsverflechtung Ost-, Mittel- und Südosteuropas. Stuttgart, 1971.
"Weltbank." Jahresbericht, 1972.
Wilczynski, J. "Multilateralization of East-West Trade." Economia internazionale, 1968, No. 2.
Wiles, P. Communist International Economics. Oxford, 1968.
Wirtschaftsbeziehungen mit dem Osten. Cologne, Reihe Kohlhammer, 1971.
Wojciechowski, B. Rozliczenia miedzy handlem zagranicznym a przemyslem w procesie integracji [Settlements Between Foreign Trade and Industrial Enterprises in the Process of Integration]. Warsaw, 1970.
The Work of the Economic Commission for Europe (Analytical Reports), 1947-1972.
Zotschew, T. D. Die aussenwirtschaftlichen Verflechtungen der Sowjetunion. Tübingen, 1969.
———. "Der Handel zwischen den Systemen." Kieler Sonderdrucke, 1972, No. 38.
Zwass, A. "The Functions of Money in Foreign Trade." Finanse, 1963, No. 103.
———. Pieniądz dwóch rynków [Money of Two Markets]. Warsaw, 1968.

LIBRARY OF DAVIDSON COLLEGE